John Hewitt

Ancient Armour and Weapons in Europe

John Hewitt

Ancient Armour and Weapons in Europe

1st Edition | ISBN: 978-3-75234-173-7

Place of Publication: Frankfurt am Main, Germany

Year of Publication: 2020

Outlook Verlag GmbH, Germany.

ANCIENT ARMOUR

AND

WEAPONS IN EUROPE

By JOHN HEWITT

ANCIENT ARMOUR,

&c.

PART I.

By whatever race Europe may have been originally peopled, this portion of the world seems to have been swept by successive tribes of adventurers from Central Asia. The so-called "Allophylian race" was displaced by the Celts; the Sclaves then drove the Celts to the west, and the Tshuds into the cold regions of the north; and lastly, the Teutonic conquerors, dispossessing at will the nations that had preceded them, laid the foundation of that vast social empire which at present, in Europe, in America, in Asia, and in the new world of the South Seas, rules the destinies of half the globe. For the purposes of art, the long period of time at which we have so rapidly glanced has been divided into the Stone Period, the Bronze Period, and the Iron Period; names derived from the materials which were in *general* use during the progress of the various races towards civilization;—a division which, though, from its great comprehensiveness, necessarily open to some objection, seems likely to be of much use in simplifying a study hitherto embarrassing alike to the general reader, and to those whose task it is to extend the range of our knowledge.

With the nations of the Stone Period and the Bronze Period we do not purpose to occupy ourselves; not that the relics of their times are of an inferior interest, but that, in commencing with the days of the iron-workers, which for general purposes we assume to be identical with the retirement of the Romans beyond the Alps, and the domination of the northern nations in the centre and west of Europe, we feel that we have a task before us already much greater than we can hope to fulfil, either to the satisfaction of our readers, or our own. If we leave much undone, we shall endeavour, in that we do, to be exact. Modern archæology differs from the old antiquarianism especially in this,— that whatever it contributes to knowledge is required to be scrupulously true. A monkish chronicler of the fourteenth century is no longer held to be an authority for the affairs of the twelfth; an illuminated Froissart of the fifteenth century is no more permitted to supply us with portraits of the Black Prince, or the costume of Duguesclin. Our pictures are no longer copies of copies; neither are they mere *versions* of old art. We must have line for line, point for point. This is essential, for two reasons: we are freed from the danger of any wrong interpretation of an historic fact, and we keep in view the characteristic art of the period under examination. The importance of this practice admitted, we shall be excused for stating that almost all the illustrations of this work have been drawn by the writer;—when from manuscripts, the collection and folio of the volume have been carefully recorded, so that the truthfulness of the copy may be readily tested;—after the drawings had been transferred to the wood, they were carefully examined before the graver was permitted to commence its work; and if, in spite of every precaution, some unlucky error would at last creep in, the mistake was always rectified with new engraving.

The chief evidences for the military equipment and usages of the Teutonic conquerors of Europe, from the period of the dismemberment of the Roman empire to the great triumphs achieved by the Normans in the eleventh century, are the writers of those times, the miniatures which decorate their works, and the graves of these ancient races; which last have of late years yielded a wondrous harvest of valuable memorials, illustrating as well the domestic practices of their occupants, as their warlike array. If these three classes of monuments are useful in supplying each other's deficiencies, still more valuable do they become to the archæologist and the historian, by the confirmation which they mutually afford to each other's testimony. A few discrepancies indeed occasionally appear on points of minute detail; and it is in the pages of the historians and chroniclers that these are generally found: but when we consider the difficulty of the transmission of knowledge in those days, and the errors that may have crept in from the negligence of book-copyists through so many successive generations, the wonder is, not that something has been left obscure, but that so much has been faithfully transmitted to our times.

The various sons of Odin, whether settled in Germany, in Gaul, in Iberia, in Scandinavia, or in Britain, bore a strong resemblance to each other, both in their military equipment, and in such tactics as they possessed. If we find one branch of this vast family combating the Romans with more than usual art, or conducting a campaign with larger strategical views than their fellows, we must attribute it rather to the superior skill of a particular leader, or to their having borrowed some valuable hints from the practice of their opponents, than to any essential difference between this or that tribe of Teutons,—between the dwellers on the right bank of the Rhine and the dwellers on the left bank,—between those whose huts were on the flats of the Waal, and those who had built their cabins in the valleys of the Loire. Such differences as have been observed, we shall point out in our progress; but we are inclined to believe that, as collections are augmented and comparisons extended, resemblances will be found to increase, and differences to diminish.

Among the writers who afford us information on the early weapons and mode of warfare of that branch of the Teutonic family which acquired the name of Franks, there are three whose testimony is of especial value to us; and we must again remark, that what was particularly true of the Franks was generally true of the Anglo-Saxons, and of all the cognate tribes which traversed Europe as conquerors. These three writers are—Sidonius Apollinaris, bishop of Auvergne, who, in the fifth century, wrote his Panegyric of the Emperor Majorian; Procopius, the secretary of Belisarius, who lived in the sixth century, and was an eye-witness of the facts he records; and Agathias, a Greek historian, who flourished in the seventh century. "The Franks," says Sidonius, describing the defeat of their king Clodion by the Roman general Aetius, "are a tall race, and clad in garments which fit them closely. A belt (*balteus*) encircles their waist. They hurl their axes (*bipennes*) and cast their spears (*hastas*) with great force, never missing their aim. They manage their shields with much address, and rush on their enemy with such velocity, that they seem to fly more rapidly than their javelins (*hastas*). They accustom themselves to warfare from their earliest years, and if overpowered by the multitude of their enemies, they meet their end without fear. Even in death their features retain the expression of their indomitable valour:—

'Invicti perstant, animoque supersunt
Jam propè post animam.'"

Procopius, describing the expedition of the Franks into Italy in the sixth century, tells us:—"Among the hundred thousand men that the king (Theodobert I.) led into Italy, there were but few horsemen, and these he kept about his person. This cavalry alone carried spears (*hastas*). The remainder were infantry, who had neither spear nor bow, (*non arcu, non hastâ armati,*) all their arms being a sword, an axe, and a shield. The blade of the axe was large, its handle of wood, and very short. At a given signal they march forward; on approaching the adverse ranks they hurl their axes against the shields of the enemy, which by this means are broken; and then, springing on the foe, they complete his destruction with the sword[3]."

Agathias, in the seventh century, writes:—"The arms of the Franks are very rude; they wear neither coat-of-fence nor greaves, their legs being protected by bands of linen or leather. They have little cavalry, but their infantry are skilful and well disciplined. They wear their swords on the left thigh, and are furnished with shields. The bow and the sling are not in use among them, but they carry double axes (πελέκεις ἀμφιστόμους,) and barbed spears (ἄγγωνας.) These spears, which are of a moderate length, they use either for thrusting or hurling. The staves of them are armed with iron, so that very little of the wood remains uncovered[4]. The head has two barbs, projecting downwards as far as the shaft. In battle, they cast this spear at the enemy, which becomes so firmly fixed in the flesh by the two barbs, that it cannot be withdrawn; neither can it be disengaged if it pierce the shield, for the iron with which the staff is covered prevents the adversary from ridding himself of it by means of his sword. At this moment the Frank rushes forward, places his foot on the shaft of the spear as it trails upon the ground, and having thus deprived his foe of his defence, cleaves his skull with his axe, or transfixes him with a second spear[5]."

We here see that the usual arms of the Franks at this time were the axe, the sword, the spear, of two kinds, and the shield. Body-armour is not worn by the soldiery at large; and the chief device of the assailant is to deprive his adversary of the aid of his shield, in order that no obstacle may stand between his brawny arm and death. The provision of cavalry is small, and the few horsemen that are found appear rather as a body-guard to the prince than as an ingredient of the army. The evidences above quoted are borne out, not alone by the contents of the Teutonic graves, but by other passages of ancient writers. Gregory of Tours, in the sixth century, tells us that Clovis, reviewing his troops soon after the battle of Soissons, reprimanded a slovenly soldier, by telling him, "There is no one here whose arms are so ill kept as yours: neither your spear (*hasta*), nor your sword (*gladius*), nor your axe (*bipennis*), is fit for service[6]." This author adds a new weapon to the Frankish soldier's equipment, in which he is equally supported by the evidences from the graves. They carried also, he tells us, a dagger, which was worn suspended from the belt. Tacitus, as early as the second century, describes with great exactness the spear-javelin named by Agathias. The whole passage is so curiously illustrative of our subject, that we venture to quote it:—"Rari gladiis, aut majoribus lanceis utuntur, hastas, vel ipsorum vocabulo *frameas*, gerunt, angusto et brevi ferro, sed ita acri et ad usum habili ut eodem telo, prout ratio poscit, vel cominùs vel eminùs pugnent: et eques quidem scuto frameaque contentus est: pedites et missilia spargunt, pluraque singuli, atque in immensum vibrant, nudi aut sagulo leves, nulla cultus jactatio: scuta tantum lectissimis coloribus distinguunt: paucis loricæ, vix uni alterive cassis aut galea."—(*Germania.*)

In the long and fierce contention between the North and the South,—between the rugged Goth and the polished Roman,—it could not but happen that an adroit captain of the ruder host would avail himself of the greater skill of his adversaries; that every campaign would teach some new formation, that every battle would disclose some useful stratagem: weapons would be improved, enriched, and augmented in their variety; the defensive armour of the leaders would extend to their subordinates; while the leaders, to retain their distinction, would be induced to render their panoply more splendid and more costly. We find, therefore, in the poems and chronicles of this later time, constant mention of rich arms and armour; and in the capitularies of Charlemagne especially, we get a glimpse of the improvements in northern warfare. "Let each count," commands the emperor, "be careful that the troops he has to lead to battle are fully equipped; that they have spear, shield, a bow with two strings, and twelve arrows, helmet, and coat-of-fence[7]." We here see the soldiery adding to their defensive appointments the casque and lorica, and to their offensive arms the bow and arrows. The equipment of Charlemagne himself has been handed down to us in the contemporary description of the Monk of Saint Gall. The head of the monarch was armed with an iron helmet,—"his iron breast and his shoulders of marble were defended by a cuirasse of iron." His arms and legs were also covered with armour; of which the cuissards appear to have been composed of the jazerant-work so much in vogue at a later period: "coxarum exteriora: in eo ferreis ambiebantur bracteolis[8]." The followers of the prince, adds his biographer, were similarly defended, except that they dispensed with the cuissards, which were inconvenient on horseback.

The proportion of cavalry continued to increase, as we clearly see from this phrase in a capitulary of *Charles le Chauve*:—"Ut pagenses franci qui caballos habent, aut habere possunt, cum suis comitibus in hostem pergant." By the clause, "aut habere possunt," it appears evident that some effort was expected to be made in order to extend this force.

Under Clovis and his immediate successors, (sixth century,) the Frankish army seems to have been pretty strictly limited to that race. But later, the Burgundians, and then the Germans, and at length the Gauls themselves, were admitted to the service. The troops were levied in the various provinces, and bore their names; as the Andegavi, the Biturici, the Cœnomanici, the Pictavi. Their leaders were the king, the dukes, and the counts. The Church lands were bound to furnish their contingent of armed men. The exempts were the very young, the old, the sick[9], and the newly married for the term of one year[10]. The provinces not only furnished the fighting men, but their arms, clothing, and a supply of food. "We order," says another of the capitularies of Charlemagne, "that, according to *ancient custom*, each man provide himself in his province with food for three months, and with arms and clothing for half a year[11]." It may be inferred from this order, that the prince trusted, for the last three months' sustenance of his troops, to the maxim always so much in favour with conquerors, that war should be made to maintain war.

In England, the Teutonic adventurers, when by many a fierce battle they had established a footing, and by the league of many a tribe they had united themselves into a large and powerful community, seem to have divided their society into two classes,—the Eorl, or noble, and the Ceorl, or freeman. "Before the time of Canute," remarks Mr. Kemble, "the ealdorman, or duke, was the leader of the *posse comitatus*, or levy *en masse*, as well as of his own followers[12]." The only superior dignities were the king and archbishop. The subordinate commands were held by the royal officers, who led the nobles and their retainers; the bishops' or abbots' officers, who were at the head of the Church vassals; and the sheriffs, who conducted the *posse comitatus*[13]. No distinct intimation of the dress of the ealdorman has come down to us, but he probably wore a *beáh*, or ring, upon his head, the *fetel*, or embroidered belt, and the golden hilt which seems to have been peculiar to the noble class. The staff and sword were probably borne by him as symbols of his civil and criminal jurisdiction[14]. But the new constitution introduced by Canute reduced the ealdorman to a subordinate position. Over several counties was now placed one eorl, or earl, (in the Northern sense, a jarl,) with power analogous to that of the Frankish dukes. The king rules by his earls and húscarlas, and the ealdormen vanish from the counties. Gradually this old title ceases altogether, except in the cities, where it denotes an inferior judicature, much as it does among ourselves at the present day[15].

The *húscarlas* were a kind of household troops, variously estimated at three thousand or six thousand men. They were formed on the model of the earlier *comites*, but probably not organized as a regular force till the time of Canute. To this prince, living as he was among a conquered and turbulent people, the maintenance of such a band, always well armed, and ready for the fray, was of the first necessity. Their weapons were the axe, the halbard, and the sword; this last being inlaid with gold. From the collocation of names among the witnesses to a charter of the middle of the eleventh century, we may infer that the *stealleras*, or marshals, were the commanding officers of the húscarlas[16]. In imitation of the king, the great nobles surrounded themselves with a body-guard of húscarlas, and they continued to exist as a royal establishment after the Conquest.

Like his ancestors, the ancient Germans, of whom Tacitus tells us, "nihil neque publicæ neque privatæ rei nisi armati agunt," the Anglo-Saxon freeman always went armed; a circumstance, however, that proves, not so much the extent of his freedom, as the smallness of his civilization. The ancient Egyptians, on the contrary, always went unarmed; and in the *Kristendom's Saga* we read, that among the Icelanders, about 1139, so great was the security, that "men no longer carried weapons at a public meeting, and that scarcely more than a single helmet could be seen at a judicial assemblage[17]."

The mode of raising ships among the Anglo-Saxons we learn from an entry in the Saxon Chronicle under the year 1008:—"This year the king commanded that ships should be speedily built throughout the nation; to wit: from three hundred hides, and from ten hides, one vessel; and from eight hides, a helmet and a coat-of-fence."

On especial occasions, the ships of war appear to have been decorated in a very costly manner; as we may gather from the present of Earl Godwin to Hardecanute, described by William of Malmesbury:—"Hardecanute looking angrily upon Godwin, the earl was obliged to clear himself by oath. But, in hopes of recovering entirely the favour of the king, he added to his oath a present of the most rich and beautiful kind. It was a ship with a beak of gold, having on board eighty soldiers, who wore two bracelets on either arm, each weighing sixteen ounces of gold. They had gilt helmets; in the right hand they carried a spear of iron; on the left shoulder they bore a Danish axe; in a word, they were equipped with such arms, as that, splendour vying with terror, might conceal the steel beneath the gold[18]."

The military system of the Danes in their own country, and of their Scandinavian brethren, may be gathered from what we have told of the changes wrought in England by King Canute. By the laws of Gula, said to have been originally established by King Hacon the Good, in 940, whoever possessed the sum of six marks, besides his clothes, was required to furnish himself with a red shield of two boards in thickness (*tuibyrding*), a spear, an axe or a sword. He who was worth twelve marks was ordered to procure in addition a steel cap (*stál-hufu*); whilst he who was worth eighteen marks was obliged to have a double red shield, a helmet, a coat-of-fence or gambeson (*bryniu* or *panzar*), and all usual weapons (*folkvopn*).

Italy, always the theatre of the most sanguinary wars, torn and wasted by the troops of pope and of emperor, and of its own citizens contending against each other; invaded and overrun by barbarian neighbours,—by the Hungarians on the north, and by the Saracens on the south,—presented a *mélange* of warlike usages and warlike equipment in which the East and the West, the North and the South became intermingled in such a manner as to give to the whole country the appearance of a vast military masquerade; an *imbroglio* which, in our time, it would be a useless attempt to resolve into its original elements. In the eleventh century, the consuls of the cities, succeeding to the functions which had been enjoyed by the dukes and counts, commanded the troops of their respective districts, and marched at their head, whether the expedition was undertaken under the banner of the emperor, or the result of a private dissension between two rival cities. The forces employed in these services differed in nothing from those of the west of Europe; the strength of the host consisted of the heavy-armed knights with lance and target, while the communal levy fought with such weapons as they could best wield or most easily obtain. The Hungarians, who overran the country as far as the Tiber on the north, and the Saracens, who harried the land to the south of that river, acted in small bodies of light cavalry, compensating by the rapidity of their movements for the inferior solidity of their armament. Before the expeditions of these marauders, the Italian cities had been open; but their depredations at length (that is, about the close of the ninth century,) caused the citizens to construct walls, to organize a communal militia for the defence of their homes, and to place officers selected from their own body at the head of their little armies.

From very early times, and almost throughout the middle ages, the clergy are found occasionally taking part in warlike enterprises;—one principal reason of which may have been, that, by personally heading their contingent, they escaped from the exactions and caprices of the vicedomini. Their presence in battle and siege is proved, not only by the direct testimony of cotemporary writers, but by the prohibitions that from time to time were issued against the practice. From Gregory of Tours we learn, that at the siege of Comminges by the Burgundian monarch, the bishop of Gap often appeared among the defenders of the town, hurling stones from the walls on the assailants. Hugh, abbot of St. Quentin, a son of Charlemagne, was slain before Toulouse, with the abbot of Ferrière; and at the same time, two bishops were made prisoners. The Saxon Chronicle, under the year 1056, says:—"Leofgar was appointed bishop. He was the mass-priest of Harold the earl. He wore his knapsack during his priesthood until he was a bishop. He forsook his chrism and his rood, his ghostly weapons, and took to his spear and his sword after his bishophood; and so went to the field against Griffin, the Welsh king: and there was he slain, and *his priests with him*." At the Council of Estines, in 743, it is forbidden "to all who are in the service of the Church to bear arms and to fight, and none are to accompany the army but those appointed to celebrate mass, to hear confessions, and to carry the relics of the saints." The Council of Soissons, in 744, records a similar prohibition against the abbots: —"Abbates legitimi hostem non faciant, nisi tantum homines eorum transmittant." The capitularies of Charlemagne contain similar ordinances: the priests are forbidden to combat "even against the pagans." The Anglo-Saxon clerics seem to have been no less belligerent than their neighbours; and Mr. Kemble sums up this part of the question in the following words:—"Though it is probable that the bishop's *gerefa* was bound to lead his contingent, under the command of the ealdorman, yet we have ample evidence that the prelates themselves did not hold their station to excuse them from taking part in the just and lawful defence of their country and religion against strange and pagan invaders. Too many fell in conflict to allow of our attributing their presence on the field merely to their anxiety lest the belligerents should be without the due consolations of religion; and in other cases, upon the alarm of hostile incursions, we find the levies stated to have been led against the enemy by the duke and bishop of the district[19]."

If there were Churchmen whom it was difficult to restrain from fight and foray, there were, on the other hand, laics who sought to escape the service by donning the cowl or chasuble. A capitulary of Charlemagne was necessary to prevent certain "liberi homines" from becoming either priests or monks, in order to avoid the military duties attached to their station[20].

The matrons of the North appear occasionally to have taken part in the defence of their country. William of Jumièges, describing the resistance of the Normans to the attack of the English in 1000, writes:—"Sed et fœminæ pugnatrices, robustissimos quosque hostium vectibus hydriarum suarum excerebrantes." Wace, noticing the same event, says:—

"Li vieilles i sont corues,
O pels, o maches, o machues,
Escorciécs è rebraciées[21]:
De bien férir apareillées."

And the English sailors, on their return after the defeat of their soldiery, themselves describe them as—

"Granz vieilles deschevelées,
Ki sembloent fames desvées[22]."

As we have before seen, the tactics of the Northern nations were borrowed in a great measure from the Romans. As early as the time of Tacitus, the Germans disposed their troops in the form of the *cuneus*, or wedge: "Acies per cuneos componitur."—(*Germania*.) And in the account given by Agathias of the battle of the Casilinus in 553, we are told that the wedge was still the arrangement adopted for the central division of the Frankish army, while the remainder was marshalled in two wings[23].

When a force of infantry had to contend against an army in which many horse were employed, they sought by serried ranks and by a favourable position to obtain the advantage over their enemy. This was the plan of the English at Hastings. A trench was before them,—

"En la champaigne out un fossé"—*Wace, Roman de Rou.*

Behind which, says the *Carmen de bello Hastingensi,*—

"Anglorum stat fixa solo densissima turba."—v. 451.

And Henry of Huntingdon: "quasi castellum, impenetrabile Normannis." And again, Malmesbury: "All were on foot, armed with battle-axes; and, covering themselves in front by the junction of their shields, they formed an impenetrable body, which would have secured their safety that day, had not the Normans by a feigned flight induced them to open their ranks, which till that time, *according to their custom*, were closely compacted[24]."

As early as the middle of the eleventh century, it was sought to familiarize the Anglo-Saxons with the equestrian mode of warfare of their neighbours, the Normans. In 1055 the alien captain of the garrison of Hereford, Raulfe, directed the English to serve on horseback; which, says the chronicler, was contrary to their usage: "Anglos *contra morem* in equis pugnarejussit[25]."

Omens in the earlier times, saintly relics in the later, were held in the highest estimation for the assurance of victory. The ancient Germans, as we learn from Cæsar, consulted their matrons as to the lucky hour for them to engage battle, and would not advance till the moon was propitious[26]. At the battle of the Casilinus, already noticed, some of the German auxiliaries of the Franks were unwilling to engage because their augurs had declared the moment to be unfavourable[27]. Gregory of Tours notices the custom of the Christian kings of France to seek a lucky omen from the services of the Church; and recounts that Clovis, arriving in Touraine on his expedition against Alaric, sent his retainers to the church in which the body of Saint Martin was deposited, in order to notice the words that should be uttered on their entry within the sacred walls. The king's satisfaction was extreme when the courtiers reported the passage of the eighteenth Psalm: "Tu mihi virtute ad bellum accinctos meos adversarios subjicis[28]."

Harold's "lucky day" was Saturday; on which he therefore fixes, to measure his strength with Duke William. Saturday was his birthday, and his mother had frequently assured him that projects undertaken on that day would bring him good fortune:—

> "Guert, dist Heraut,——
> Jor li assis à Samedi,
> Por ço ke Samedi naski.
> Ma mere dire me soleit
> Ke à cel jor bien m'aveindreit."
> *Rom. de Rou*, l. 13054.

Saintly relics were carried in procession to insure a successful expedition, or worn about the person of the combatant, or enclosed in a feretory and set up on the field of battle. Pope Gregory the Great included among the presents which he sent to Childebert II., certain relics which, worn round the neck in battle, would defend him from all harm: "quæ collo suspensæ a malis omnibus vos tueantur[29]." When Rollo, duke of Normandy, besieged Chartres, the bishop assembled the clergy and people, and—

"Traist horz entre sis mainz, d'une châsse ù elfu,
La kemise à la Virge.

Reliques è corz sainz fist mult tost avant traire,
Filatieres è testes et altres Saintuaires[30]:
Ne lessia croix, ne châsse, ne galice[31] enaumaire.

Li Eveske meisme porta *por gonfanon*
Li plus chières reliques par la procession."

The effect of all this upon Rollo was most startling:—

"Quant Rou si grant gent vei, si s'en est esbahi
De la procession ki de Chartres issi:
Des relikes k'ils portent, è des cants k'il oï;
De la Sainte Kemise ke la Dame vesti,
Ki Mere è Virge fu——
N'i osa arester, verz sis nés[32] tost s'enfui;
E, come pluséors distrent, la véue perdi.
Mez tost la recovra et asez tost gari."—

Rom. de Rou, vol. i. p. 81.

William the Conqueror and his barons, wanting a wind to invade England, addressed themselves to the monks of S. Valery; and—

"——unt tant li covent préié
Ke la châsse Saint Valeri
Mistrent as chams sor un tapi.
Al cors saint vinrent tuit orer
Cil ki debveient mer passer:

Tant i out tuit deniers offert,
Tot li cors saint en ont covert.
Emprez cel jor, asez briement,
Orent bon oré[33] è bon vent."—*Rom. de Rou*, ii. 146.

But the most curious accumulation of these "saintuaires" was on the field of Hastings, where Duke William had a portable altar, enclosing divers relics of saints and martyrs, other relics being suspended round his neck; while before him was borne a sacred standard which had been blessed by the Pope, and on his finger was placed a ring, (also sent by "the apostle,") in which was set, according to some evidences, one of the hairs of St. Peter; according to others, one of his teeth[34]:—

"L'Apostoile (li otréia,)
Un gonfanon li envéia;
Un gonfanon et un anel
Mult precios è riche è bel:
Si come il dit, de soz la pierre
Aveit un des cheveuls Saint Pierre."

Or, following another manuscript of the *Roman de Rou*,—

"——de soz la pierre
Aveit une des denz Saint Pierre."

In these days, when the shock of armies was not accompanied by the thunder of cannon, when the silent flight of the arrow, the hum of the sling-stone, or the whirr of the javelin, were all that preceded the hand-to-hand conflict, no small account was made of the various war-cries of opposing chieftains. And not only war-cries, but even songs, were employed to encourage the assailants or intimidate the foe; of which the Song of Roland, sung by Taillefer on the field of Hastings, is an example in the memory of every reader. Snorro, in the Heimskringla, has preserved a fragment of the improvised verses sung by Harold Harfagar, as, mounted on his black charger, he passed along the line of his troops previous to the battle of Stanford-Bridge[35]. The pagan Northmen invoked their divinities,—a practice that was continued, according to the chronicle of Wace, to the middle of the eleventh century; for, of Raoul Tesson at the battle of Val-des-Dunes, he writes:—

"De la gent done esteit emmie[36]
Poinst li cheval, criant *Turaïe*[37]

13

> Cil de France crient *Montjoie*.
> Willame crie *Dex aïe*:
> C'est l'enseigne de Normendie.
> E Renouf crie o grant pooir,
> *Saint Sever, Sire Saint Sevoir.*
> E Dam As Denz[38] va reclamant,
> *Saint Amant, Sire Saint Amant.*"
>
> > *Rom. de Rou*, ii. 32, seq.

In the fight between Lothaire, king of France, and Richard I., duke of Normandy,—

> "Franceiz crient *Monjoe*, è Normanz *Dex aïe*:
> Flamenz crient *Asraz* è Angevin *Valie*:
> E li Quens Thibaut *Chartres et passe avant* crie."—
>
> > *Ibid.*, i

At the field of Hastings, the English—

> "*Olicrosse* sovent crioent,
> E *Godemite* reclamoent.
> *Olicrosse* est en engleiz
> Ke Sainte Croix est en franceiz;
> E *Godemite* altretant
> Com en frenceiz Dex tot poissant."—*Ibid.*, ii. 213.

To complete our sketch of the Anglo-Saxon warrior, we may add that he wore both beard and moustache, neither of which were in vogue among the soldiers of Duke William. Wace has not omitted this point. The Normans—

> "N'unt mie barbe ne guernons[39],
> Co dist Heraut, com nos avons."—*Rom. de Rou*, ii. 174.[40]

Let us now examine a little more in detail the arms, offensive and defensive, of the various Northern tribes, at whose military institutions and practices we have taken so rapid a glance.

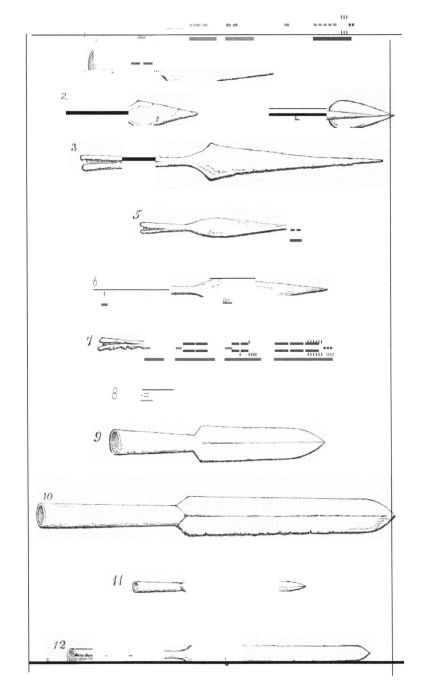

PLATE II.

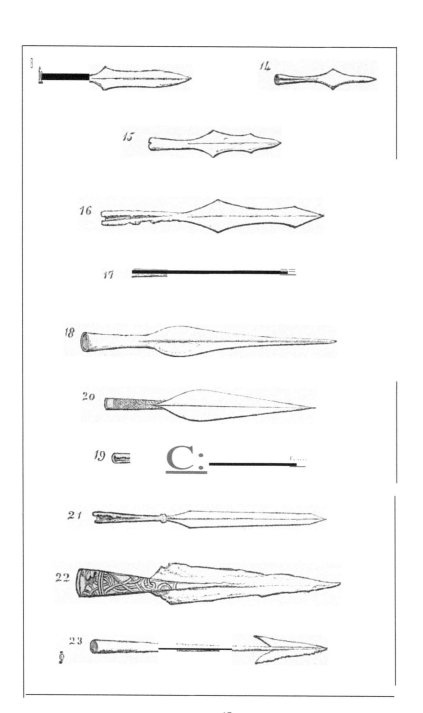

PLATE III.

The SPEARS seem to have been of two kinds: the longer spear in use among the cavalry, or to be employed[Pg 22]
[Pg 23]
[Pg 24] against them; and the shorter kind, which, as we have seen, might serve either as a javelin, or for the thrust at close quarters. In the accompanying groups of spear-heads, found in graves in different parts of Europe, we have collected the principal varieties of form[41]: the leaf-shaped, the lozenge, the spike, the ogee, the barbed, and the four-edged. These forms are infinitely varied in the monuments of the time, by giving to the weapons more or less of breadth or of slenderness. The blades are always of iron, and those found in England have a longitudinal opening in the socket. Their length is various, but they usually range from ten to fifteen inches. In the cemetery at Little Wilbraham, Cambridgeshire, the smallest found was two and a half inches, the longest eighteen inches[42]. In the Ozingell cemetery (in Kent), they occur of twenty-one inches in length[43]. The spear-heads of this period found in Ireland differ but little from the examples discovered in England and on the Continent. Those from the Ballinderry find, observes Mr. Wakeman, "are singularly like specimens found at Ozingell." In Anglo-Saxon interments, the spears occur in much greater numbers than any of the other weapons. The cemetery at Little Wilbraham produced thirty-five spears, but only four swords; and the axes, in all similar explorations, are of still greater rarity. These usual types of the spear-head found in Great Britain closely resemble those discovered in the graves of France, Germany, Denmark, and Switzerland. Numerous examples of them will be found figured in the Abbé Cochet's work[44], in Lindenschmit's Selzen Cemetery[45], in Worsaae's Copenhagen Museum[46], and in Troyon's *Tombeaux de Bel-Air.*

One of the first things that strikes the student in turning over the illuminated manuscripts of the Anglo-Saxons, and comparing their pictures with the relics procured from the graves, is the great frequency in the paintings of the barbed spear or *angon*, and its extreme rarity in real examples. We have already seen, in the description of Agathias, that this weapon was employed with fearful effect by the Franks in the seventh century; and the constant occurrence of it in the vellum-paintings of a later date, leaves us no room to doubt that it was a familiar form to our Teutonic ancestors. Yet its occurrence in the graves is of the greatest rarity. We have given, in our plate of spears, figure 17, a specimen of the barbed javelin, forming part of the Faussett Collection, found in 1772 in a grave on Sibbertswould Down, in Kent. Its length is eleven inches. Figure 23 in the same plate is from Mr. Wylie's paper in the Archæologia, (vol. xxxv.); the original, of iron, and in length sixteen inches, was found in a Norwegian tumulus. Mr. Wylie has also engraved another example, preserved in the *Musée de l'Artillerie* at Paris, said to have been procured from a Merovingian grave. In the Abbé Cochet's work (Plate XVI.) is figured another specimen, from a grave at Envermeu, the length of which is five inches; the barbs spreading out widely on each side, exactly in the manner of the royal "broad-arrow." Several examples are given in Worsaae's Copenhagen Museum, p. 69; one of which differs from the rest in having the barb on one side only, the other side being leaf-shaped. The barbed spear or javelin has also been found at Mainz, Darmstadt, and Wiesbaden[47]; but in all cases it occurs in very small proportion to the other weapons discovered.

The four-edged spear-head is of still greater rarity. In the graves opened by Mr. Wylie at Fairford, in Gloucestershire, one of these curious weapons was obtained; which we have copied from the volume describing this find[48], in our plate of spears, fig. 18. It is of iron, sixteen and a half inches in length, and two inches across at the broadest part. "It reminds one," remarks Mr. Wylie, "of the spear of Thorolf in Eigil's Saga:" "*Cujus ferrum duas ulnas longum, in mucronem quatuor acies habentem, desinebat.*" These four-edged weapons are of the highest antiquity;—compare those of the Egyptians, figured and described in Sir Gardner Wilkinson's work[49].

Another variety, found at Douvrend, and figured at page 283 of *La Normandie Souterraine*, has a leaf-shaped blade with recurved hooks at the socket end. Mr. Wylie has given this example in his paper in the Archæologia, (vol. xxxv. p. 48,) and considers it to be the weapon named by Sidonius as forming part of the Frankish warrior's equipment: "*lanceis uncatis, securibusque missilibus dextræ refertæ.*" Four other examples of this spear were found in the valley of the Eaulne[50].

Occasionally the spear-head was formed with its two sides on different planes; with the object, as it would appear, of giving a rotary motion to the weapon when used as a javelin. Two examples of this construction are described and engraved in the account of the excavations, by Mr. Akerman, at Harnham Hill, near Salisbury[51].

The spear-head was generally attached to its shaft by means of rivets passing through the socket into the wood beneath. Sometimes, in lieu of the socket, there was a spike at the base of it, which was driven *into* the wood, as in one of the Livonian examples, now in the British Museum, and figured in Dr. Bähr's work, *Die Gräber der Liven*. Sometimes, again, a ferule of bronze or iron was added to the socketed spear-head at its junction with the staff, as in the example in Mr. Rolfe's museum, at Sandwich, obtained from the Ozingell graves, and figured on our Plate II., fig. 6. In this instance the ferule was of bronze. One of iron occurred in the cemetery at Linton Heath, Cambridgeshire, (figured in Archæol. Journal, vol. xi. p. 106). In manuscript illuminations the spear-head of the Anglo-Saxons is constantly represented with one or more cross-bars at the base of the blade. A spear of iron having a cross-piece of analogous form was found among Anglo-Saxon relics near Nottingham in recent excavations, and has been added to the Tower Collection. It is engraved in the Archæological Journal, vol. viii. p. 425. Similar examples are figured in the Illustrated Catalogue of Mr. Roach Smith's Museum, p. 103.

The shaft itself appears to have been generally of ash. Portions of the wood have been found at Wilbraham, at Ozingell, at Northfleet, and other places. Some of that from Northfleet, having been examined by Professor Lindley and by Mr. Girdwood, has been pronounced to be undoubtedly ash[52]. The general use of this wood is strikingly confirmed by several passages in "Beowulf," that curious Anglo-Saxon poem which the concurring opinion of the best Northern scholars has assigned to the close of the eighth century:—

"Their javelins piled together stood,
The seamen's arms, of ashen wood."—*Line* 654.

And again, line 3535:—

"Thus I the Hring-danes
for many a year
governed under heaven
and secured them with war
from many tribes
throughout this earth
with spears and swords."
(*Æscum and ecgum.*)

In this passage, *æscum*, ash, is put for the spear itself. Mr. Roach Smith has collected several other instances of a similar kind. "In Cædmon, the term *æsc-berend*, or spear-bearer, is applied to a soldier." In the fragment of the poetical "History of Judith" we have *æsc-plega*, the play of spears, as a poetic term for a battle. So we have *æsc-bora*, a spear-bearer; and in the Codex Exoniensis, *æsc-stede*, a field of battle. And again, in "Beowulf:"—

"*Eald Æsc-wiga.*"
Some old spear-warrior[53].

In the eleventh century we find the ashen spear again mentioned. Robert of Aix, describing the knights his companions in the First Crusade, says: "Hastæ *fraxineæ* in manibus eorum ferro acutissimo præfixæ sunt, quasi grandes perticæ[54]." The Abbé Cochet, however, describes the remains of a lance-shaft found at Envermeu as being of oak; black with age, and of an extreme hardness[55].

The staves were sometimes of a rich and costly character. The heriot of the Anglo-Saxon Wulfsige consisted of two horses, one helmet, one byrnie, one sword, and a spear twined with gold[56].

The spear-staves deposited in the graves are necessarily of the shorter kind: the length of the entire weapon being about six feet; a fact easily ascertained by measuring the distance from the blade to the iron shoe, where that is found. This iron shoe is generally a hollow spike, into which the wood was fitted; as in that of the "Fairford Graves," Plate xi.; the one from Northfleet, (figured in the Journal of the Archæological Association, vol. iii.); and another in the Faussett Collection, found at Ash-by-Sandwich. Sometimes it was a button, to be driven into the shaft by means of a nail issuing from its centre. An example of this variety is engraved in the *Nenia Britannica* of Douglas.

Those who used the shorter spear or javelin were provided with several of these weapons, which they hurled successively at the enemy. In Harleian MS., No. 603, folio 30[57], may be seen a spearman holding three lozenge-headed javelins. Cædmon's Paraphrase (Archæologia, vol. xxiv. Plate LV.) has a figure carrying three barbed javelins (*angones*). In Harl. MS., 603, folio 56[b], the Destroying Angel has three barbed spears, one of which is represented in its flight, another poised in the right hand, ready to follow, while the third is held in the left hand, to be employed in its turn. This curious example has been figured by Mr. Akerman, to illustrate his paper, "On some of the Weapons of the Celtic and Teutonic Races," in vol. xxxiv. of the Archæologia.

Vegetius (lib. i. c. 2.) tells us that, in his day, the barbarians were armed with two or three javelins, a weapon which had fallen into disuse among the Romans. In the Bayeux tapestry there are figures of the Anglo-Saxons furnished with three or four of these missiles. Even in the graves of these people, the spears are sometimes found in pairs. Sir Henry Dryden, in his explorations at Marston Hill, in Northamptonshire, met with two warriors having two spears each. And the Hon. Mr. Neville found at Little Wilbraham, in Cambridgeshire, another example of a similar kind. The Wilbraham Cemetery disclosed another curious usage. Where cremation had been employed, spear-heads (and knives also) were in several cases discovered in the urns. Kings as well as their followers were buried with their weapons beside them. The spear-head found in the tomb of Childeric, which is of lozenge form, is engraved in the *Milice Françoise* of Father Daniel. This tomb was discovered in 1655, and the weapons found in it are preserved in the Imperial Library at Paris[58].

A singular usage appears to have prevailed when the spear and the axe were deposited in the same grave. The spear in this case was reversed,—the point at the feet of the warrior. Examples of this practice have been observed in Normandy, at Mondorf, and at Selzen[59]. At Wilbraham, spear-heads were found at the feet[60].

The pagan Northmen sought to enhance the value of their arms by referring their fabrication to weapon-smiths of a preternatural power. The Christianized Germans of the tenth century obtained a similar result by the employment of iron from the reliquary. At the coronation of the Emperor Otho the Great, in 961, Walpert, archbishop of Milan, presided at the solemnities: the prince placed on the altar of Saint Ambrose all the royal insignia; the lance, of which the head had been forged out of one of the nails of the true cross, the royal sword, the axe, the belt, and the royal mantle. After some intervening ceremonies, he was again armed with the weapons which had been laid upon the altar, and the archbishop placed on his head the iron crown of

Lombardy[61].

Not the least interesting among the many singular objects discovered by the Abbé Cochet in his researches in Normandy, is the little silver coin containing the portrait of "un guerrier frank debout." In his right hand the warrior carries his lance, while the left appears to hold the well-known round target of his time. This curious little relic is engraved on page 359 of the *Normandie Souterraine*.

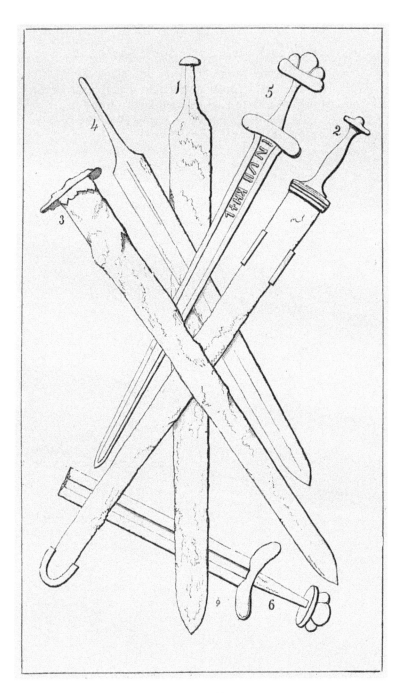

PLATE IV.

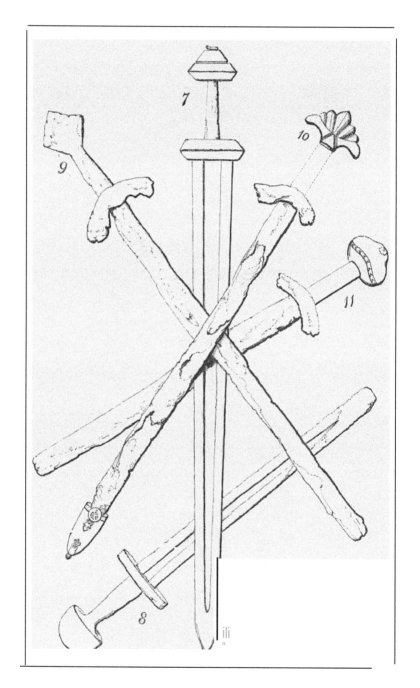

PLATE IV.

The SWORDS of the ante-Norman period may be divided into three classes: the earlier broadsword without cross-piece, straight, double-edged, and acutely pointed; the later sword, similar in fashion to the above, but having a guard, or cross-piece; and the curved weapon with a [Pg 32]

[Pg 33]

[Pg 34] concave edge, called in Anglo-Saxon the *seax*; the *sica* of classical times. The first has become familiar to us from the numerous examples procured from the graves of France, Germany, Switzerland, Denmark, and England. This type agrees exactly with the description left us by Sidonius Apollinaris; who, recording a victory obtained by the Franks over the Goths, has this passage: "Alii hebetatorum cæde gladiorum latera dentata pernumerant. Alii *cæsim atque punctim* foraminatos circulos loricarum metiuntur[62]." We have engraved, figure 1 of our plate of swords, a fine specimen of this kind of weapon, which was found among the "Fairford Graves." It is nearly three feet in length (the usual size of these swords), and when dug up, had fragments of the wood and leather which once formed its scabbard, still adhering to the iron. Other examples discovered in England are engraved in Mr. Neville's "Saxon Obsequies," Mr. Akerman's "Pagan Saxondom," and in the account of the Ozingell Cemetery[63]. German specimens appear in the "Selzen Cemetery," Swiss in the *Tombeaux de Bel-Air*, Danish in the "Copenhagen Museum," p. 66, and Frankish in *La Normandie Souterraine*. The Irish swords are shorter than others of this date, —not exceeding thirty inches,—as we learn from the researches of Mr. Wakeman[64]. That this sword of the earlier Iron Period resembled the anterior bronze sword in being without cross-piece, seems clear from two facts. Firstly, no such provision (except in one or two isolated cases) is found to accompany the weapons disclosed by the graves; secondly, it has been remarked, that in many instances, where the wood of the handle and that of the sheath remain, they approach so closely together, that there is no space left for any intervening appendage.

The sword with cross-piece appears to belong to the later Iron Period. When real examples are found in this country, and in others early Christianised, they are generally dredged from the beds of rivers, or turned up among old foundations; though in states where paganism held a longer sway, they are obtained from the graves. Two very early English specimens are figured in the "Pagan Saxondom:" one found at Gilton, in Kent, and now in Mr. Rolfe's Museum; the other found at Coombe, in Kent, and preserved in the collection of Mr. Boreham. The cross-piece in these examples has projected but little beyond the edges of the blade. From specimens given in our plates, and from the numerous representations of Anglo-Saxon manuscripts, we see that the guard eventually became a much more prominent feature of the Northern brand.

The third variety of the Anglo-Saxon sword, the *seax*, which Mr. Kemble[65] defines to be "ensis quidam curvatus," is apparently that old Thracian weapon, the *sica*, which among the Romans was in such little repute, that *sicarius* came to mean a bandit, or an assassin. The Anglo-Saxon curved sword never appears in their book-paintings, and has not been found in their graves. But in the Copenhagen Museum is a weapon which seems exactly to answer this description of the Northern *seax*. It is engraved in Mr. Worsaae's "Illustrations of the Copenhagen Museum," p. 97, fig. 384.

The handle of the earlier sword appears often to have been a mere haft, like that of our knives; sometimes it had a pommel. The later sword-handle consisted of grip, pommel, and cross-piece. The grip seems to have been commonly of wood, and it is not unusual to find portions of this wood still adhering to the tang of those swords which have been recovered from the graves. Part of such a hilt, found at Northfleet, in Kent, was submitted to the examination of Professor Lindley, and pronounced to be pine. Mr. Worsaae is of opinion that the Danish swords had the handle covered with "wood, leather, bone, or horn; which, however, is now consumed[66]." Mr. Wakeman tells us that some of the Ancient-Irish iron swords "have been found with the handle of bone remaining." Generally the cross-bar was straight; but sometimes it curved towards the blade; as in Cott. MSS., Tiberius, C. vi. fol. 9; Cleopatra, C. viii., in many places; in that fine sword found in the river Witham, and preserved in the British Museum; in the sword discovered in a tumulus in Lancashire (engraved in Archæol. Journal, vol. vi. p. 75); and in the examples given in our plate of swords, figs. 9, 10, 11, from Dr. Bähr's Livonian Collection. These cross-pieces of metal were often, as well as the pommels, richly decorated. The specimen from the Witham, named above, has both pommel and guard, which are of iron, inlaid with gold and copper in a pattern of lozenges. The most usual forms of the pommel were trefoil, cinquefoil, hemispherical, round, and triangular. To some a little ring was added, probably to attach a sword-knot; as in the example already noticed from Gilton, and figured in the "Pagan Saxondom." Of the other kinds named above, the first four occur constantly in the miniatures of Anglo-Saxon books, and it is difficult to understand on what grounds the swords with foliated pommels, when found in this country, are so generally assigned to the Danes. The triangular pommel is more rare. In our plate, fig. 7, we give an example in an ancient Norwegian sword in the possession of Dr. Thurnum. It is entirely of iron, measuring 3 feet, 1½ inches. A sword of similar form is engraved in Worsaae's "Copenhagen Museum," p. 97.

That the sword-hilts were occasionally of a costly character, we have the concurring testimony of ancient charters, poets, chroniclers, and of the graves. The poetical Edda records that Gunnar, a *regulus* of Germany, replied to the messenger of Attila,—"Seven chests have I filled with swords; each of them has a hilt of gold: my weapon is exceedingly sharp; my bow is worthy of the bench it graces; my byrnies are golden; my helmet and white shield came from the hall of Kiars[67]." Kiars was a *regulus* of Gaul. In "Beowulf" (line 1338), the "Great Prince" delivers into the keeping of his servant "his ornamented sword, the costliest of blades" (*irena cyst*). Again: "The son of Healfdene gave to Beowulf a golden ensign, as the reward of victory; a treasure with a twisted hilt, a helm and byrnie, a mighty valued sword many beheld borne before the warrior." (Line 2033.) At line 3228, we have "the hilt variegated with treasure;" and afterwards (line 3373,) we read of a "sword, the costliest of irons, with twisted hilt, and variegated like a snake." In this passage, both sword and simile are curiously illustrative of the ornamental art of the Anglo-Saxons, of which so many examples have come down to us. A document of the early part of the tenth century, given in Mr. Thorpe's "Anglo-Saxon Laws[68]," distinguishing between the *eorl* and the *ceorl*, declares, that if the latter "thrive so well, that he have a helm and byrnie, and a sword ornamented with gold, if he have not five hides of land, he is notwithstanding a ceorl." We have already seen that Canute's huscarlas were armed "with axes, halbards, and swords inlaid with gold." Eginhard tells us that the belt of Charlemagne was "of gold or silver, and the hilt of his sword was made of gold and precious stones." And of the splendid galley fitted out by Earl Godwin, as a present to Hardiknut, we are told that the warriors had "swords whose hilts were of gold."

Among the heriots enumerated by Mr. Kemble[69], that of Beorhtric, about 962, includes a sword worth eighty mancuses of gold. And Duke Ælfheah was possessor of another of the same value. In the will of prince Æthelstan, dated 1015, is named "a silver-hilted sword which Woolfricke made." Guillaume de Jumièges and Dudon de S. Quentin tell us that Richard the First, duke of Normandy, rewarded the services of two knights by presenting to each a sword whose hilt of gold weighed four pounds, and a bracelet of gold of the same weight. In illuminated manuscripts of this period, the mountings of swords are generally coloured yellow, implying probably a surface of gold, whether from thin plates of that metal, or from gilding. In the Fausset Collection is the bronze pommel of a sword, which has been richly gilt. The mountings of another in the British Museum are inlaid with gold. In Mr. Rolfe's possession are examples both in gilded bronze and of silver. In Denmark, hilts have been found "partly of silver, or inlaid with silver, or with gold chains attached to them[70]." Other Danish swords were surrounded with chains of gold, or covered with plates of gold and silver; and swords with handles entirely of silver have also been discovered[71]. Coloured beads appear sometimes to have formed part of the decorations of the Anglo-Saxon sword. Mr. Neville remarks, in his description of the relics found at Wilbraham, that "an immense blue-and-white perforated Bead accompanied three out of the four swords, probably as an appendage to the hilt or some part of the scabbard." On Plate xxi. of his "Saxon Obsequies" he has figured two of these beads: one is an inch and three-quarters in diameter, the other an inch and a quarter. Occasionally, runic or Latin inscriptions appear upon these weapons. In "Beowulf" this usage is noticed:—

> "So was on the surface
> of the bright gold
> with runic letters
> rightly marked
> set and said,
> for whom that sword,
> the costliest of irons,
> was first made."—*Line* 3373.

Mr. Rolfe had the good fortune to become the possessor of a sword-pommel thus "rightly marked." It is of silver, and was found at Ash-by-Sandwich. The runes occupy one side only of the pommel, the other having zigzag and triangular ornaments. This curious relic has been figured in the "Archæological Album," "Pagan Saxondom," and in Mr. Wright's "Celt, Roman, and Saxon." Professor Thomsen of Copenhagen informs the writer of these pages that, in Denmark, swords of the latest pagan period have been found, having runic inscriptions formed by letters of iron let into the iron blade. In the Tower collection may be seen a sword of somewhat later date, in which also is exhibited this curious practice, of inserting letters of iron into an iron blade. Among the swords found in Ireland, attributed to the Scandinavian settlers in that country, instances have occurred of inscriptions "in Latin letters[72]." In the Northern Sagas, frequent mention is made of the swords of their heroes being marked with runes; and the evidences we have adduced are of no small value in shewing the correctness of these writings as regards the ordinary usages of the time.

A further distinction was conferred on the swords of the great heroes of the North;—they were honoured with particular names. In the Wilkina Saga we read of "the sword called *Gramr*, which is the best of all swords," with which Sigurdr slays the cunning smith, Mimer; and again, of the weapon named *Naglhringr*, obtained for Dietrich of Bern, by the dwarf Alpris, (c. xvi.) Vermund the Wise armed his son Uffe with the brand *Skrep*, none other being proportioned to his strength. That of Rolf Krage was called *Skrofnung*. In "Beowulf" (canto xxi.), we have "the hilted knife named *Hrunting*,"—

> "wæs þam hæft-mece
> Hrunting nama;"

whose "edge was iron stained with poisonous twigs, hardened in gore." And in canto xxvi. of the same poem we learn that—

> "*Nægling*, old sword and gray of hue,
> False in the fray, in splinters flew."

King Hacon the Good, Snorro tells us, "girded round him his sword called *Kuernbit*" (millstone-biter). Thorolf, in Egil's Saga, "was armed with a sword named *Lang*, a mickle weapon and good." In Magnus Barfot's Saga (cap. xxvi.), the king wore "a most sharp sword called *Leggbitr*, the hilt of which was made of the tooth of the Rosmar (walrus), and ornamented with gold." The sword *Mimung* was no whit inferior to any of these. It was forged by Weland, in a trial of skill with another celebrated weapon-smith, Amilias by name. Weland first made a sword with which he cut a thread of wool lying on the water. But not content with this, he re-forged the blade, which then cut through the whole ball of floating wool. Still dissatisfied, he again passed it through the fire, and at length produced so keen a weapon that it divided a whole bundle of wool floating in water. Amilias, on his part, forged a suit of armour so much to his own satisfaction that, sitting down on a stool, he bade Weland try his weapon upon him. Weland obeyed, and there being no apparent effect, asked Amilias if he felt any particular sensation. Amilias said he felt as though cold water had passed through his bowels. Weland then bade him shake himself. On doing so, the effect of the blow was apparent: he fell dead in two pieces[73].

The skilful weaponer was always a person of high consideration in these days. This is curiously shewn in the law of Ethelbert which enacts that "if one man slay another, he is to pay his wergyld: but not so, if the slayer happen to be the king's weapon-smith or his messenger; in that case, he is to pay only a moderated wergyld of a hundred shillings[74]."

We have already noticed the curious custom of burying the spear-head in the same vase with the bones of the Anglo-Saxon warrior. An analogous practice has been observed in Denmark; where the sword of the hero, broken into several pieces, is placed over the mouth of the urn. An example of this kind of interment is engraved in Worsaae's "Copenhagen Museum," p. 98. Occasionally the iron sword, having been softened by the fire, was bent, and in this state deposited in the grave. The Abbé Cochet remarks:—"Cet usage des sabres ployés au feu et enterrés avec les morts est très-rare chez nous: il s'est rencontré en Allemagne, en Danemark, et en Suisse, ou M. de Bonstetton en a vu un grand nombre, en 1851, dans les sépultures de Tiefenau, près Berne. Ce savant ajoute que cette coutume, plus barbare que romaine, peu connue des Helvètes, était très-fréquente chez les peuples Scandinaves. Il existe, dit-il, au musée de Schwerin plusieurs glaives en fer que l'on croit provenir des Vendes, et qui ont été rougis dans le feu et ensuite ployés. Baehr signale le même fait dans les tombes d'Ascheraden et de Segevold[75]."

The Sheaths of the swords were commonly of wood covered with leather, as we learn from the graves; and they were sometimes mounted in bronze. Figure 2 of our fourth Plate shews an example from Wilbraham, in which the locket and chape are of bronze; and the Livonian sword, Plate v. fig. 10, has an ornamented bronze chape. In the British Museum is an Anglo-Saxon blade found in a grave at Battle Edge, Oxfordshire, which retains the bronze chape and locket of its scabbard. These fitments were sometimes gilt, or even of gold. Mr. Worsaae, in his "Primeval Antiquities of Denmark," page 50, has figured the gold locket of a sword-sheath, adorned with the winding pattern so characteristic of this period. Wood and leather were the ordinary materials used in the Danish scabbards. Of the sheaths formed of these substances, which have been partially preserved to our times, the most curious example is that figured by Mr. Bateman in vol. vii. of the Journal of the Archæological Association. It was found in a barrow in Derbyshire, and is constructed of thin wood overlaid with leather, the surface of the latter being covered with a pattern of alternate fillets and lozenges. A scabbard found at Strood, in Kent, was formed externally of a substance resembling shagreen. Dr. Bähr, in *Die Gräber der Liven*, Plate xv., has engraved a dagger-sheath, which is entirely of bronze, from Ascheraden; and in the *Abbildungen von Mainzer Altherthümern* for 1852, is another bronze dagger-sheath, containing an iron dagger, which was found near Treves. Several are in the British Museum. Mr. Roach Smith has another, found in the Thames;—all of them probably belonging to the period under consideration. There is also a curious type of sword-scabbard, formed entirely of bronze, which further observation may probably shew to be of Northern make. The example here engraved was found on a moor near Flasby, in Yorkshire; it contains the blade of an iron sword. Several similar ones have been discovered. One dug up at Stanwick has been presented by the Duke of Northumberland to the British Museum. Another is engraved in Dr. Wilson's "Annals of Scotland," found near Edinburgh. A fourth, from the bed of the Isis, is figured in the Archæological Journal, vol. x. p. 259. The Earl of Londesborough has another, dredged from the Thames, which differs from the rest in having been ornamented with enamelled studs. This is engraved in vol. iii. of the *Collectanea Antiqua*. See also the Danish example, figured in Worsaae's "Copenhagen Museum," p. 66. All these bronze scabbards have contained iron blades.

No. 6.

The Sword-Belts appear to have been usually girt round the waist; the buckles and tongues of them having often been found in the graves. These fitments are generally of bronze, sometimes of copper; and the metal is not unfrequently gilt, or embossed, or enamelled. Some buckles in the Faussett collection, found in Kent, are set with garnets. The belt was occasionally worn across the body, suspended from the right shoulder; as in the fine figure in Cotton MS., Tiberius, C. vi. fol. 9. Our woodcut, No. 17, furnishes an example of the belt girt round the waist, from an illumination in Add. MS., No. 18,043.

The AXE, as we have seen, was a characteristic weapon of the Northern nations. It is not unfrequently found in the graves of these people on the

Continent, but in Anglo-Saxon interments it is of the extremest rarity. In the Wilbraham excavations, a hundred graves yielded only two axes. In the Fairford researches, not one was found in a hundred and twenty graves; and in the many Kentish barrows examined by the Earl of Londesborough in 1841, not a single specimen was obtained. The axe appears to have been of three principal forms: the "taper axe," the broad axe, and the double-axe, or bipennis. The pole-axe and the adze-axe were varieties of these. The battle-axe was also called *francisca*, from the favour with which it was regarded by the Franks. Isidorus (lib. xviii. c. 8.) tells us of "Secures quas Hispani ab usu Francorum per derivationem *franciscas* vocant."

Examples of the Anglo-Saxon taper-axe, from the Ozingell Cemetery, are given in figures 1 and 2 of our Plate. Figures 3 and 4, found in Ireland, fig. 6, from Selzen in Germany, and fig. 9, from Livonia, closely resemble the Kentish ones. Fig. 8, from Livonia, differs chiefly in having a prolongation at the back. Specimens of the taper-axe found in France are given in Plates vii., ix., and xi. of *La Normandie Souterraine*; and Danish examples occur at pages 68 and 96 of Worsaae's "Copenhagen Museum." Some of the axe-heads dug up in Denmark exhibit a very curious transitional construction; the blade being of copper edged with iron. Another axe in the[Pg 46]

[Pg 47] Copenhagen Museum, "of the very earliest times of the iron period," is inscribed with runes. The axe found in the tomb of Childeric is of the "taper" form already described; it is represented in Plate ii. of Daniel's *Milice Françoise*. We have already, by the passages from Sidonius and Procopius, seen how the sons of Odin commenced their attack by hurling their axes at the foe. A curious illustration of this practice of throwing the axe is afforded by a charter of Canute, granting to the monks of Christ Church, Canterbury, the port-dues of Sandwich, "from Pepernesse to Mearcesfleote, as far as a taper-axe can be thrown on the shore from a vessel afloat at high water[76]:" swā feorr swā mæȝ ān taper-æx beon ȝeworpen ū of ðam scipe ūp on dæt land.

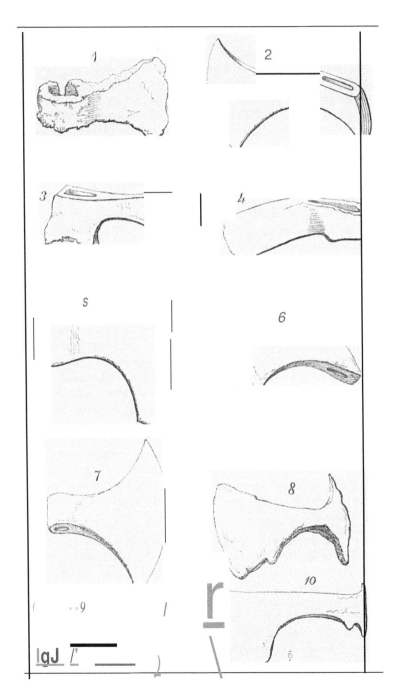

PLATE VII.

Figure 10 of our Plate, from Livonia, offers a variety from the axe already described, in having an angle in its under line. A similar contour is found in examples discovered in Normandy, and figured on Plate VII. of the Abbé Cochet's work. The broad-axe is seen in our figures 5 and 7; the first from Selzen, the other from Livonia. Compare the Frankish specimen engraved at page 233 of *La Normandie Souterraine*. Others have been found in England.

The single-axe used by the Anglo-Saxons in battle does not seem to have differed in form from those employed in woodcraft; as may be seen by referring to the Calendar contained in Cotton MS., Julius, A. vi., faithfully copied in Shaw's "Dresses and Decorations." Indeed, it is probable that the blade which had felled an oak was often called upon to strike down an enemy. Manuscripts do not frequently give pictures of the battle-axe; but examples occur in Cott. MS., Cleop., C. viii., and in the Anglo-Saxon Benedictional of the Library of Rouen.

The double-axe is of still more rare occurrence in book-paintings. It appears in two places in Harleian MS., No. 603, but this is a work not earlier than the close of the eleventh century. In the graves, the bipennis has never been found at all; neither is it seen in the hands of the Anglo-Saxons in the Bayeux Tapestry. But if the bipennis of the true classical form, that is, having two vertical blades, has not hitherto been seen among the varied contents of the Northmen's graves, a very singular variety of this implement has been discovered among the tombs of the Valley of the Eaulne. It is a kind of adze-axe, the one blade being vertical, the other horizontal. It was found by the Abbé Cochet in the cemetery of Parfondeval, and has been engraved in his work, p. 306, and in the *Archæologia*, vol. xxxv., p. 229. The adze form of one of the blades would seem to indicate rather an artificer's tool than a warrior's weapon, and the Abbé tells us that the peasants have still such an implement, which they call their *bisaiguë* (p. 307). We may remember, however, that an authority for the military use of the horizontal blade exists in the effigy at Malvern[77].

The Pole-axe is the almost universal form of this arm in the Bayeux tapestry. Not only the Saxon soldiery, but Harold, and even Duke William himself, are armed with this fearful weapon. Indeed, for a force of infantry, as the English were, contending against cavalry, no other kind of axe could have been of much service. Wace, whose minute descriptions, wearisome enough to the general reader, are invaluable to the archæologist, has not lost sight of the long-handled axes of the islanders. He has even given us the particular dimension of the head,—"ki fu d'acier:"—

"——un Engleiz vint acorant:
Hache noresche[78] out mult bele,
Plus de *plain pié* out l'alemele[79].

—— la coignie
K'il aveit sus el col levée,
Ki mult esteit *lonc enhanstée*[80]."

Rom. de Rou, ii. 225.

And again, line 13536:—

"Un Engleiz od une coignie,
Ke il aveit, *lungue emmanchie*,
L'a si féru parmi li dos
Ke toz li fet croissir les os."

The same Master Wace has recorded his objection to the Northern axe; that, requiring both hands to wield it, the weapon cannot be used effectively with the shield:—

"Hoem ki od hache volt férir,
Od sez dous mainz l'estuet tenir[81].
Ne pot entendre à sei covrir,
S'il velt férir de grant aïr[82].
Bien férir è covrir ensemble,
Ne pot l'en faire, ço me semble."

Rom. de Rou, ii. 262.

The handle of the Axe was of wood, traces of which have been observed in the relics obtained from the graves. In a single instance, it has been found of iron. This example occurred at Lède, in Belgium, and has been described by M. Rigollot in the *Mémoires de la Société des Antiquaires de Picardie*, vol. x.

The Guisarme is a weapon frequently mentioned by our early chroniclers and poets; but, though it is sometimes made to be identical with the pole-axe, at others it is distinguished from that arm. Wace tells us it was "sharp, long, and broad:"—

"E vos avez lances agües,
E granz gisarmes esmolues."—*Rom. de Rou*, l. 12907.

"Dous Engleiz vit mult orguillos:

37

En lor cols aveient levées
Dui gisarmes lunges è lées[83]."—*Ib.*, l. 13431.

The Statute of Arms of King William of Scotland (1165-1214) enacts: "Et qui minus habet quam XL. solidos, habeat Gysarm, quod dicitur Hand-axe[84]." From another Scottish ordinance we learn that the hand-axe was a long-handled weapon. The Provost of Edinburgh in 1552 directs: "Because of the greit slauchteris done in tyme bygane within the burgh, and apperendlie to be done, gif na remeid be provydit thairto; that ilk manner of persone, occupyaris of buthis or chalmeris in the hie-gait, that they have lang valpynnis[85] thairin, sic as handex, Jedburgh staif, hawart jawalyng[86], and siclyk lang valpynnis, with knaipschawis[87] and jakkis; and that they cum thairwith to the hie-gait incontinent efter the commoun bell rynging[88]."

No. 8.

Knives of various sizes are constantly found in the Northern graves. The smaller were evidently for domestic purposes, for they are discovered in female interments as well as in those of the other sex. But the larger kind appear to have been used as daggers. They have been more frequently observed in the continental tombs than in those of our island; and, as they very rarely appear in the pictures of the Anglo-Saxons, we may conclude that they formed no necessary part of the equipment of these warriors. A fine example of this weapon is given on our ninth Plate (fig. 1,) from the Ozingell Cemetery. It is sixteen inches in length, of iron, and is provided with a cross-piece. In the following group from the Anglo-Saxon and Latin Psalter of the Duc de Berri, in the Paris Library, the spearman's adversary appears to be employing exactly such an instrument as the example from the Kentish grave[89]. Figure 2 in our Plate is a two-edged dagger of iron from the Faussett [Pg 52]
[Pg 53] collection. It was found near Ash-by-Sandwich, and measures ten inches in the blade. Figures 3 and 4 are Ancient Irish. The first is the ordinary type of this weapon, of which many have been found. The second is

remarkable from the retention of its handle, which is of wood, and ornamented with carving. Both these are from Mr. Wakeman's paper on Irish Antiquities in vol. iii. of the *Collectanea Antiqua*. Figures 5 and 6 are German examples, from the Selzen graves. The first is very remarkable from the ring at the extremity of the tang. In Denmark, daggers have been found of a transitional period, the bulk of the blade being of bronze, edged on both sides with iron. Other Danish examples are given in Mr. Worsaae's "Copenhagen Museum," pages 66 and 97. In Dr. Bähr's explorations in Livonia, a dagger of iron was discovered with its bronze sheath. (See *Die Gräber der Liven*, Plate xv.) Gregory of Tours, in the sixth century, mentions in several places that the Frankish soldiers carried large knives at their belts; and there seems no reason to doubt that the examples from the graves are the very "cultri validi" of the historian. Of these Frankish war-knives, several specimens are figured in the *Normandie Souterraine*. They closely resemble those found in Germany, Switzerland, Denmark, and England. The handles appear to have been of wood. One of the Frankish examples still had portions of the wooden haft remaining[90]. Other specimens of the Northern *cultelli* will be found collected on Plate LVIII. of the second volume of the *Collectanea Antiqua*. Some of these weapons appear to have been inlaid with copper or other metal; for which purpose one or more incised lines are formed near the back of the blade. An Anglo-Saxon knife found in excavations in the city of London, and engraved (fig. 3.) in the Plate of the *Collectanea Antiqua* already noticed, still retains the bronze inlaying in the channels of its blade.

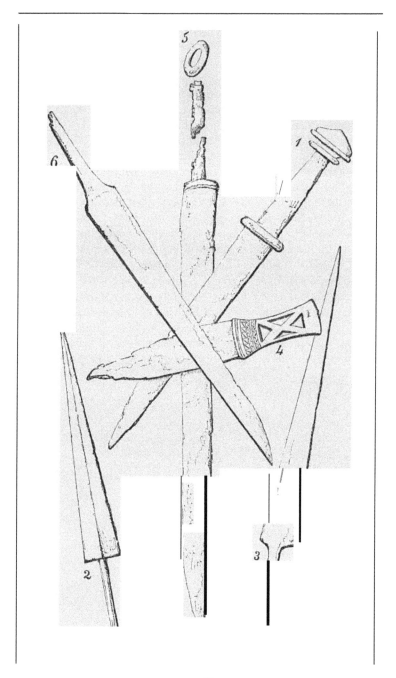

PLATE IX.

A curious variety of the war-knife is in the collection of Mr. Roach Smith, of which the single edge is straight, or nearly so, and the point formed by a diagonal cut at the back of the blade. It is believed, in its perfect state, to have measured upwards of thirty inches; is of steel; and has on both sides a double line of the channelling already noticed[91]. A weapon of similar form appears among the Livonian antiquities now in the British Museum, and is represented on Plate XIX. of Dr. Bähr's *Gräber der Liven*.

The LONG-BOW was another weapon of this era. Agathias, indeed, has told us that the Franks used neither bow nor sling. But arrows are expressly mentioned in the Salic Law; and, to reconcile these conflicting testimonies, it has been suggested that the archery of the Salic Law is that of the chase alone. *Poisoned* arrows, however, are here named, and the hunter does not ply his art with poisoned shafts. "Si quis alterum de sagitta toxicata percutere voluerit[92]," &c. Further on, a fine is fixed for him who shall deprive another of his "second finger, with which he directs his arrow:"—secundum digitum, quo sagittatur. At a later period, the bow is especially commanded as a part of the soldier's equipment. One of the capitularies of Charlemagne directs —"that the Count be careful to have his contingent fully furnished for the field; that they have lance, shield, a bow with two strings and twelve arrows," &c. According to the testimony of Henry of Huntingdon, William the Conqueror reproached the English with their want of this weapon. The Bayeux tapestry, however, seems to authorize the belief that they were not entirely without it. (See the first group of Anglo-Saxons in Stothard's XIVth. plate.) The probability seems to be that, while the Normans employed archers in large bodies, the English merely interspersed them in small numbers among their men-at-arms. The bow, at all events, was in use among the Anglo-Saxons: it is frequently represented in manuscript illuminations, and arrow-heads have been found in the graves. Figures 1, 2, 3 and 4 in our Plate are from Kentish interments. The first two form part of the Fausset collection; the others, figured in the *Nenia Britannica*, were found on Chatham Lines. The whole are of iron. Pictorial examples of the Anglo-Saxon bow, arrows, and quiver may be seen in Cotton MSS., Cleop., C. viii., Claudius, B. iv., Tiberius, C. vi., and in the fine *Prudentius* of the Tenison Library. See also Strutt's *Horda*, vol. i. plate XVII. Arrow-heads of iron have also been found in France, Denmark, Germany, Switzerland, and Livonia. Figures 5 and 6 of our Plate are examples from the cemetery at Selzen in Rhenish Hesse; figs. 7 and 8 from Livonian graves. With the latter was also found part of a quiver. The Abbé Cochet[93] has engraved and described specimens found in France, and M. Troyon notices Swiss examples in his paper in the *Archæologia*, vol.

xxxv., and Plate xvII. Compare also Archæological [Pg 56]
[Pg 57] Journal, vol. iii. pp. 119, 120. In the Suabian graves at Oberflacht, bows also were found. See *Archæologia*, vol. xxxvi. Among the figures of the ivory carving forming the cover of the "Prayer-book of Charles the Bald" are two archers, each holding a leash of barbed arrows; the arrows very clearly represented. This curious sculpture, illustrating the lvii[th]. Psalm, (a favourite subject with the middle-age artists,) has been carefully engraved in the sixth volume of the *Revue Archéologique*. The original is in the Imperial Library at Paris.

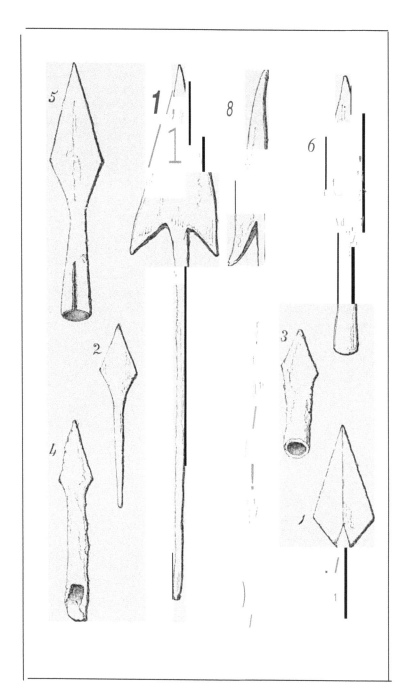

PLATE X.

These were the usual weapons of the Northern nations: these are seen in their pictures, are named in their laws, are described in their Sagas, are found in their graves. But other arms appear to have been of occasional employment: the mace, the pike, the sling, the stone-hammer, the "morning-star," the fork, and the bill. The Mace is seen in the hands of the Anglo-Saxons (as well as of the Normans) in the Bayeux tapestry; and it seems not unlikely that those dentated hoops of bronze[94] which have been found both in England and on the Continent were the heads of similar weapons; for it must not be forgotten that, even in the "Iron Period," objects of bronze continued in use. From the inexhaustible Wace we learn that the "vilains des viles" who joined Harold's army,—

> "Tels armes portent com ils trovent:
> Machues portent è granz pels[95],
> Forches ferrées[96] è tinels[97]."—*Line* 12840.

It will be remembered that the mace is a weapon of the most remote antiquity, and is found, almost identical in form with those of the Northern nations, among the monuments of the ancient Egyptians and Assyrians.

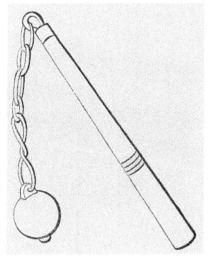

No 11.

The Stone-Hammer appears to have been employed by the troops of Harold. William of Poictiers says: "Jactant cuspides ac diversorum generum tela, sævissimas quasque secures, et *lignis imposita saxa*[98]." Of the Bill, an example occurs in the fine Anglo-Saxon Benedictional of Rouen: it closely resembles the common long-handled hedging-bill of our own day. The Morning-star, an instrument formed of a ball of metal (sometimes spiked) attached by a chain to a short staff, after the manner of a whip, is believed to have been another of the arms of this period. Dr. Bähr found the head of one of these in his Livonian researches; a complete one, of bronze, (here engraved) was discovered at Mitau. Professor Thomsen mentions also a bronze specimen, in his account of the Copenhagen Museum. The Sling, according to the opinion of the Père Daniel, was employed by the Franks in intrenched positions and beleaguered towns[99]. This ancient instrument, which is found in Egyptian[100] and Assyrian[101] monuments, was certainly in use among the Anglo-Saxons, whether for warfare or the chase alone, it is not easy to determine. The figure here engraved is that of David, from the Anglo-Saxon and Latin Psalter of Boulogne. See also the slinger in Strutt's *Horda*, Plate xvii., from Cotton MS., Claudius, B. iv., and Plate iii. of Stothard's Bayeux Tapestry. In the Copenhagen Museum are sling-stones, "either with a groove cut round the middle, or with two grooves cut cross-wise; having, in the latter case, the shape of a ball somewhat flattened." It does not appear that the Northern nations used leaden pellets; as the Greeks and Romans did, inscribing them with a thunderbolt, or some quaint sentence, as "Take this."

No 12.

It will have been observed, from several passages already cited, that the use of poisoned weapons is imputed to the Northern tribes of this period. In "Beowulf," and elsewhere, we read of poisoned swords, poisoned arrows, and poisoned daggers; and, however rare may have been the employment of such terrible ministers, it does not seem permitted us to deny altogether their existence. The famous sword of Beowulf,

"Hrunting nama,"

had its edge "stained with poisonous twigs." This, indeed, is the evidence of a poet: but the Salic Law, as we have seen, speaks of "sagittæ toxicatæ[102]." And Gregory of Tours tells us, of Fredegonda: "Fredegundis duos cultros ferreos fieri præcipit, quos etiam caraxari profundiùs et veneno infici jusserat, scilicet si mortalis adsultus vitales non dissolveret fibras vel ipsa veneni infectio vitam possit velociùs extorquere[103]." And again, the same writer speaks of these poisoned daggers, or *scramasaxi*: "Cum cultris validis quos vulgò scramasaxos vocant, infectis veneno, utraque latera ei feriunt[104]."

No 13.

Let us now examine, as far as we are enabled to do so, what was the Teutonic warrior's defensive equipment. The structure of the Body-armour can only be inferred from indirect evidences; for the vague terms of the writers, such as *lorica* and *byrnie*, and the rudely conventional forms of the painters, who indicated a tree by a cluster of three or four leaves, and a coat-of-fence by a few circles penned on the parchment or punched on the bronze, afford us little help in determining with exactness how the armour-smith achieved his task. It is curious that the best testimony we obtain is that of the poets. A simile or an epithet lets in more light than all the limners and all the historians. It seems clear that in the earlier days of Northern rule, none but leaders wore body-armour; but, as years rolled on, and prosperity increased, the subaltern ranks affected this distinction. As we have already shewn (page 38), the Ceorl vied with the Eorl in the richness and completeness of his equipment; and at length, under the rule of Charlemagne, the troops of the Count, as we have seen, are *all* required to have defensive armour: "Omnis homo de duodecim mansis, bruniam habeat." Those who had not this amount of land, clubbed together and furnished amongst them the panoply in which one of their number went forth to the host. Was this *byrnie* of interlinked chain-mail? The Anglo-Saxon poem of "Beowulf" may throw some light on the question:—

"The war-byrnie shone, hard (and) hand-locked (*heard hond-locen*); the bright ring-iron sang in their trappings when they proceeded to go forward to the hall, in their terrible armour."—*Canto* i. *line* 640.

"Beowulf prepared himself, the warrior in his weeds, he cared not for life: the war-byrnie, twisted with hands (*hondum ge-broden*), wide and variegated with colours, was now to try the deep," &c.

Canto xxi. *line* 2882.

In Canto xxii. we have,—"the war-dress, the locked battle-shirt." ... "On his shoulder lay the twisted breast-net (*breost-net broden*) which protected his life against point and edge." ... "his war-byrnie, his hard battle-net (*here-net hearde*)."

If there is meaning in words, surely "the *twisted* breast-net," the "hard battle-*net*," the "*locked* battle-shirt," the "byrnie *twisted* with hands," the "war-byrnie, hard and *hand-locked*," can mean nothing but the hauberk of interlinked chain-mail; that garment which, we have so often been told, came to us at some unknown time, from some unknown people, dwelling in some unknown region of the East. If this fabric, which, for brevity, we will call chain-mail, came from the East, where are the eastern monuments that exhibit it? It is not seen in Egyptian, Assyrian, nor Indian sculptures or paintings; and the triumph-scenes of these nations represent in great diversity the numerous tribes of Asia. The same origin has been given to Cannon; but every one who has made any research in this direction knows that the Oriental derivation of this engine has not the smallest foundation in fact[105]. In the Volsunga Saga, a work of the eleventh century, we read that "Sigurd's sides so swelled with rage that the rings of his byrnie were burst asunder;" which could scarcely have happened (adds Von Leber, who notices this passage,) with a garment made of rings sewn contiguously[106]. The well-known enigma of Bishop Aldhelm, written in the eleventh century, so curiously illustrates our inquiry, that we shall be pardoned for reprinting it. It is headed "De Lorica:"—

"Roscida me genuit gelido de viscere tellus:
Non sum setigero lanarum vellere facta:
Licia nulla trahunt, nec garrula fila resultant:
Nec croceâ seres texunt lanugine vermes:
Nec radiis carpor, duro nec pectine pulsor:
Et tamen, en, vestis vulgi sermone vocabor.
Spicula non vereor longis exempta pharetris."

Roy. MS., 15, A.
xvi.

A *lorica* formed of metal, without the aid of any texture of wool or of silk, could scarcely be anything else than a coat of chain-mail. We may further refer to the Bayeux tapestry (Stothard, Plate xvi.), where the *pillards* are appropriating the armour of the slain. The last figure in the second border of that plate is stripping the hauberk over the head of a fallen warrior; and, in thus turning it inside out, discloses the interior of the garment, which exhibits the ring-work exactly in the same manner as it is seen on the outside of others. At a later period, a similar evidence is afforded by the sculptured monumental effigies; the overlapping folds of the hauberk shewing the ring-work on the inside as well as on the outside. Figures of the thirteenth century in the Temple Church and in St. Saviour's Church, London, offer illustrations of this fact. Further instances may be found at Stowe-Nine-Churches in Northamptonshire, and at Aston, Warwickshire; and probably no English county is without similar examples. Compare also the curious fragment of chain-mail found at Stanwick, Yorkshire, and now deposited in the British Museum.

The defence made of iron rings, of which Varro attributes the invention to the Gauls, appears to be no other than the hauberk of chain-mail:—"Lorica a loris, quod de corio crudo pectoralia faciebant, postea succuderunt Galli e ferro sub id vocabulum, ex annulis, ferream tunicam." Whoever may have been the inventors of this armour, the probability seems to be that it came into use gradually: from its costliness and rarity, leaders only could at first obtain it; that, as handicraft improved, and the efficiency of the defence became acknowledged, its adoption was extended, and its costliness diminished. The notion, that in the thirteenth century the hauberk of chain-mail came suddenly and generally into use, is against all known precedent, and contrary to the natural course of human inventions.

Other kinds of body-armour were worn at this time. Charlemagne, as we have seen, was defended by a kind of jazerant-work. Ingulphus tells us that Harold, finding the heavy armour of his troops an incumbrance in their mountain warfare with the Welsh, clothed them in a defence of leather only. Something similar is seen in this figure from Cotton MS., Cleop., C. viii.

The coat here seems to be of hide, with the fur left upon it; a dress still in use among some of the Cossack soldiers of Russia. Wace appears to describe this garment, where, recounting the death of Duke Guillaume Longue-Espée by the traitorous Fauces, he says:—

> "Fauces leva l'espée ke soz sez *peaux* porta,
> Tel l'en dona en chief ke tot l'escervela."—*Rou*, i. 138.

No 14.

Armour of padded-work, a defence of a very high antiquity, and of a very wide adoption, was also probably in vogue; and also coats covered with scale-work; but these are difficult to be identified in the monuments of the time. The hauberks of the Anglo-Saxons at the battle of Hastings are remarked to have been both short and small:—

> "Corz haubers orent è petis,
> E helmes de sor lor vestis."—*Wace.*

In Anglo-Saxon illuminations, a very large majority of the fighting men appear to have no defensive armour at all but the helmet and shield; as in this example from a MS. of *Prudentius*, of the eleventh century, in the Tenison Library. The leg-bands seen on these figures, and on many others of the same period, were in common use among the soldiery. It is a fashion of which we find an early example in the *calceus patricius* of the Romans, and a remnant in the chequered hose of the Scottish Highlanders. Those of the Anglo-Saxons were generally wound round the leg, and then turned down and fastened below the knee. Sometimes they were tied in front; as may be seen in the Ethelwold Benedictional; and compare Stothard's Bayeux Tapestry, Plate iv. Henry of Huntingdon, who wrote in the beginning of the twelfth century, gives us incidentally the full arming of a warrior of the eleventh[107]. When Sigeward, duke of Northumberland, found death approaching him, not on the field of battle, but in the peaceful chamber, he exclaimed: "Quantus pudor me tot in bellis mori non potuisse, ut vaccarum morti cum dedecore reservarer. Induite me saltem lorica mea impenetrabili, præcingite gladio, sublimate galea: scutum in læva, securim auratam mihi ponite in dextra, ut militum fortissimus modo militis moriar. Dixerat: et ut dixerat, armatus honorifice exhalavit."

No 16.

In an age when missiles were much in use; javelins, arrows, and the stones of the mangona and of the slinger; the soldier would naturally employ his first care to the arming of his head. Consequently we find in the monuments of this period that, even when the body appears to have no defensive covering, the head is carefully protected by the helmet.

No 17.

In the beginning, even the helmet was rare among the Teutonic tribes. Tacitus tells us, of the ancient Germans: "Paucis loricæ, vix uni alterive cassis aut galea." And Agathias in the seventh century mentions that few of the Franks had helmets. Leaders, however, wore them. Dagobert, in a contest with the Saxons, received a blow which, dividing his casque, carried away a part of his hair[108]. And when his father, Clotaire II., came to his relief, this latter prince placed himself on the bank of the Veser, announcing his arrival to the Saxon

51

leader by taking off his helmet and displaying his long locks[109]. In the time of Charlemagne, as we have seen from his capitularies, the count is required to furnish troops who are provided with helmets. The fashion of these headpieces we learn from various vellum-paintings of a little later date. We find them to have been hemispherical, conical, of the Phrygian form, combed, and crested: sometimes of a complicated make, with a sort of crocketed ridge[110]; sometimes terminating in a kind of fleur-de-lis[111]. The figure here given from Add. MS., 18,043, a Psalter of the tenth century, affords a good example of the combed helmet. The personage represented is Goliath; and it may be necessary to add, in order to understand the girding of the sword, that the warrior presents his back to us. In lieu of the combed crest, the figure of a boar, sacred to the god Freya, was often placed on the helmets of the pagan Teutons; a practice which at length became so general, that the word *eofor* (boar) was poetically used for the casque itself. Thus, in "Beowulf:" "He commanded them to bring in the boar, an ornament to the head, the helm lofty in war:"—

"eofor heáfod-segn
heaþo-steápne helm," &c.—*Line* 4299.

Again: "The white helm covered the hood of mail, … surrounded with lordly chains, even as in days of yore the weapon-smith had wrought it, had wondrously furnished it, had set it round with the shapes of swine, that never after brand nor war-knife might have power to bite it." (l. 2895.)

Here we see the particular object of this device: it was to act as a holy charm. In Canto 15, the boar seems also to be implied; and in this instance it is "fastened to the helm with wires." "About the crest of the helm, the defence of the head, it held an amulet fastened without with wires, that the sword, hardened with scouring, might not violently injure him when the shield-bearing warrior should go against his foes." Tacitus, in the *Germania*, has a passage curiously illustrating this superstition. The Æstii, he says, "Matrem Deum venerantur: insigne superstitionis, formas aprorum gestant. Id pro armis omnique tutelâ, securum Deæ cultorem etiam inter hostes præstat." Mr. Bateman, in opening a barrow in Derbyshire, was fortunate enough to meet with one of these Northern helms surmounted with the boar crest. The casque is made of iron and horn, with silver-headed rivets. The hog is of iron, having eyes of bronze. See Mr. Bateman's "Antiquities of Derbyshire" for a more full account of this curious relic[112]. The practice of adorning the helmet with a crest is of a very high antiquity, and is first observed among the Asiatics. The Shairetana, first enemies, then allies, of the Egyptian Pharaohs, "wore a helmet ornamented with horns, and frequently surmounted by a crest, consisting of a ball raised upon a small shaft, which is remarkable from being the *earliest instance of a crest*[113]." In the Assyrian monuments, the crested helmet is of frequent occurrence; the form of the crest being generally that of a fan, or of a curved horn, or a kind of crescent, with its cusps turned downwards. See Layard's "Nineveh and its Remains," for examples of all these.

No 18.

In addition to the "white" (or polished) helmet named in a former extract from "Beowulf," we have, at line 5,226, a "brown-coloured" one, (*brun-fagne helm*). This may have been of leather, of iron bearing the stain of years, or even of bronze. On several occasions, relics of bronze have been disinterred which have every appearance of being the framework of helmets. These metal frames—for they occur of iron as well as of bronze—are presumed to have been fixed over a cap of leather. The example here engraved was found in 1844, on the skull of a skeleton exhumed on Leckhampton Hill, near Cheltenham. The material is bronze, but worked very thin. At the summit is a ring, and on one side appears a portion of the chain which seems to have fastened it beneath the chin. The ring may have served to attach a tufted ornament, or a grelot. A Livonian headpiece, engraved on Plate v. of Dr. Bähr's work, has a boss at the summit exactly similar to this, but with the addition of a grelot fixed to the ring. The bronze fragments found by Sir Henry Dryden in a grave at Souldern, Oxfordshire, appear to have formed part of a helmet like that before us[114]. The example of iron, already noticed, discovered by Mr. Bateman, is also of framework, though somewhat differing in pattern from the Leckhampton relic. Another iron framework helmet, of the thirteenth century, was found in an old fort in the Isle of Negropont, and is figured by Hefner in Plate LXIII. of his *Trachten*. Compare also Plate XXXIV., Part ii., of the same book[115]. The secretum engraved in vol. vii. of the Archæological Journal, page 305, is of analogous character: as are also the so-called Spider Helmets, and the "skulls for hats;" examples of which may be seen in the Tower Armories. But the most curious illustration of the purpose of the bronze relic represented in our woodcut, is the helmet proposed for the Royal Artillery in 1854. The metal framing of this was identical in arrangement with the ancient defence; consisting of a hoop encircling the head and two semicircular bands, crossing each other at the crown, and surmounted by a metal knob. The metal in this case was brass, and it did not greatly differ in substance from the ancient bronze. The cap beneath was of felt. In Anglo-Saxon illuminations, it is not unusual to see headpieces in which bands of gold-colour traverse a ground of different hue; and it seems not improbable that these examples may represent the kind of helmet under consideration. Similar banded casques occur in the Bayeux tapestry, in the pictures of the Painted Chamber at Westminster, and in other monuments. See also Archæol. Journ., vol. xii. p. 9.

The bronze helmet has also been discovered in Scotland. Dr. Wilson tells us that "part of a rudely-adorned helmet of bronze was found in Argyleshire[116]." Another bronze headpiece is preserved in the Copenhagen Museum, and Professor Thomsen mentions similar ones, "overlaid with gold." (Manual.)

A helmet of wood is mentioned by Wace as being worn by one of the Anglo-Saxon combatants at the battle of Hastings:—

> "Un helme aveit tot fait de *fust*,
> Ke colp[117] el chief ne recéust.
> A sez dras[118] l'aveit atachié,
> Et envirun son col lacié."

A Norman knight attacked him:—

> "Sor li helme l'Engleiz féri,
> De suz les oils[119] li abati,
> Sor li viare[120] li pendi,
> E li Engleiz sa main tendi,
> Li helme voleit[121] suz lever,
> E son viaire delivrer;
> E cil li a un colp doné,
> E sa hache à terre chaï[122]."

In book-illuminations of this period the helmet is frequently coloured yellow, which may either signify bronze or gilding. A crown is sometimes added, not in the case of kings alone, but of distinguished personages generally. One of the crowned figures in our woodcut, No. 13, represents the patriarch Abraham. The nasal appears to have been given to the helmet about the end of the tenth century: of which an early example is furnished in the figure of a warrior in Cotton MS., Tiberius, C. vi. fol. 9, a work of this period. By the middle of the next century, its adoption has become general, and in the Bayeux Tapestry it is worn equally by Norman and Saxon.

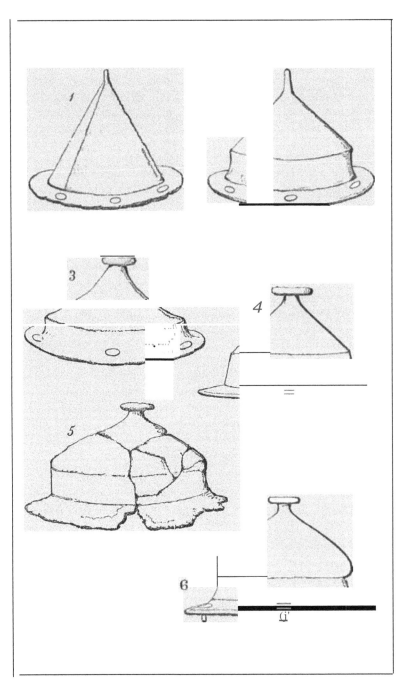

PLATE XIX.

To a soldiery with whom body-armour appears to have been a secondary consideration, the SHIELD would be of the first consequence. We find, therefore, the Northern warrior seldom unaccompanied by this useful defence. Leader and retainer, horseman and foot-soldier,—all are equipped with the target. Its form was usually round, though in the pictures, being seen in profile, it often has the appearance of an oval. And, as the plump-cheeked houris of the East were called "moon-faced damsels," so the round targets of the Teutons were named by the poets "moony shields." They were convex, and in the centre was a boss of metal, generally terminating in a button or in a spike, but sometimes without either. The spiked shield was no doubt used as an offensive arm. The buttons are sometimes plated with silver, or tinned, as are the heads of the rivets remaining in the edge of the umbo. Across the hollow of the boss was fixed a handle of wood covered with iron; and by this handle the shield was held at arm's length, the hand entering the hollow of the boss: see woodcut, No. 13. In the Wilbraham Cemetery was found the umbo of a shield to[Pg 73]
[Pg 74] which the handle was still attached by its rivets. (See fig. 10 of our xxth plate.) The shield was sometimes strengthened with strips of iron fixed across the inside; these strips being prolongations of the handle just described. Such a shield-handle was found at Envermeu by the Abbé Cochet, and is figured on Plate XVI. of his work. In this example the handle has a *single* strip on each side, running towards the edge of the shield. A similar one was found in a Merovingian cemetery near Troyes. In a Frankish grave at Londinières was discovered a variety of this type, in which the strips proceeding from the handle were *three* on each side, radiating towards the rim. This very curious example is engraved in the *Normandie Souterraine*, Plate VIII. Others were found in the recent excavations in the Isle of Wight.

The body of the shield was usually of wood; the lime having a marked preference. Thus, in "Beowulf[123]," the heroic Wiglaf "seized his shield, the yellow lindenwood" (*geolwe linde*). And a spell preserved in Harl. MS., 585, f. 186, has:—

> "Stod under linde
> under leohtum scylde:"

"I stood under my linden shield, beneath my light shield." In the Anglo-Saxon poem of "Judith:"—

> "The warriors marched:
> the chieftains to the war,
> protected with targets,

with arched linden shields."
(*hwealfum lindum*[124].)

In a fragment on the battle of Maldon:—

"Leofsunu spake
and lifted his linden shield."
(*and his linde ahof*[125].)

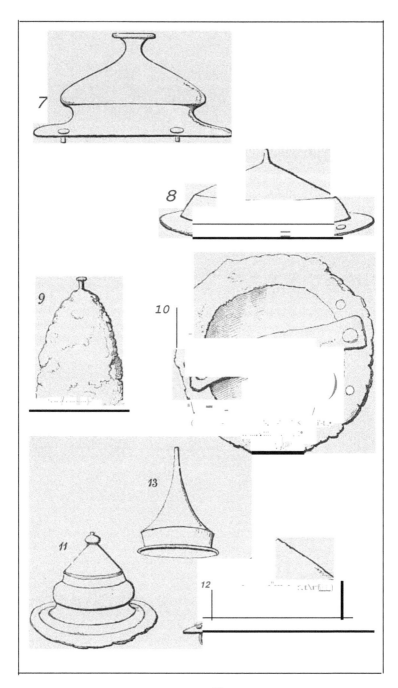

PLATE XX.

And the Saxon Chronicle tells us, in recounting the defeat of Anlaf in 937, how King Athelstan and his heroes

"the board-walls clove:
and hewed the war-lindens."

Leather was sometimes used in the construction of shields, as we learn from the Laws of Æthelstan, which forbid the employment of sheepskins for this purpose under a penalty of thirty shillings. In an example from the cemetery at Linton Heath, Cambridgeshire, the leather covering seemed to have been stretched over the iron umbo as well as over the wooden surface of the shield[126]. The edge was protected by a rim of metal. Portions of these rims have been found in the graves, both in England and on the continent; and as they present segments of circles, become of use in determining the shape of the shields themselves. In the Museum of Schwerin is an example of the metal rim which is complete: it is circular, and the central boss is also present.

The oval shield appears in a few examples only. One was found among the graves explored at Oberflacht, in Suabia; another is figured by Silvestre, (vol. i. pl. CXLIV.) from a Longobardic miniature of the eleventh century; and a third occurs in the Bayeux Tapestry, Plate XVI. The surface of the Northern shields was painted in various fanciful devices, sometimes heightened with gilding. And, as Christianity was embraced by the various Northern tribes, the cross became a frequent decoration. The encomiast of Queen Emma, in describing the fleet of Canute the Great, says: "Erant ibi scutorum tot genera, ut crederis adesse omnium populorum agmina. Si quando sol illis jubar immiscerit radiorum, hinc resplenduit fulgor armorum, illinc vero flamma dependentium scutorum[127]."

Among the devices, there is nothing of a heraldic character, and even as late as the time of the Bayeux Tapestry, as Stothard has well remarked, "we do not find any particular or distinguished person twice bearing the same device[128]."

In the accompanying figure from Cotton MS., Cleopatra, C. viii., we observe that the Anglo-Saxon horseman carried his shield, when not in use, slung at his back. The knights of the fourteenth century carried their helmets in the same manner, as may be seen in the fine manuscript of the *Roman du Roi Meliadus*, Additional MSS., 12,228. Besides the ordinary Northern shields, we sometimes find them represented of so large a size as to cover the whole person. In Harleian MS. 2,908, fol. 53, are two such, but perhaps mere exaggerations of the draughtsman. Shields of this kind were, however, certainly in use in the East at an early date, and may be seen in Egyptian,

Assyrian, and Indian monuments[129].

No. 21.

It has been conjectured that the bronze coatings of shields which have from time to time been discovered in this country, and commonly attributed to the Ancient Britons, may belong to the Anglo-Saxon period: while we admit this probability, we must not forget that they have not yet been found in the Anglo-Saxon graves.

The shields placed in the graves were the ordinary "lindens," of which no part commonly remains but the metal boss and handle. The chief varieties of forms offered by the bosses will be found in our Plates xix. and xx., figs. 1 to 10; all from English tombs[130]. Similar relics have been dug up in Scotland; of which No. 11 in our Plate offers an example. This was procured from a tomb in the county of Moray, accompanied with fragments of oak and remains of the hero's horse and its bridle. See Dr. Wilson's "Archæology of Scotland," to which we are indebted for this specimen. On the continent similar objects have been found, differing but slightly from our own examples. No. 12 is from the cemetery at Selzen, in Rhenish Hesse. No. 13 is from a Danish tomb. See also the examples given in Worsaae's Copenhagen Museum, p. 68. The shields of the Danes appear to have been ornamented with gold and colours, the favourite hue being red. In Sæmund's poetical "Edda" we read of a "red shield with a golden border," and Giraldus de Barri tells us that the Irish "carried red shields, in imitation of the Danes." Some of the Danish shields, like the weapons, were inscribed with runes[131]. In the tumulus opened at Caenby, in Lincolnshire, believed to have been that of a Danish viking, part of a wooden shield was procured, ornamented with plates of silver and bronze, bearing the serpentine and scroll patterns so characteristic of this period. These fragments are engraved in the seventh volume of the Archæological Journal.

The *guige* or strap by which the target was occasionally suspended from the combatant's neck, leaving the hands free to direct the steed or ply the weapon, appears (at least during the later days of Saxon rule) to have been in use among our countrymen, as well as with their Norman neighbours. Of Harold's nobles, Wace tells us:—

"Chescun out son haubert vestu,
Espée ceinte, *el col l'escu.*"—*Rom. de Rou*, ii. 213.

And in the Bayeux Tapestry, the kite-shield thus fixed may be seen on the English side.

The place occupied by the shield in the graves of the Frankish, Germanic, and Scandinavian heroes is by no means uniform. It has been found on the breast, on the right arm, upon the knees, and beneath the head. It is by the position of the umbo in the grave that this fact has been exactly ascertained. Examples will be found in the Ozingell Cemetery, in the explorations at Harnham Hill (*Archæologia*, vol. xxxv.), in the Selzen find, in the *Normandie Souterraine*, and in the account of the cemetery at Linton Heath (Archæol. Journ., vol. xi. p. 108).

The Horse furniture of the Northern cavalry appears to have been usually very simple. By referring to our engravings, Nos. 16 and 21, it will be seen that the saddle was provided with girth, breastplate, and crupper, the latter being fixed to the sides of the saddle: pendent ornaments are attached to the bridle, breastplate, and crupper. From the poem of "Beowulf" we learn that the war-horse was occasionally furnished with much costliness:—

"Then did the Refuge of warriors command eight horses, ornamented on the cheek, to be brought into the palace: … on one of which stood a saddle variegated with work, made valuable with treasure: that was the war-seat of a lofty king when the son of Healfdene would perform the game of swords."—*Canto* 15.

A donation of the Anglo-Saxon king Ethelbert affords another example:
—"Missurum etiam argenteum, scapton aureum, item *sellam cum freno aureo gemmis exornatam*, speculum argenteum, armilaisia oloserica, camisiam ornatam prædicto monasterio gratanter obtuli[132]."

No. 22.

As it was an occasional practice to bury the horse of the hero in the same grave with his master, the metal portions of the fitments have been preserved to our time. Examples of stirrups may be seen in the *Annaler for Nordisk Oldkyndighed*, in Worsaae's Copenhagen Museum, and in *Die Gräber der Liven*: all these are of a single piece, having a loop for the attachment of the leather. The bits are of two kinds,—snaffles with rings at the sides, and snaffles with long cheeks. The example here given is from a Kentish barrow opened by the Earl of Londesborough. A similar one is in the Livonian collection of the British Museum. Compare also the York volume of the Archæological Institute, page 29; Worsaae's Copenhagen Museum, pp. 70, 95 and 96; and M. Troyon's paper in the *Archæologia*, vol. xxxv. p. 396, and Plate xviii. The snaffle with cheeks was found among the Wilbraham relics[133], and occurs also in the Selzen Cemetery[134]. A very curious variety, in which the snaffle is of iron, while the cheeks are of bronze richly foliated, was discovered in an old fort at Lough Fea, in Ireland, and is engraved in the third volume of the Archæological Journal. In a tumulus opened in Denmark were found the remains of a bridle which had been covered with thin plates of silver.

A good example of the Anglo-Saxon Saddle, seen without the rider, occurs in Cotton MS., Claudius, B. iv.; which has been engraved by Strutt in the *Horda*. See also our cut from Cleopatra, C. viii. (page 77) where the breastplate, crupper, and single girth are very clearly made out.

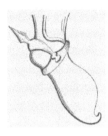

No. 23.

The Spur of this period consisted of a single goad, sometimes of a lozenge form, sometimes a plain spike. The shanks were straight. The following illustration of the lozenge goad is from the bronze monument of Rudolf von Schwaben, in the Cathedral of Merseburg, a work of the eleventh century[135]. A very similar example, dug up in railway excavations near Nottingham, has lately been added to the Tower collection. This is of iron. Compare the Swiss specimen engraved by M. Troyon in vol. xxxv. of the *Archæologia*, Plate xvii. This also has a lozenge goad, but the neck of the spur is much longer. A Livonian example in the British Museum has the goad in the form of a plain quadrangular spike. The conical spike is seen among the Danish relics figured on pages 70 and 95 of Mr. Worsaae's "Copenhagen Museum." A very curious variety was found in the excavations of the Anglo-Saxon cemetery at Linton Heath, and is figured in the eleventh volume of the Archæological Journal. The buckles in this specimen, instead of being attached to the strap, form part of the spur itself; being contrived at the ends of the shanks.

Among the many curious usages revealed by the examination of the ancient tombs, not the least singular is the practice of burying the equestrian warrior with a single spur. This fact has been noticed, not alone among the pagan Northmen, but as late as the thirteenth century; and it does not rest on the doubtful evidence of careless observers, but has been vouched by the testimony of skilful and practised archæologists. It has been further remarked that the spur, in all such cases, is attached to the left heel. M. Troyon, in his excavations in the Colline de Chavannes, Canton de Vaud[136], found three spurs, all of different sizes, which he therefore concludes "ont appartenu chacun à des cavaliers différents." At Bel-Air, near Lausanne, this gentleman found an interment where a single spur had been fixed to the left heel of the entombed warrior. And in a note to his interesting memoir on the exploration of the Colline de Chavannes, he says: "J'ai retrouvé quelquefois des éperons dans des tombes antiques, mais le mort n'en portait jamais qu'un seul, qui était fixé au pied gauche." The similar instance which has been noticed in an interment of the thirteenth century is that recorded in the fourth volume of the Archæological Journal, page 59. A knight of the Brougham family, found buried in the chancel of the church at Brougham, in Westmoreland, had a single iron spur "round the left heel." "No spur was found upon the right heel." This knight presented the further singularity of having been buried cross-legged[137].

However highly his steed might be prized by the Northern warrior, it was not alone in feats of horsemanship that he was required to excel. The youthful Grymr, in the old poem of "Karl and Grymr," "as he grew up, was accustomed to make his sword ruddy in the warlike play of shields; to climb the mountains; to wrestle; to play well the game of chess; to study the science of the stars; to throw the stone; and to practise such other sports as were held in estimation."

Olaff Trygvason, according to an old Norwegian chronicle quoted by Pontoppidan, "could climb the rock of Smalserhorn, and fix his shield on the top; he could walk round the outside of a boat upon the oars, while the men were rowing; he could play with three darts, throwing them into the air alternately, and always keeping two of them up: he was ambidexter, and could cast two darts at once with equal force; and he was so famous a bowman that none could equal him." At a little later date, Kali, an earl of the Orkneys, boasts of his acquirements:—"I know," says he, "nine several arts. I am skilful at the game of chess, I can engrave runic letters, I am expert at my book, I can handle the tools of the smith, I can traverse the snow on wooden skates, I excel in shooting with the bow, I ply the oar with address, I can sing to the harp, and I compose verses[138]."

In the tenth century, Richard, duke of Normandy "—

— sout en Daneiz, en Normant[139] parler:
Une chartre sout lire, è li parz deviser:
Li pere l'out bien fet duire è doutriner.
De tables è d'eschez sout compaignon mater:
Bien sout paistre[140] un oisel è livrer è porter:
En bois sout cointement è berser[141] è vener.
As talevas[142] se sout bien couvrir è moler[143],
Mestre pié destre avant è entre d'els dobler:
Talons sout remuer è retraire è noxer,
Saillir deverz senestre è treget[144] tost geter:
C'est un colp damageux ki ne s'en seit garder,
Mais l'en ne s'i deit lungement demorer."

Roman de Rou, vol. i. p.
126.

Of the STANDARDS in use at this period, the notices that have reached us are neither numerous nor clear. In Asser's "Life of King Alfred" we read, that the Christian English gained a signal victory over the pagan Danes in Devon, slaying their king, and capturing "among other things, the standard called Raven; and they say that the three sisters of Hingwar and Hubba, daughters of Lodobroch, wove that flag and got it ready in one day[145]. They say, moreover, that in every battle, wherever that flag went before them, if they were to gain the victory, a live crow would appear flying on the middle of the flag; but if they were doomed to be defeated, it would hang down motionless. And this was often proved to be so." (Sub an. 878.) The Danish chronicles and sagas, however, make no mention of this Raven standard. Mr. Worsaae ("Danes in England") gives the engraving of a coin of Anlaf, on which he recognises the national device, and finds it again in that figure of a bird on one of the flags of the Bayeux tapestry; "for it is very natural," he says, "that the Scandinavian vikings, or Normans, who had achieved such famous conquests under Odin's Raven, should continue to preserve this sign,"&c.

Ancient evidences are not agreed as to the Anglo-Saxon standard used at the battle of Hastings. William of Poitiers describes it as "memorabile vexillum Heraldi, hominis armati imaginem intextam habens ex auro purissimo." Malmesbury follows him: "vexillum—quod erat in hominis pugnantis figura, auro et lapidibus arte sumptuosa contextum."

In the Bayeux tapestry this design does not appear, but the old Dragon Standard, derived by the Northern nations from the Romans. And it will be observed that the dragon of Harold is not a picture painted on a flag; but, like the Roman *draco*, a figure fixed by the head to a staff, with its body and tail floating away into the air. Compare the representations on the Trajan and Antonine columns, and in the Bayeux tapestry. The dragon is found also among the continental Saxons. Of Witikind we are told: "Hic arripiens Signum, quod apud eo habebatur sacrum, leonis atque *draconis* et desuper aquilæ volantis insignitum effigie[146]," &c. And this device of a dragon appears to have been in use till at length displaced by the more exact distinctions of hereditary heraldry.

The well-known custom mentioned by Plot, of the inhabitants of Burford, in Oxfordshire, carrying the figure of a dragon yearly "up and down the town in great Jollity, to which they added the Picture of a Giant," in memory of a victory over Ethelbald, king of Mercia, in which this prince lost his "Banner, whereon was depicted a Golden Dragon;" seems entitled to greater consideration than most of the customs of old times. The Dragon Standard of the Anglo-Saxons is a fact substantiated by many monuments; and the portraying a vanquished enemy under the lineaments of a hideous giant, is a practice which has had the sanction of all times and all nations.

A very curious kind of flag occurs in the Anglo-Saxon manuscript of *Prudentius* in the Tenison Library. It is suspended from a horizontal bar near the spear-head, after the manner of a sail looped up to its yard, and from the side hangs a kind of fringe. It decreases below, presenting altogether a triangular form, and seems to be the same object as that figured by Mr. Worsaae, from a coin of Anlaf, in his "Danes in England."

The celebrated *Carrocio* or Car Standard of the Italians appears to have been invented during the war between the Milanese and the Emperor Conrad, about 1035, by Heribert, the archbishop of Milan. This car had four wheels, and was drawn by four yoke of oxen, caparisoned in red. The chariot itself was red: in the midst of it was a tall red mast, surmounted by a golden globe, and bearing the banner of the city: beneath the banner was a large crucifix, of which "the extended arms appeared to bless the troops." A kind of platform in front of the *carrocium* was occupied by a company of chosen heroes, elected for its especial defence; while, on a similar platform behind, the trumpets of the army contributed by their inspiriting strains to give confidence to all around. Before leaving the city, mass was solemnised upon the platform of the chariot, and not unfrequently a chaplain was assigned to accompany it into the field of battle, and to give absolution to the wounded. This device of the Milanese was soon imitated by others of the Italian cities, and with all it was held to be in the last degree humiliating to abandon the *carrocio* to the enemy[147]. Other origins have, however, been given to the Car Standard. It has been attributed to the Saracens; and the monk Egidius ascribes its invention to the Duke of Louvain, who caused the banner which had been embroidered by the Queen of England to be placed in a superb chariot drawn by four oxen. The Italians have a large balance of evidence on their side.

Of the various kinds of "GYNS" in use, the notices are not very distinct. And a chief source of the vagueness arises from the circumstance that, as the earliest chroniclers wrote in Latin, they applied the names of Roman engines to instruments which probably differed both in form and principle from their ancient prototypes. Tacitus, indeed, tells us that the barbarians borrowed these engines from those of the Romans; deserters or prisoners from whose ranks taught to the Northmen the art of their construction. But there seems good reason to believe that the motive principle of the classic periers, *torsion*, was no longer in use among the middle-age engineers: their instruments consisting of a lever furnished at one extremity with a sling and at the other with a heavy weight; the sudden liberation of the latter contributing the force necessary to propel the stone from the sling. See this subject fully discussed in the second volume of the *Études sur l'Artillerie* of the Emperor of the French; and compare the evidences furnished by monuments of the twelfth and thirteenth centuries, given in later pages of this work.

In 585, we learn from Gregory of Tours, that the Battering Ram and the Testudo were employed by the Burgundians in the siege of Comminges[148]. This Tortoise, or screen for the propellers of the Ram, is described by the translator of Vegecius in 1408 under the name of the "Snayle or Welke[149]:" "For, righte as the snaile hath his hous over hym where he walkethe or resteth, and oute of his hous he shetethe his hede whan he wolle, and draweth hym inne a-yene, so doth this gynne." In the ninth century we obtain considerable light on this subject from the curious description of the Siege of Paris, written in Latin verse by Abbo, a monk of St. Germain-des-Prez, who was an eye-witness of the events he records. He names the Musculus and the Pluteus, both of which were contrivances to shelter the besiegers while at work; the Balista and Mangana, machines for casting large stones; the Catapulta, which cast both stones and darts; the Terebra, a spiked beam for boring into the walls; and the Falarica, a gyn throwing darts to which burning substances were affixed; a terrible instrument in those days, when the roofs of houses were almost invariably covered with thatch.

The Moveable Towers formed of wood, in imitation of those of the Romans, and placed by the walls of city or castle in order to bring the assailants to a level with the defenders, are first mentioned in medieval annals under the eleventh century; but they play no conspicuous part in the military history of these days till the succeeding century, when their employment appears to have been frequent. In 1025, Eudes, comte de Chartres, is said to have used the Moveable Tower in besieging the Castle of Montbrol, near Tours; and so high was it, that it overtopped the keep-tower of the fortress[150].

In the east of Europe, the Greek Fire had been known as early as the year 673; when, according to the historians of the Lower Empire, Callinicus, the philosopher, taught the use of it to the Greeks. He himself had probably derived the knowledge of this composition from the Arabians; for, though powder acting by *detonation* (and consequently cannon) appears to have been first produced in Europe, and that not earlier than the beginning of the fourteenth century, the Asiatics had the use of powder that would *fuse* at a very early date. The Greek Fire was discharged from tubes, which could be turned in any direction. The Princess Anna Comnena, in the *Alexiad*, describes its use, as it was employed by the Emperor Alexis against the Pisans, from tubes fixed at the prow of his vessels:—"They (the Pisans) were astonished to see fire, which by its nature ascends, directed against them, at the will of their enemy, downwards and on each side." The receipt for the composition of the Greek Fire may be found in the Treatise of Marcus Grecus. The terrors of these early fire-mixtures were enhanced by the belief that not only they, but the flames kindled by them, were inextinguishable by water: "de quibus fit incendiarium quod ab aqua non extinguitur[151]." The

Greek Fire did not, however, reach the west of Europe till a much later period. It was objected against its use, that such an agent was contrary to the spirit of religion and the nobleness of chivalry: it was felt that a weapon which could be used alike by the weak and the strong, by the humble and the powerful, might become a dangerous rival to the knightly lance and panoply.

[Pg 91]
[Pg 92]

No. 24.

PLATE XXV.

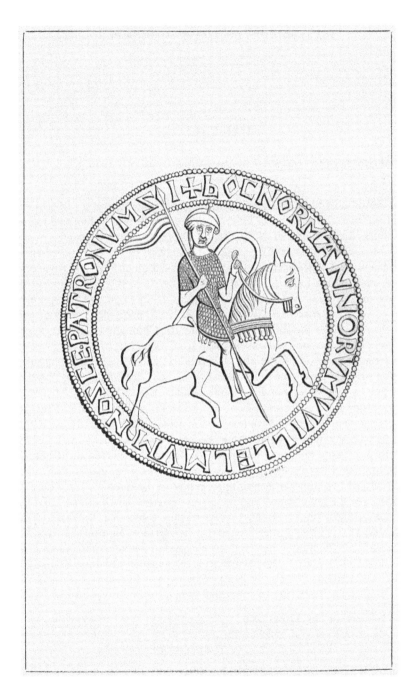

PART II.

FROM THE NORMAN CONQUEST OF ENGLAND TO THE END OF THE TWELFTH CENTURY.

For the period now to be examined, namely, from about the year 1066 to the close of the twelfth century, our chief evidences are still the illuminations of manuscripts, the writings of chroniclers and poets, tapestry-pictures, ivory carvings and metal chasings. The valuable testimonies of the graves are lost to us; but a new source of information is opened to our inquiries in the royal and baronial seals, which from the second half of the eleventh century appear in great abundance wherever the feudal system is in vogue. Among these various evidences, there are two which, for our particular purpose, are especially valuable,—the Bayeux tapestry and the Chronicle of Robert Wace. There seems to be no reasonable doubt of this tapestry having been embroidered at the close of the eleventh century; and whoever has carefully examined it, will be at once convinced that it was wrought, not by courtly ladies, but by the ruder hands of the ordinary tapestry-workers. Curious analogy is found in the decorations of *subsellæ* of a somewhat later date[152]. The especial value of the Chronicle of the Dukes of Normandy is in the minuteness with which Wace delights to describe the incidents of knightly achievement. Taking his crude facts from William of Jumièges and Dudo of St. Quentin, he fills up their outlines with unwearying elaboration. Not content with drily noting the gathering of a host or the issue of an onslaught, he tells us how the levies came into the camp "by twos, and by threes, and by fours, and by fives," and with what weapons they contended, the material of their staves, and the length and breadth of their blades. He himself lived so near the time of which he writes, and the changes in the interval were so few, that his descriptions have, in most instances, the exactness of those of an eye-witness. The incidents of Duke William's Conquest of England he learns from the lips of his own father, who lived probably in the eleventh century:—

> "—— jo oï dire à mon pere:
> Bien m'en sovint, maiz varlet ere."
> *Roman de Rou*, l. 11564.

We must still, however, keep in view that Wace, like all writers and

70

illuminators of the middle-ages, does not hesitate to fill up his pictures from the scenes around him; so that, while we concede him a large measure of authority, especially for the events near his own time, we must on some occasions withhold our confidence, when his testimony is not in accordance with evidence which is strictly cotemporary.

With the feudal system was introduced a scheme of military rank which was altogether distinct from social position. Esquire, knight, and banneret had no necessary connection with prince, baron, or private person. The heir of a crown might be but an esquire; a fortunate soldier often became a knight. The esquire was the aspirant to knightly honours, and patiently served his apprenticeship to arms in the court of his prince or the hall of some neighbouring baron. At the age of twenty-one he was eligible to knighthood: he became, if he had property enough to support the dignity, a knight-bachelor: "s'il a bien de quoi maintenir l'estat de chevalerie; car aultrement ne lui est honneur, et vault mieulx estre bon escuyer que ung poure chevalier[153]." In the field, the knight's contingent was led under a Pennon, a flag that differed from the square Banner of the banneret in being pointed at the fly. The dignity of the Knight Banneret required a retinue of at least fifty men-at-arms with their followers, so that it could only be enjoyed by the rich. The chronicles of the middle-ages are full of examples in which the knight who has distinguished himself on the field of battle declines this dignity on the plea of inadequate funds. When accepted, the Pennon of the knight was often at once converted on the spot into a Banner; as in the instance recorded by Olivier de la Marche:—"Si bailla le Roi d'Armes (de la Toison d'Or) un couteau au Duc (de Bourgogne), et prit le pennon en ses mains, et le bon Duc, sans oster le gantelet de la main senestre, fit un tour autour de sa main de la queue du pennon, et de l'autre main coupa ledit pennon et demeura quarré; et la Banniere faite[154]." Froissart offers several similar instances.

The feudal Levy was conducted on the very simple principle, that they who held the land should defend the land, and contribute to the king's army in proportion to the extent of their holdings. Those who could not serve in person, as clerics and ladies, were bound to furnish substitutes. The various contingents due from the vassals were carefully recorded in rolls; and in the *Milice Française* of Père Daniel is preserved a curious note of such a roll, of the time of Philippe Auguste, in which the contributors to the host are arranged in the following order: archbishops, bishops, abbots, dukes, earls, barons, castellans, vavassors, knights-banneret, and knights[155]. The usual time of service at this period was forty days: any further attendance was voluntary, and was probably much dependent on the prospect of booty.

That knight and esquire were not necessarily of gentle blood, might be proved by numerous ancient evidences: one or two may suffice. Matthew Paris, under the year 1250, tells us that the king "gave a charter of the liberty of warren in the land of Saint Alban's to a certain knight named Geoffry, although not descended from noble or knightly ancestors." This knight had obtained the privilege "from having married the sister of the king's clerk, John Maunsell." The "lady's name was Clarissa, and she was the daughter of a country priest, but exalted herself in her pride above her station, to the derision of all." Froissart, in the fourteenth century, gives us the history of Jacques le Gris, the bosom-friend of the Earl of Alençon,—"qui n'étoit pas de trop haute affaire, mais un écuyer de basse lignée qui s'étoit avancé, ainsi que fortune en avance plusieurs; et quand ils sont tous élevés et ils cuident être au plus sûr, fortune les retourne en la boue et les met plus has que elle ne les a eus de commencement[156]."

In fact, numerous exceptional cases might be adduced on almost every point of knightly usage, and to chronicle the whole would be a labour of many pages. A detail of such usages (the education of the varlets, the probation of the knights, the ceremonies of investiture, and the institutions of the various brotherhoods) is by no means within the province of this work. A large amount of information on these points will be found in the *Mémoires sur l'ancienne Chevalerie* of St. Palaye, and in the various works of Ducange; from whose pages numerous references will lead the more critical investigator to a wide range of valuable authorities. An able sketch of the Feudal System, as it existed in Italy, appears in the first volume of Sismondi's *Républiques Italiennes au Moyen-âge*, p. 80, sq.

Besides the feudal troops already noticed, there was a more general levy, when any pressing danger menaced the state. Thus, in 1124, Louis le Gros met the threatened invasion of the Emperor Henry V. by raising an army of more than 200,000 men[157]. And under Philippe le Bel, we have an ordinance calling upon all his subjects, "noble and non-noble, of whatsoever condition they be, between the ages of eighteen and sixty," to be ready to take the field. A similar provision was found in England. The *Posse Comitatûs*, which was under the command of the sheriffs of the various counties, included every freeman capable of bearing arms between the ages of fifteen and sixty. In 1181, Henry II. fixed an assize of arms, by which all his subjects, being freemen, were bound to be in readiness for the defence of the realm, "Whosoever holds one knight's fee shall have a coat-of-fence (*loricam*), a helmet (*cassidem*), a shield, and a lance; and every knight as many coats, helmets, shields, and lances, as he shall have knights' fees in his domain. Every free layman, having in rent or chattels the value of sixteen marks, shall have a coat-of-fence, helmet, shield and lance. Every free layman having in chattels ten marks, shall have a haubergeon (*halbergellum*), iron cap and lance (*capelet ferri et lanceam*). All burgesses and the whole community of freemen shall have each a 'wambais,' iron cap, and lance. On the death of any one having these arms, they shall remain to his heir. Any one having more arms than required by this assize, shall sell or give them, or so alienate them, that they may be employed in the king's service. No Jew shall have in his custody any coat-of-fence or haubergeon (*loricam vel halbergellum*), but shall sell it or give it, or in other manner so dispose of it that it shall remain to the king's use. No man shall carry arms out of the kingdom, or sell arms to be so carried. None but a freeman to be admitted to take the oath of arms (*et præcepit rex, quod nullus reciperetur ad sacramentum armorum nisi liber homo*[158])." In this curious document it will be remarked that the old national weapon, the axe, is altogether omitted; and the bow, which afterwards became so effective an arm among the infantry of this country, is equally unnoticed. The extensive levy indicated in these passages was clearly that of the so-called *Arrière-ban*, the *Milice des Communes*, or *Communitates Parochiarum*; troops who marched under the banners of their respective parishes. For in an ordinance of Charles VI. of France, in 1411, we find the *ban* and *arrière-ban* very exactly defined:—"Mandons et convoquons par devant nous, tous noz hommes et vassaulx tenant de nous, tant en fiefs qu'en arrière-fiefs: et aussi des gens des bonnes villes de notre royaume qui out accoustumé d'eulx armer par forme et manière de arrière-ban[159]."

As the vassals were not always disposed to exchange hawk and hound for lance and destrier, and as kings found themselves but ill-served by barons who had become almost as powerful as themselves, a plan was devised, by which both were relieved from this embarrassment of feudal relations. The vassal compounded by a money-payment called Scutage for the service due to his lord; and the lord, with the proceeds of this shield-tax, obtained the aid of foreign soldiery. Henry II. in England, and Philip Augustus in France, employed these mercenaries, who were called Coterelli, Rutarii, Bascli, and Brabantiones, names derived from their condition or country[160]. William the Conqueror, Wace tells us, had mercenary troops mixed with his feudal followers:—

"De mainte terre out soldéiers:
Cels por terre, cels por déniers."—*Rom. de Rou*, l. 13797.

Again:—

"Dunc vindrent soldéirs à lui:
Et uns è uns, è dui è dui,
E quatre è quatre, è cinc è sis,
E set è wit, è nof è dis:
E li Dus toz les reteneit:

73

Mult lor donout è prameteit.

Alquanz soldées demandoent,
Livreisuns è duns covetoent."—*Line* 11544.

Besides the troops enumerated above, the King's Body-guard became a corps of some celebrity at the close of the twelfth century. Philip Augustus is said to have instituted this corps in the Holy Land, to protect his person from the machinations of the Old Man of the Mountain; and in imitation of his ally, Richard of England embodied a similar force. The *Servientes armorum, Sergens d'armes*, or *Sergens à maces*, were armed *cap-à-pie*, and besides their distinctive weapon, the mace, carried a bow and arrows[161], and of course a sword. In the fourteenth century they had a lance[162]. In the beginning of the fifteenth century, as we learn from the curious incised stones[163] formerly placed in the church of their brotherhood, St. Catherine-du-val, at Paris, and now preserved in the Church of St. Denis, the *sergens d'armes* were still clad in complete armour, their weapons being a mace and sword. The number of these guards at their first institution is not clear, but in the time of Louis VI. of France they were *reduced* to a hundred. It must be borne in mind that the name of *serviens* or *sergent*, as applied to military persons, had a much wider signification than this of a body-guard. It often included all beneath the dignity of a knight.

The Archers in the army of William the Conqueror fulfilled those duties of preliminary fight which at a later period fell to the lot of the musquetiers, and in our own day have passed to the cannonier. The Norman bowmen are the first of the invading troops to set foot on English soil:—

"Li archiers sunt primiers iessuz:
El terrain sunt primiers venuz.
Dunc a chescun son arc tendu,
Couire et archaiz el lez pendu.
Tuit furent rez è tuit tondu,
De cors dras furent tuit vestu."—*Rom. de Rou*, l. 11626.

These shaven and shorn, short-coated archers, with their quivers hung at their side, are exactly reproduced in the Bayeux tapestry (Plates XIII., XV., and XVI.):—

"La gent à pié fu bien armée:

Chescun porta arc et espée.
Sor lor testes orent chapels,
A lor piez liez lor panels.
Alquanz unt bones coiriés,
K'il unt à lor ventre liés.
Plusors orent vestu gambais,
Couires orent ceinz et archais.

Cil a pié aloient avant
Serréement, lors ars portant."—*Line* 12805.

From this curious passage it appears that the archers of William were not a particular and distinctly organized corps, but that *all the foot* were armed with the bow. The caps and boots are clearly portrayed in the Bayeux tapestry; and from this valuable monument we obtain an exact confirmation of the statement of Wace, that some of the archers were clad in armour. See Plate XIII. We must observe also, that the advantage of a close formation was thoroughly appreciated at this day. The serried order of the foot noted above was also adopted by the cavalry:—

"Cil à cheval è cil à pié
Tindrent lor eire è lor compas,
Serréement lor petit pas,
Ke l'un l'altre ne trespassout,
Ne n'aprismout ne n'esloignout.
Tuit aloent serréement,
E tuit aloent fièrement."—*Line* 12825.

In Plate XIII. of the Bayeux tapestry, we find an archer who carries his quiver, not "el lez pendu," but slung at his back, so that the arrows present themselves at the right shoulder. In Plate XVI. we have a mounted archer joining a group of knights in the chase of the discomfited Saxons; from which we may venture to infer, that on the rout of an enemy it was the practice of such bowmen as could obtain horses, to act with the cavalry in the pursuit of the flying foe.

GREAT SEAL OF WILLIAM RUFUS.

No. 26.

If the Norman archers were for the most part clad in "cors dras," the horsemen were fully furnished in the choicest military equipment of the day: —

> "Dunc issirent li Chevalier,
> Tuit armé è tuit haubergié[164]:
> Escu al col, healme lacié:
> Ensemble vindrent al gravier[165],
> Chescun armé sor son destrier.
> Tuit orent ceintes les espées,
> El plain vindrent lances levées.
> Li Barunz orent gonfanons,
> Li chevaliers orent penons."—*Rom. de Rou*, l. 11639.

76

"Chevaliers ont haubers è branz,
Chauces de fer, helmes luizanz,
Escuz as cols, as mains lor lances."—*Line* 12813.

In the south, military science was already so far advanced that a Code for the discipline of troops had been established. The rules laid down by the Emperor Frederic for the control of his army in Italy in 1158, have been preserved by Radevicus of Frisinga[166], and are given by Sismondi[167].

Wherever the feudal system had taken root, a similar arming and similar tactics prevailed. The military

"Chevals quistrent et armes à la guise franchoise,
Quer lor semblout è plus riche è plus cortoise."

But in the border-nations of Europe, where the old liberties of Celt and Teuton still lingered, the fashions of war were very different. In Ireland, in Scotland, in Wales, and in the Scandinavian North, the heroes were by no means clad in the pattern of the Bayeux tapestry. From Giraldus Cambrensis we learn that the Irish in the twelfth century wore no body-armour. In riding they used neither saddle nor spur. Their shields were circular, and painted red. Helmets they had none. Their weapons were a short spear, javelins, and an axe. The axes, which they had derived from the Norwegians and Ostmen, were excellently well steeled. "They make use of but one hand when they strike with the axe, extending the thumb along the handle to direct the blow; from which neither the helmet can defend the head, nor the iron folds of the armour the body; whence it has happened in our time that the whole thigh of a soldier, though cased in well-tempered armour, hath been lopped off by a single blow, the limb falling on one side of the horse, and the expiring body on the other. They are also expert beyond all other nations in casting stones in battle, when other weapons fail them, to the great detriment of their enemies[168]." The bow not being in use among the Irish of this time, and consequently there being nothing to oppose to the distant attack of the Norman archers, the havoc made by these latter troops was terrific; so that Giraldus, in his chapter, "Qualiter Hibernica gens sit expugnanda," recommends that in all attacks upon them, bowmen should be mixed with the heavy-armed force.

The Welsh also retained their old mode of warfare:—

"Gens Wallensis habet hoc naturale per omnes
Indigenas, primis proprium quod servat ab annis,"

says Guillaume le Breton. "They are lightly armed," writes Giraldus Cambrensis, "so that their agility may not be impeded; they are clad in haubergeons (*loricis minoribus*), have a handful of arrows, long lances, helmets, and shields, but rarely appear with iron greaves (*ocreis ferreis*). Fleet and generous steeds, which their country produces, bear their leaders to battle, but the greater part of the people are obliged to march on foot over marshes and uneven ground. Those who are mounted, according to opportunity of time and place, both for the retreat and advance, easily become infantry. Those of the foot-soldiers who have not bare feet, wear shoes made of raw hide, sewn up in a barbarous fashion. The people of Gwentland are more accustomed to war, more famous for valour, and more expert in archery, than those of any other part of Wales. The following examples prove the truth of this assertion. In the last assault of Abergavenny Castle, which happened in our days, two soldiers passing over a bridge to a tower built on a mound of earth, in order to take the Welsh in the rear, their archers, who perceived them, discharged their arrows, penetrating an oaken gate which was four fingers thick: in memory of which deed, the arrows are still preserved sticking in the gate, with their iron piles seen on the other side.... Their bows are made of wild elm, unpolished, rude, and uncouth, but strong; not calculated to shoot an arrow to a great distance, but to inflict very severe wounds in closer fight[169]." Guillaume le Breton, in describing the Welsh troops who accompanied Richard Cœur-de-Lion into France, deprives them of defensive armour altogether:—

"Nec soleis plantas, caligis nec crura gravantur:
Frigus docta pati, nulli oneratur ab armis,
Nec munit thorace latus, nec casside frontem[170]."

But he allows them a greater variety of weapons on this occasion than is found in the account of Giraldus:—

"Clavam cum jaculo, venabula, gesa, bipennem,
Arcum cum pharetris, nodosaque tela vel hastam."

The *gesa* of this passage is the often-mentioned *guisarme*. The *nodosa tela* is not so clear, but may have been a dart with a ball at the end; the object of which ball was to arrest the javelin when, sliding through the hand, it had inflicted its wound, so that it might be employed afresh. Such weapons were used by the ancient Egyptians[171], and are still employed in the manner mentioned above by the Nubians and Ababdeh.

Hoveden, describing the battle of Lincoln in 1141, and the disposition of the Earl of Chester's army, says: "On the flank, there was a great multitude of Welshmen, better provided with daring than with arms."

In Scotland, two leading influences were at work. The highlanders adhered to their old habits and their old arms with a pertinacity which has not been extinguished even in our own day. The round shield ornamented with knot-work subsisted to the field of Culloden, and the dagger with its hilt of the same pattern, is still in vogue. But in the south of Scotland the fashions of

France and of England had made great inroads; especially advanced by the crowds of discontented nobles of Saxon and of Norman blood, who sought in the court of the Scottish king solace for their misfortunes, or revenge for their wrongs. Thus in the seal of Alexander I. (1107-1124,) we find that monarch wearing the hauberk with tunic and the nasal helmet, and armed with lance and kite-shield, exactly as seen in the monuments of his more southern cotemporaries. This equipment, however, was only found among the leaders of their hosts, and even they did not always think fit to adopt the new fashion. Thus, at the battle of the Standard, in 1138, the Earl of Strathearne exclaims: —"I wear no armour, yet they who do will not advance beyond me this day."

FROM THE GREAT SEAL OF ALEXANDER I., KING OF SCOTLAND.

No. 27.

This Battle of the Standard, so called from the *Carrocium*, or Car-standard, which was brought into the field by the English, affords us a good insight into the warfare of the Scots of this day. Let us remember, however, that it is an English chronicler who records the fight. Roger of Hoveden tells us that the bishop[172] who accompanied the English army, addressing the troops previous to the engagement, said of the Scots: "They know not how to arm themselves for battle; whereas you, during the time of peace, prepare yourselves for war, in order that in battle you may not experience the doubtful contingencies of warfare.... But now, the enemy *advancing in disorder*, warns me to close my address, and rushing on *with a straggling front*, gives me great

80

reason for gladness." At the end of his speech, "all the troops of the English answered, 'Amen, Amen.'"

"At the same instant the Scots raised the shout of their country, and the cries of 'Albany, Albany!' ascended to the heavens. But the cries were soon drowned in the dreadful crash and the loud din of the blows. When the ranks of the Men of Lothian, who had obtained from the king of Scotland, though reluctantly on his part, the glory of striking the first blow, hurling their darts and presenting their lances of extraordinary length, bore down upon the English knights encased in armour, striking, as it were, against a wall of iron, they found them impenetrable. The archers of King Stephen, mingling among the cavalry, poured their arrows like a cloud upon them, piercing those who were not protected by armour. Meanwhile the whole of the Normans and English stood in one dense phalanx around the standard, perfectly immoveable. The chief commander of the Men of Lothian fell slain, on which the whole of his men took to flight. On seeing this, the main body of the Scots, which was contending with the greatest valour in another part of the field, was alarmed and fled. Next, the king's troop, which King David had formed of several clans, as soon as it perceived this, began to drop off: at first, man by man, afterwards in bodies; the king standing firm, and being at last left almost alone. The king's friends seeing this, forced him to mount his horse and take to flight. But Henry, his valiant son, not heeding the example of his men, but solely intent on glory and valour, bravely charged the enemy's line, and shook it by the wondrous vigour of his onset. For his troop was the only one mounted on horseback, and consisted of *English and Normans who formed a part of his father's household*. His horsemen, however, were not long able to continue their attacks against soldiers on foot, cased in armour, and standing immoveable in close and dense ranks; but, with their lances broken, and their horses wounded, were compelled to fly. Rumour says that many thousands of the Scots were slain on that field, besides those who, being taken in the woods and standing corn, were put to death. Accordingly, the English and Normans happily gained the victory, and with a very small effusion of blood." The standard which gave to this battle of Cuton Moor its popular name, was formed of a mast placed on a car, having at its summit a silver pix containing the Host, and beneath, three banners, those of St. Peter, St. John of Beverley, and St. Wilfrid of Ripon.

The equipment of the Scandinavian heroes in the twelfth century has come down to us in several cotemporary writings. The author of the *Speculum Regale*, an Icelandic chronicle of this period, instructs his son in his military duties: when combating on foot, he is to wear his heavy armour, namely, a byrnie, or thick panzar[173] (*thungann pannzara*), a strong shield (*skiold*) or buckler (*buklara*), and a heavy sword. For naval actions the best weapons are long spears, and for defence, panzars made of soft and well-dyed linen cloth, together with good helmets (*hialmar*), pendant steel caps (*hangandi stálhufur*), and broad shields[174]. The directions for a knight's equipment are more minute: Let the horseman use this dress: first, hose made of soft and well-prepared linen cloth, which should reach to the breeches-belt (*broka-belltis*); then, above them, good mail-hose (*bryn-hosur*), of such a height that they may be fastened with a double string. Next, let him put on a good pair of breeches (*bryn-brækur*), made of strong linen; on which must be fastened knee-caps made of thick iron and fixed with strong nails. The upper part of the body should first be clothed in a soft linen panzar (*blautann panzara*), which should reach to the middle of the thigh; over this a good breast-defence (*briost biorg*), of iron, extending from the bosom to the breeches belt; above that a good byrnie, and over all a good panzar of the same length as the tunic, but without sleeves. Let him have two swords,—one girded round him, the other hung at his saddle-bow; and a good dagger (*bryn-knif*). He must have a good helm, made of tried steel, and provided with all defence for the face (*met allri andlitz biaurg*); and a good and thick shield suspended from his neck, especially furnished with a strong handle. Lastly, let him have a good and sharp spear of tried steel furnished with a strong shaft[175]. It will be remarked that the body is here clothed in four different garments, one over the other; which appear to be the *tunic*, reaching to mid-thigh; the breast-defence of iron (whether formed in a single piece, or of several smaller plates, does not appear); the *hauberk* of the chain-mail, and the *gambeson*, a quilted coat, made in this instance without sleeves. Besides the weapons named above, the axe was still in favour among the Northern warriors. By the ancient laws of Helsingia, every youth on attaining the age of eighteen, was bound to furnish himself with five kinds of warlike equipment: a sword, an axe, a helmet (*jernhatt*), a shield, and a byrnie or a gambeson. A spirited passage of Giraldus Cambrensis brings the Norwegian troops vividly before us. Describing their attack upon Dublin, about 1172, he has: "A navibus igitur certatim erumpentibus, duce Johanne, agnomine *the wode*, quod Latine sonat insano vel vehementi, viri bellicosi Danico more undique ferro vestiti, alii loricis longis, alii laminis ferreis arte consutis, clipeis quoque rotundis et rubris, circulariter ferro munitis, homines tam animis ferrei quàm armis, ordinatis turmis, ad portam orientalem muros invadunt." The round painted shields edged with metal will bring to remembrance the similar defences of the Anglo-Saxons; and in the laminated cuirass we see another instance of the *jazerant* armour worn by Charlemagne. In King Sverrer's *Saga*, written towards the close of the twelfth century, by the abbot of Thingore in Iceland, and others, from the narrative of the king himself, we have a curious passage: "Sverrer was habited in a good byrnie, above it a strong gambeson (*panzara*), and over all a red surcote (*raudan hiup*[176]). With these he had a wide steel hat (*vida stálhufu*), similar to those worn by the Germans; and beneath it a mail cap (*brynkollu*), and a 'panzara-hufu.' By his side hung a sword, and a spear was in his hand[177]." From this description it seems clear that those singular broad-rimmed helmets found occasionally in monuments of the twelfth, thirteenth, and fourteenth centuries, and more frequently in later times; of which examples occur among the sculptures of the tomb of Aymer de Valence, in Westminster Abbey, and on the great seal of Henry III., king of Spain; were introduced into the north and west of Europe through Germany; the Germans, on their part, probably deriving them from the Italians; to whom this form of headpiece had come down from the well-known *petasus* of classic times. The *panzara-hufu* was probably a quilted coif worn under the steel hat. Compare Willemin, vol. i., Plate CXLIII.; and see our woodcut, No. 56.

The Prussians in the twelfth century differ but little in their appearance from the Anglo-Saxon warrior of the preceding age. They wear the tunic, reaching to the knees, and belted at the waist; but, in lieu of leg-bands, have tight hose. They have spears little exceeding their own height, and the shield they carry is a mean between the kite and the pear-shape. We derive these particulars from the curious figures of the bronze doors of Gnesen Cathedral, given by Mr. Nesbitt in the ninth volume of the Archæological Journal, (p. 345); the subject represented being the Legend of Saint Adalbert. Hartknoch (*De Rebus Prussicis*) tells us that the arms of the Prussians were clubs, swords, arrows, spears and shields, and their dress consisted of a short tunic of linen or undyed woollen cloth, tight linen chausses reaching to the heels, and shoes of raw hide or bark.

Throughout the period which we are now investigating, the Clergy not unfrequently appear in knightly equipment at siege and battle. But in order to avoid an infringement of *the letter* of the canons, which forbade them to stain their hands with human blood, they armed themselves with the mace or bâton. At the battle of Hastings, Odo, bishop of Bayeux,—

> "Un haubergeon aveit vestu
> De sor une chemise blanche:
> Lé fut li cors, juste la manche.
> Sor un cheval tot blanc séeit:
> Tote la gent le congnoisseit:
> Un baston teneit en son poing."—*Rom. de Rou*, l. 13254.

In the disorders of Stephen's reign, the prelates appear to have been still more frequently trespassers on the canons of the Church; for the author of the *Gesta Stephani* exclaims, "The bishops, the bishops themselves, I blush to say it,—

not all of them, but many, bound in iron, and completely furnished with arms, were accustomed to mount war-horses with the perverters of their country, to participate in their prey." Everyone will remember the answer attributed to Richard Cœur-de-Lion, who, when the pope required him to release from captivity his spiritual "son," the bishop of Beauvais, sent back the hauberk in which the prelate had been taken, adding, in the words of the history of Joseph: "This have we found: know now whether it be thy son's coat or no." The monk of St. Edmund's, Jocelin of Brakelond, tells us under the year 1193: "Our abbot, who was styled 'the Magnanimous Abbot,' went to the siege of Windsor, where he appeared in armour, with *other abbots* of England, having his own banner, and retaining many knights at heavy charges; being more remarkable there for his counsel than for his piety. But we cloister-folks thought this act rather dangerous, fearing the consequence, that some future abbot might be compelled to attend in person on any warlike expedition."

On other occasions, however, the clergy fulfilled in the field duties more in harmony with their peaceful calling,—attending the wounded or consoling the dying. At the battle of Hastings, the Norman priests gathered together on a hillock, where, during the contest, they offered up prayers for their companions:—

> "Li proveire è li ordené
> En som un tertre sunt monté,
> Por Dex préier è por orer."—*Wace*, l. 13081.

And frequent injunctions forbade these holy men from joining in military exploits. Among the decrees of the synod of Westminster, promulgated in 1175, we read: "Whoever would appear to belong to the clergy, let them not take up arms, nor yet go about in armour. If they despise this injunction, let them be mulcted with the loss of their proper rank[178]."

The TACTICS of this period are pretty clearly exemplified by the proceedings of Duke William at the field of Hastings. The army was divided into three corps:—

> "Normanz orent treiz cumpaignies,
> Por assaillir en treiz parties."

The hired troops were placed in the first division, to bear the brunt of the fight:—

> "Li Boilogneiz é li Pohiers[179]
> Aureiz, è *toz mes soldéiers*."

The second consisted of the Poitevins and Bretons,

> "E del Maine toz li Barons."

The third corps was the largest:—

"E poiz li tiers ki plus grant tint."

And this, led by William himself, appears to have held the position of a reserve:—

"E jo, od totes mes granz genz,
Et od amiz et od parenz,
Me cumbatrai par la grant presse,
U la bataille iert plus engresse[180]."

The battle was opened by the archers:—

"Cil a piè aloient avant
Serréement, lor ars portant."

The charge of the horse, as is well known, was preceded by the feat of Taillefer, to whom the duke had accorded the privilege of striking the first blow. The charge of the knights was at this time, and long after, made in a single line, or *en haie*, as it was called; the attack in squadrons being a much later practice. The Normans acted against their opponents as well by the weight of the horse as by dint of weapons. One knight—

"Assalt Engleiz o grant vigor
Od la petrine du destrier:
En fist maint li jortresbuchier,
Et od l'espée, al redrecier,
Véissiez bien Baron aidier."—*Line* 13491.

Another—

"——un Engleis ad encuntré,
Od li cheval l'a si hurté,
Ke mult tost l'a acraventé,
Et od li piez tot défolé[181]."—*Line* 13544.

Spare horses and arms are provided for distinguished leaders:—

"Li Dus fist chevals demander:
Plusors en fist très li[182] mener.
Chescun out à l'arçon devant
Une espée bone pendant.
E cil ki li chevals menerent
Lances acérées porterent."—*Line* 12699.

In the crusades, the European knights occasionally, though very rarely, contended on foot; and the Princess Anna Comnena remarks that the French men-at-arms, so terrible on horseback, are little dangerous when dismounted[183].

To disorder the enemy's ranks by a simulated flight appears to have been a favourite stratagem of the Normans. Duke William Sans-peur used this device against the Germans before Rouen:—

"Li Normanz par voisdie[184] s'en alerent fuiant,
Por fere desevrer cels ki vindrent devant;
Et Alemanz desrengent, si vont esperonant:
As portes de Roen la vindrent randonant[185]."

Wace, l. 3972.

The similar incident of the battle of Hastings is in the recollection of all:—

"Normanz aperchurent è virent
Ke Engleiz si se desfendirent
E si sunt fort por els desfendre,
Peti poeint sor els prendre:
Privéement unt cunseillié,
Et entrels unt aparaillié,
Ke des Engleiz s'esluignereient,
E de fuir semblant fereient."—*Line* 13311.

Another device of Duke William on this eventful day was to assail the English by a downward flight of arrows, for he had found that the shields of his opponents had secured them from the effects of a direct attack: "Docuit etiam dux Willielmus viros sagittarios ut non in hostem directe, sed in aëra sursum sagittas emitterent cuneum hostilem sagittis cæcarent: quod Anglis magno fuit detrimento[186]."

War-cries were still in vogue, and saintly relics and emblems were regarded with a veneration commensurate with the power of the Church and the confiding credulity of the soldiery. The sacred symbol of the Cross is seen constantly on the shields of the knights; and one of the barons of Rufus, on departing for the Crusades, tells the king that his shield, his helmet, his saddle, and his horses, shall all be marked with this holy device[187]. It was even found useful to enrol mock-saints in the armies contending against the enemies of the faith. Thus, in the contest between the Saracens in Sicily and Count Roger, about the year 1070, Saint George mounted on a white horse is seen to issue from the Christian ranks, and head the onslaught on the unbelievers:—"Apparuit quidem eques splendidus in armis, equo albo insidens, album vexillum in summitate hastilis alligatum ferens, et desuper, splendidem crucem et quasi a nostrâ acie progrediens. Quo viso nostri hilariores effecti Deum Sanctumque Georgium ingeminando ipsum

86

præcedentem promptissimè sunt secuti[188]." It is perhaps unnecessary to say that the narrator of this incident gives it in implicit belief of the saintly character of the splendid knight.

Not saints alone, but necromancers were occasionally attached to military expeditions. Such an auxiliary, according to Wace, accompanied Duke William in his expedition to England:—

> "Un clers esteit al Duc venuz
> Ainz ke de Some fust méuz:
> D'Astronomie, ço diseit,
> E de nigromancie saveit:
> Por devinéor se teneit,
> De plusurs choses sortisseit."—*Line* 11673.

Having predicted a safe voyage to William, and the prediction having been fulfilled, the duke remembered him of his *nigromancien*, and desired that search might be made for this learned clerk. But the poor fellow had himself been drowned in the passage:—

> "En mer esteit, ço dist, néiez,
> Et en un nef perilliez."

On which the duke wisely remarks:—

> "Malement devina de mei,
> Ki ne sout deviner de sei."

Adding:—

> "Fol est ki se fie en devin,
> Ki d'altrui ovre set la fin,
> E terme ne set de sa vie:
> D'altrui prend garde è sei s'oblie."

GREAT SEAL OF KING HENRY THE FIRST.

No. 28.

In examining the BODY-ARMOUR of the period under review, though we find some change in the adaptations of the old fabrics,—of the quilted-work, of the interlinked chain-mail, of the scale and jazerant,—there appears to be only one piece which is entirely new,—the so-called *Plastron de fer*, a breastplate that was worn beneath the gambeson or other armour that formed a general covering for the body. In a preceding passage from the *Speculum Regale*, we have read of a breast-defence of iron, extending from the throat to the waist, which may have been the breastplate in question. But a passage of Guillaume le Breton more exactly defines this contrivance. In the encounter between Richard Cœur-de-Lion (then earl of Poitou), and Guillaume des Barres:—

"Utraque per clipeos ad corpora fraxinus ibat,
Gambesumque audax forat et thoraca trilicem
Disjicit: ardenti nimium prorumpere tandem

88

Vix obstat ferro fabricata patena recocto,
Qua bene munierat pectus sibi cautus uterque."
Philippidos,
lib. iii.

A further evidence of this additional arming of the breast may be derived from the present practice of the East, where quilted coats-of-fence have a lining of iron plates at that part only. In the museum of the United Service Institution may be seen Chinese armours of this construction.

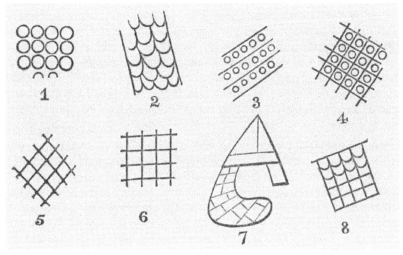

No. 29.

Though from written testimonies we learn that the fabrics already enumerated were in use, and that the materials of the defences were iron, leather, horn, and various kinds of quilting, it is by no means easy to identify these structures in the pictorial monuments of the day. Nothing perhaps can more strongly mark this fact, than the diversity of interpretation that has been given to the armours in the Bayeux tapestry by some of the latest and most critical investigators of the subject. Von Leber sees in them a contrivance of leather and metal bosses: "ein Lederwamms mit aufgenähten Metallscheiben oder Metallbukeln[189]." M. Allou attires the warrior in a "vêtement particulier formé d'anneaux ou de mailles de fer, ou bien de petites pièces de même métal assemblées à la manière des tuiles ou des écailles de poisson[190]." In the *Bulletin Monumental* of the Société Française, vol. xi., page 519, we have: "On croit distinguer, d'après l'indication de la broderie, des disques en métal appliqués sur une jaque de cuir." Mr. Kerrich[191] considers the coats marked with rounds as chain-mail. M. de Caumont has remarked that "in the Bayeux

89

tapestry some of the figures are in chain-mail, and others in a kind of armour composed apparently of metallic discs sewn to a leathern *jaque*[192]." In the following we have collected the various modes of indicating the armour in this tapestry, and it must be confessed that to appropriate each is no easy task. It is indeed rather from a comparison with numerous other monuments, than from the testimony of these examples alone, that one is able to form any opinion as to the fabrics intended; and even at last the conclusion *must* be doubtful, and may be erroneous. From analogous representations of various dates, however, it seems likely that the figures 1 and 2 are intended for interlinked chain-mail; Nos. 3 and 4 for jazerant-work (armour formed of small plates fastened by rivets to a garment of cloth or canvas); Nos. 5 and 6 appear to be plain quilted defences; No. 7 seems only a rude attempt to represent the quilted coif; No. 8 is one of many examples where different markings are used on the same garment. In some instances, the markings copied above are so strangely intermixed in the same dress, that one is led to doubt if, in any case, each differing pattern is intended to represent a different kind of armour.

If from the tapestries we turn to the seals of this period, we shall find a similar difficulty in appropriating the armours represented. The modes of marking the defences are four. One of these is a sort of honeycomb-work, formed by a number of small, shallow, circular apertures, leaving a raised line running round their edges, so as to give a reticulated appearance to the surface. See woodcuts 42 and 43. This texture seems to represent interlinked chain-mail. A second mode consists of a series of lines crossing each other, so as to form a trellis-work of lozenges.

GREAT SEAL OF KING STEPHEN.

No. 30.

The great seal of King Stephen here given affords an instance of this method. Compare also woodcut No. 41. This, if not another conventional mode of representing interlinked chain-mail, may be intended for quilted armour. A third kind of engraving presents a number of raised half-circles covering the surface of the hauberk. See woodcut No. 26. This, though often described as scale-armour, seems to be no more than the ordinary chain-mail, the difficulty of representing which threw the middle-age artists upon a variety of expedients to obtain a satisfactory result. In the fourth method, lines of half-circles placed contiguously cover the whole exterior of the garment; and that this is another mode of indicating chain-mail is clearly proved by the similar work found on monuments of all kinds, even to the sixteenth century. See woodcut No. 1, fig. 1.

From this glimpse at the seals and tapestries, (and the illuminated manuscripts of the period contribute similar testimony,) we may gather that the artists of this day had no uniform method of depicting the knightly harness; so that, instead of endeavouring to find a different kind of armour for every varying pattern of the limners, we should rather regard the varied patterns of the limners as so many rude attempts to represent a few armours. In the following sketch we have collected some of the methods in use at various times to indicate the ordinary interlinked chain-mail.

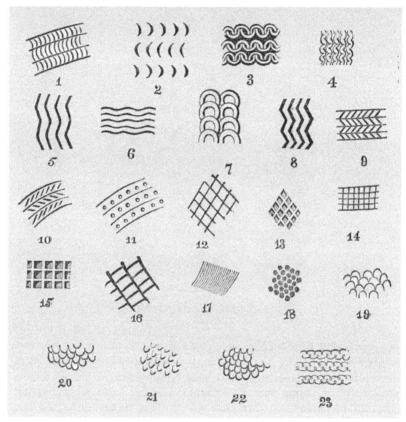

No. 31.

Figure 1 is the most usual, and is found from the twelfth century to the sixteenth. See woodcut No. 1, the seal of King Richard I. Late examples occur in the brass of Sir William Molineux, 1548[193]; in the sculptured effigy of Sir Giles Daubeny in Westminster Abbey; and in the statue of Sir Humfrey Bradburne, on his monument in Ashborne Church, Derbyshire, 1581. Fig. 2 is seen on our woodcuts 32, 37, and 53, from manuscript miniatures: it occurs in sculpture among the effigies of the Temple Church, London. Fig. 3 is of frequent appearance. See woodcut No. 59. The most ancient monumental brass extant, that of Sir John D'Aubernoun, (woodcut 55,) also exhibits this mode of indicating the armour. Fig. 4 occurs in the brass of Sir Richard de Buslingthorpe, c. 1280, figured by Waller, Part x. Fig. 5 is from one of the effigies in the Temple Church: the lines are undulating channels in the stone. Fig. 6 is from the sculptured effigy of Rudolf von Thierstein, at Basle: engraved in Hefner's Costumes, part ii., Plate XLI. Fig. 7 occurs on the monumental statue of Sir Walter Arden, in Aston Church, Warwickshire[194]. Fig. 8 is found in early woodcuts: as in the *Morte d'Arthur*, printed by Wynkyn de Worde in 1498. Fig. 9: an early example of this marking occurs in Willemin's *Monuments Inédits*, vol. i., Plate 30; a late one (sixteenth century) in the incised slab of a Bagot, in the church of Blithfield, Staffordshire. Fig. 10: a variety of the foregoing. See Hefner's *Trachten*, part i., Plate LXV., and part ii., Plate XXXIV. Fig. 11: from an ivory chess-piece of the thirteenth century: woodcut No. 69. The lines are incised, the rounds are punctured. Fig. 12 is a very frequent pattern. It appears in the Bayeux tapestry, in manuscript miniatures, and in ivory carvings. See the chess-piece engraved in *Archæologia*, XXIV. 238, from the Isle of Lewis; and compare the figures of that very curious Asiatic roll in the Museum of the Royal Asiatic Society. Fig. 13: this trellis-work is common in seals of the twelfth century. See our woodcuts No. 30 and 41. The lozenges are slightly sunk, the fillets in relief. Fig. 14: found in the Bayeux tapestry; in the *Bible de St. Martial* of the Imperial Library of Paris, twelfth century; and in Add. MS., 15,277, of the fifteenth century, where the mailing is expressed throughout in this manner. The Asiatic roll named above has it also. Fig. 15: from the statuette of "Sir de la Tremouille," 1514, in the collection at Goodrich Court. The figure is of steel, and the squares appear to have been formed by a punch. Fig. 16: from the sculptured effigy of a Berkeley in Bristol Cathedral. The markings are channels in the stone. Fig. 17: from Roy. MS., 14, E. iv. The mailing in this volume is expressed by close, fine lines: the manuscript is of the fifteenth century. Fig. 18: the honeycomb-work found on early seals. The great seal of King Stephen (woodcut 42) affords a good example. The rounds are depressed, the edges have a reticulated appearance. Figs. 19 and 20: from the illuminations of a Sanscrit MS. in the British Museum, (Add. MSS., 15,295-7.) These very curious volumes abound in armed figures, which are large, and carefully finished. Fig. 21: from Egerton MS., No. 809, twelfth century; and Add. MS. 15,268, of the thirteenth century. Fig. 22: from Harleian MS., 2803. This differs but little from fig. 20; but fig. 20 has more of the *scale* form, while this is rather of *ring*-work. Fig. 23 is a marking found in early etchings, and very well represents the texture of chain-mail.

As we have already seen, the Body-armours which may most safely be assigned to early Norman times are chain-mail, quilted-work, jazerant, scale, and a small proportion of plate used as an additional protection to the breast: the materials, iron, leather, and horn, with wool, tow, or cotton for quilting pourpointed defences. The ordinary series of body-garments worn by the knight are the Tunic, the Gambeson and the Hauberk. The Surcoat, though found in some rare instances at the close of the twelfth century, does not become a characteristic part of the knightly equipment till the thirteenth century.

The Tunic appearing from beneath the hauberk may be seen in the seals of Alexander I. of Scotland, and of Richard I. of England, (cuts 1 and 27,) and in the accompanying group from Harleian Roll, Y. 6, the "Life of Saint Guthlac," a work of the close of the twelfth century. Compare also woodcuts 34, 35, and 40. We have already had written notice of this garment in the "blautann panzara" of the *Speculum Regale.* Wace gives it also to Bishop Odo, for the field of Hastings:—

> "Un haubergeon aveit vestu
> De sor une chemise-blanche."

The Gambeson (or Wambasium[195],) was a quilted garment, used either alone, or with other armour. This defence is as early as the Ancient Egyptians, and figured examples of it may be seen in Sir Gardner Wilkinson's work, Plate III., and cut 46, (ed. 1837). From a curious passage of the *Chronicon Colmariense* we learn that it was stuffed with wool, tow, or old rags: —"*Armati* reputabantur qui galeas ferreas in capitibus habebant, et qui *wambasia*, id est, tunicam spissam ex lino et stuppa, vel veteribus pannis consutam, et desuper *camisiam ferream*, id est vestem ex circulis ferreis contextam." An ancient authority quoted by Adelung has also: "vestimenti genus, quod de coactili ad mensuram et tutelam pectoris humani conficitur, de mollibus lanis," &c.

As the sole armour of the soldier, the gambeson is mentioned both by Wace and Guillaume le Breton. The former tells us, in his description of the troops of Duke William preparing for the fight:—

"Plusors orent vestu gambais."—*Rom. de Rou*, l. 12811.

The latter says:—

"Pectora tot coriis, tot gambesonibus armant."—*Philipp.*, lib. ii.

These were probably foot-troops; but a document of the next century shews us that horsemen were sometimes armed in the wambais only. In 1285, land in Rewenhall, Essex, is held by Eustace de Ho, "per serjantiam inveniendi unum hominem equitem cum uno gambesone in exercitu Dom. Regis, cum contigerit ipsum ire in Wallia, sumptibus suis propriis per XL. dies[196]." It seems likely that many of these quilted coats-of-fence were reinforced by plates of iron over the breast, as in the pourpointed armours of the East in the present day. As an additional reason for considering the defences of gamboised work to be those indicated by the cross-lines of the ancient vellum-pictures, we may mention that the garments thus marked are occasionally tinted in various colours. Thus, the figures in a Massacre of the Innocents, in Cotton MS., Caligula, A. vii., are painted with red, blue, green, and buff; and another in Count Bastard's work, from a French manuscript of the twelfth century, has the garment marked with stripes of red[197]. The "Aketon" appears to be but another name for the gambeson.

No. 33.

The Hauberk was the chief knightly defence. It reached to the knees; the skirt sometimes opening in front, sometimes at the sides. The sleeves usually terminated at the elbow, but occasionally extended to the wrist. Sometimes the hauberk reached as high as the neck only, but more generally it was continued so as to form a coif, leaving only the face of the knight exposed to view. In many examples in the Bayeux tapestry, it is furnished with a kind of pectoral, the construction of which has not been ascertained: in other cases, the whole surface is of a uniform structure. In this rude but curious little figure from Harleian MS., 603[198], a work of the close of the eleventh century, probably executed in France, we have a good example of the hauberk of the period, with its short sleeves, and the skirts open in front for convenience of riding. This is exactly the hauberk of the Bayeux tapestry, though more clearly depicted here than in the needle-work of the tapestry. The rounds on the surface appear to be a conventional mode of representing chain-mail. The figure is that of Goliath, to whom therefore has been given the long beard and round target of the pagan Northmen. He wears, however, the conical nasal helmet of the knightly order.

In this example, from Cottonian MS., Nero, C. iv. fol. 13, written in France, about 1125, we have a curious instance of the hauberk with lateral openings at the skirt. It is remarkable also for the manner in which the sword is carried partially beneath the hauberk; a contrivance seen also in the Bayeux tapestry, (Plate VI.,) and of which analogous examples will be found throughout the middle-ages. In the figure before us, it will be observed that the defence is continued over the head as a coif or hood, and is surmounted by the usual conical nasal helmet, or "Casque Normand." The subject of which this forms part, is the Massacre of the Innocents. The stigma of a moustache is therefore added, in the same spirit as the beard was given to Goliath in the preceding example.

The continuous Coif to the hauberk is seen constantly in the Bayeux tapestry, (Stothard, Plates x. to xiii.). It occurs also on many of the seals of the twelfth century, (see our cuts, No. 27, 43 and 44;) and in vellum-paintings of this time, (see cuts 32, 34, 37 and 38). The hood of mail made separately from the hauberk does not appear till the thirteenth century. The short sleeves of this garment are seen in our woodcuts 25, 32 and 38. Examples of the long-sleeved hauberk occur in cuts 28, 37, 42 and 43.

The Haubergeon, as the name indicates, was a smaller hauberk; though it does not appear by the pictorial monuments of the middle ages in what it especially differed from the latter defence. While Duke William, preparing for the battle of Hastings,—

"Sun boen *haubert* fist demander;"

Bishop Odo—

"Un *haubergeon* aveit vestu."

The Duke was armed with lance and sword; the Prelate—

99

"Un *baston* teneit en son poing."

All which seems to shew that Odo was equipped as a light-armed fighter. And perhaps we may gather from the prominent notice accorded to his "white tunic," that it was the *shortness* of the haubergeon which caused that garment to be so particularly remarked. In documents of the thirteenth century, the haubergeon is distinguished from the hauberk and gambeson, taking its place between them. Thus the Statute of Arms of 1252 directs every man, according to the rate of his lands and chattels, to provide himself with the *lorica*, or with the *habergetum*, or with the *perpunctum*. And the Statute of Winchester, in 1285, makes the same distinction. From Guillaume Guiart we learn that this garment was of mail:—

"Armez de cotes a leurs tailles,
Et de bons hauberjons a mailles."—*Sub an.* 1304.

And the Teloneum S. Audomari has: "Lorica, iv. denar.; Lorica minor, quæ vulgo *Halsbergol* dicitur, ii. den."

Body-armour of Leather is found throughout the middle ages. According to Wace, some of the Norman soldiers in the Conqueror's train had defences of this material fastened to their breasts:—

"Alquanz unt bones coiriés,
K'il unt à lor ventre liés."—*Line* 12,809.

And Guillaume le Breton in the "Philippidos" has,—

"Pectora tot *coriis*, tot gambesonibus armant;"—

while a passage cited by Ducange shews us that, sometimes at least, this cuirass was of leather boiled in oil; a material much in vogue in the middle-ages, under the name of "cuir boulli:"—

"Cuirie ot bonne, qui fust de cuir boilly."

A good example of the Scale-armour worn occasionally about the close of the eleventh century is afforded in the following group, given by Hefner[199] from a vellum-painting in his possession. The armour in the original is silvered, and the pendent scales of the foremost figure are ornamented with bosses of gold. The tunics are white, shaded with blue. The Princess Anna Comnena tells us that some of the French knights at this period were clothed in scale-armour[200].

The material of the scale-armour is occasionally Horn. In the twelfth century, the Emperor Henry V. clothed a body of his troops in an impenetrable scale-armour of horn: "So trug im Jahre 1115 eine Schaar im Heere Heinrichs V. undurchdringliche Harnische von Horn[201]." And in the poem of "Wigalois," written about the close of the twelfth century, we have a curious description of this horn-mail worn over the hauberk and richly adorned with gold and precious stones:—

"Ein brunne het er an geleit
Uber einen wizzen halsperch.
Daz was heidenischez werch
Von *breiten blechen hurnin*;
Mit golde waren geleit dar in

101

Rubin, und manec edel stein
Der glast da wider einander schein
Saffire und berillen."

No. 36.

The accompanying little figure from Harleian MS., No. 603, fol. 13vo., appears to wear a defence of scale-work, but of what material it is difficult to say. The original is a pen-drawing only: the manuscript, of the close of the eleventh century. The figure is further curious for the mantle fastened at the right shoulder by a fibula.

From the monuments of this time, it does not appear that leg-defences were general. In the Bayeux tapestry they are accorded only to the most distinguished personages: in these cases, they are generally marked with rounds, as the hauberks are, probably indicating chain-mail. In this tapestry, three other modes of clothing the leg are seen: in some figures the crossing lines forming lozenges are found, which we have assumed to be pourpointerie; in others appear the fasciæ, or winding bands, which we have already observed among the Anglo-Saxons: and in many, the chausses are merely represented of a single colour, as red, blue, or yellow; which does not seem to imply armour of any kind. Wace makes mention of iron chausses:—

"Chevaliers ont haubers è branz,
Chauces de fer, helmes luizanz."—*Line* 12,813.

They are seen in the great seals of Richard the First, (cut 1,) and in other monuments of the twelfth century. In this curious group of David and Goliath, from a German manuscript in the British Museum, dated 1148[202], we have a singular example of studded chausses: the chain-work of the hauberk being marked in rows of half-circles, and coloured grey in the original, the chausses marked in rounds, and silvered, it becomes clear that the latter garment is of a different construction from the coat. From its being elastic, as shewn at the foot, it probably was a defence of pourpointerie, the bossed rivets being for the purpose of keeping the quilting in its place.

PLATE XXXVII.

No. 38.

Such defences are frequently seen in monuments of the fourteenth century, and real armour of this fabric will be found among the Eastern examples in the Tower collection and the United Service Museum. Where the chausses are not of a defensive construction, the warrior has commonly short boots, similar to those seen on the figure of David in the foregoing woodcut. In the following example they are of a more ornamental character than usual; and the chausses in this figure are also of a peculiar fashion. The subject is from Harl. MS. 2803, written about 1170, and represents Goliath. The short boot occurs likewise on the seals of William the Conqueror and of Alexander I. of Scotland, (cuts 25 and 27). See also examples from illuminated manuscripts in our engravings 32, 34 and 36. At the close of the eleventh century, the fashion of the boots ran into an excess which much disturbed the equanimity of churchmen and chroniclers. "Then," says Malmesbury, under the reign of William Rufus, "was there flowing hair and extravagant dress; and then was invented the fashion of shoes with curved points." (Bk. iv. c. 1.) This device is said to have originated with Fulk, earl of Anjou, who sought thus to hide a deformity of his feet. Ordericus Vitalis, who gives us the information, adds, that the fashion soon spread, and the shoemakers made their wares with points like a scorpion's tail: "unde sutores in calceamentis quasi caudas scorpionum, quas vulgo *Pigacias* appellant, faciunt." This not being enough, a fellow of the court of Rufus,—"Robertus quidam *nebulo* in curia Rufi Regis,"—filling the peak with tow, twisted it round in the form of a ram's horn; a fancy much approved by the courtiers, who distinguished the inventor of the fashion with the surname of Cornardus. (Eccl. Hist., lib. viii.)

No. 39.

Examples of the Mantle worn over the armour are somewhat rare. The two following illustrations, from monuments of the twelfth century, exhibit this arrangement. The first is from a sculptured doorway of Ruardean Church, in Gloucestershire, and represents St. George. The cloak is here fastened by a fibula in front. The second subject is from an enamel preserved at the Louvre. The patriarch Abraham, armed as a knight, with hauberk and nasal helmet, has his mantle fastened at the right shoulder. Another subject from this enamel is engraved in the *Revue Archéologique*, vol. vi., page 99: Heraclius slaying Cosroes. "Eraclius Rex" is armed exactly like the figure of Abraham before us, and though engaged in the decollation of the infidel monarch, still retains the flowing and capacious mantle. See also, for the cloak of this period, our woodcut No. 36, and "Glossary of Architecture," vol. ii., Plate LXXIII.

The characteristic Helmet of this time is the conical nasal helmet, of which we have seen examples in the close of the former period. The face-guard, or nasal, was a revival from classic days. Good examples, of Greek art, appear among the figures on the tympana of the temple of Minerva at Ægina; careful casts of which have been placed in the collection at Sydenham. The nasal helmet is found, not alone in the eleventh and twelfth centuries, but occasionally in every century down to the seventeenth. In the Bayeux tapestry it is almost universal, the nasal being much broader than that of Greek times, the crown conical, and not much raised above the head. In some cases tasselled cords appear at the back of the head-piece (see Plate XI. of the tapestry), which may have served to fasten it to the coif below; but the chief fastening of the casque was by means of laces meeting under the chin. See the seal of William the Conqueror (woodcut 25), and the excellent example in the Kerrich Collections, from a sculpture at Modena (Add. MSS., 6728, fol. 17). The round and flat-topped helmets of the twelfth century have also the nasal. Of the first an instance occurs in the seal of Patrick Dunbar, earl of March, engraved in Laing's "Scottish Seals." The second appears in the figures of the Harleian Roll, Y. 6, (woodcut 32). In seals, it is often very difficult to tell whether a nasal has existed or not, from the melting of the wax, and from this defence following so closely the line of the face. In some rare instances, a sort of peak is used instead of the nasal, not descending below the eyebrows. See Plate 65 of Hefner's "Costumes;" and compare the figure on folio 9 of Cotton. MS., Tiber., C. vi., an example of Anglo-Saxon times. To the nasal helmet, cheek-pieces and a neck-defence were occasionally added. These pieces are also found on Greek examples, and appear, too, in modern Eastern armour; as may be seen in the helmet of Tippoo Saib, preserved in the India House Museum. The casque with neck-piece appears in the Bayeux tapestry (see Plate IX.), and on the seal of Stephen de Curzun, (Cotton Charter, V. 49). The nasal helmet with neck-guard and cheek-defences occurs among the chess-pieces found in the Isle of Lewis, and now in the British Museum.

The helmets not having nasals are chiefly conical, round and flat-topped. The old combed form of Anglo-Saxon times occurs in Harl. MS. 603, fol. 13vo., a book of the close of the eleventh century. The Phrygian form appears in Harl. MS. 2800, fol. 21 of vol. ii., a work of the close of the twelfth century. The conical casque is found in the annexed seal of Conan, duke of Britanny, circa 1165: from Harl. Chart., 48, G. 40. The round-topped helmet is seen on the first seal of Richard I., (woodcut 1, fig. 1,) and in many examples in Cotton MS., Titus, D. xvi. The cylindrical or flat-topped helmet appears to have come into fashion towards the close of the twelfth century. In its earliest form it resembled that on the second seal of Richard I., (woodcut 1, fig. 2,) and the similar examples figured in Stothard's Monuments, Plate xxiv., and Surtees' Durham, vol. i. p. 24, and vol. ii. p. 139. In all these examples the casque is of one piece, having two horizontal clefts for vision, and being strengthened by bands crossing each other over the face and on the top. The Durham examples are without ornament, but the helmet of Richard has a fan-crest, ensigned in its lower portion with a lion. The seal of Baldwin, earl of Flanders, circa 1191, badly engraved by Vredius, offers another early example of the flat-topped knightly helm. The cylindrical casque common in the next century differs from this in having a *grated ventail*; by which a better supply of air could always be obtained by the warrior, and a still more abundant provision occasionally acquired by opening the ventaglia, which to this end was constructed with hinges at the side. Some varieties of the casque worn during the twelfth century may be seen in the *Archæologia*, vol. xxiv., copied by Sir Frederic Madden from the Isle of Lewis chess-pieces in the British Museum. Among these will be remarked the "Iron Hat," with its round crown and flat rim, of which we have already traced the descent from the *petasus* of classic times[203]. Sometimes the helmets are surmounted with a kind of knop or button; as in the picture given by Silvestre from a Latin Horace in the Paris Library[204]; in the seal of William the Conqueror, in the Bayeux tapestry, and in the Spanish manuscript of the year 1109 in the British Museum, (Add. MS. 11,695, fol. 194).

The fan-crest represented in the seal of Richard I. is a very early instance of a fashion which came into more favour towards the close of the thirteenth century. Fan-crests, as we have seen, were in use among the Ancient Egyptians, Assyrians, Greeks, Romans, and again among the Anglo-Saxons. But they do not appear during the rule of the Norman kings in England till the end of the thirteenth century; except in this single instance of Richard's seal. It may perhaps be doubted if the monarch ever wore such a decoration: an embellishment, perhaps, added by the seal-engraver from some monument of classic times. This seems the more likely from the fact that, in classic examples, the union of a fan-crest with a casque adorned on its sides with an animal form, is of constant occurrence. Among a thousand examples that might be cited, we may quote, as a readily accessible authority, Montfaucon's *Antiquité Expliquée*, vol. i., Plate XLII. At a later period of the middle-ages, this combination is again found: the helmet on the seal of Reinald, Graf von Geldern in 1343, has a striking resemblance to that of Richard: a lion is figured on the part surmounting the crown of the head, and over that again is placed the fan-crest. A copy of this monument may be seen in the useful series of "Ancient Seals" in the collection at Sydenham. Early examples of the casque ornamented with a heraldic device on its *surface* are offered by the enamelled tablet at Le Mans, attributed to Geoffry of Anjou, (Stothard, Plate II.,) and the effigy of "Johan le Botiler," circa 1300, engraved in our woodcut No. 74.

The Shields of this period are chiefly the kite-shaped, the triangular, and the round. The first two are sometimes flat, and sometimes bowed; the round are flat or convex. The kite-shield is of most frequent occurrence during the earlier part of the period under examination, the triangular during the latter. As the round target was most convenient for the foot-fighter, so the kite-shield, broad in its upper part, so as to cover the body of the warrior, and narrow where the leg only required to be defended, and where the position of the knight on his horse necessitated a tapering form, seems to have been most in favour with the horseman. The bowed kite-shield is very distinctly shewn in many cotemporary monuments: in Cotton MS., Titus, D. xvi., of the close of the eleventh century; in the curious pyx from the collection of the late T. Crofton Croker, Esq., engraved in the "Gentleman's Magazine" for 1833; in Harl. MS., 2895, fol. 82; in the enamelled figure attributed to Geoffry of Anjou; and in the seals of King Stephen, (woodcuts 30 and 42). The Princess Anna Comnena, at the close of the eleventh century, tells us that the shields of the French crusading knights were of this fashion:—"For defence they bear an impenetrable shield, not of a round, but of an oblong shape; broad at the upper part and terminating in a point. The surface is not flat, but convex, so as to embrace the person of the wearer; an umbo of shining brass is in the middle; and the exterior face is of metal so highly polished by frequent rubbing as to dazzle the eyes of the beholder[205]."

The flat kite-shield is not always to be identified in the drawings of the time, because the shadeless outlines of the limners may pass for either flat or bowed surfaces. But that some at least of those in the Bayeux tapestry were flat, seems clear from the soldiers using them as trays on which to set the cups and dishes of their "Prandium." (See Plate xi.) Ivory carvings also shew the flat kite-shield: the Isle of Lewis chessmen afford good examples.

As we have seen from the above passage of Anna Comnena, the old Northern fashion of the boss or umbo was still occasionally retained; but such an adjunct to a horseman's target seems rather for ornament than use. The bossed kite-shield occurs in the enamel of Geoffrey Plantagenet; in the pyx named above; and in Harl. MS. 2895, fol. 82.

GREAT SEAL OF KING STEPHEN.

No. 42.

In lieu of the convex boss, the shield has sometimes a projecting spike; as in the great seal of King Stephen, here given; and in the first seal of Richard I. It occurs also in the seals of William de Romara (temp. Hen. I.), in the office of the Duchy of Lancaster, and of a Curzun (Cotton Charter, V. 49).

About the middle of the twelfth century appears the triangular shield,—a form obtained by reducing the arched top of the kite to a straight, or nearly straight, line. This variety also was either bowed or flat; and though the earliest examples are as tall as the kite-shields of the eleventh century, the triangular target soon became much reduced in its height. The form of this defence, both the flat and the bowed kind, may be seen in the seals of Henry II. and Richard I. (cuts 1 and 44), the figures from Hefner's *Trachten*, (cut 35), and those from Harleian Roll, Y. 6 (cut 32).

The round shield is of more rare appearance. It occurs in Harl. MS. 603, of the close of the eleventh century; in the Spanish MS. of 1109, already cited; and in the Psalter of Eadwine, circa 1150. Though the circular target does not often appear in miniature paintings, it is probable that it was in frequent use among the foot troops.

The kite and triangular shields were provided with straps for attachment to the arm and for suspension round the neck. The first were called *enarmes*:—

> "Por la crieme des dous gisarmes,
> L'escu leva par les enarmes."
>> *Wace, Rom. de Rou*, l. 13,450.

> "Li Dus vit sa gent resortir:
> Par les enarmes prinst l'escu."—*Idem*, l. 13,880.

There was some variety in their arrangement, but the object was always to attach the shield to the fore-arm: the round target of the Anglo-Saxons, on the contrary, was held at arm's-length by a bar grasped by the hand. Examples of the *enarmes* of this period may be found in Plate v. of the Bayeux tapestry. See also the seal of Henry II., (woodcut 43). The *guige* or strap for suspension has already been described, as to its purpose, in our first division. It is represented in our woodcuts 32, 35, 42 and 43. By aid of the *guige*, the shield, when not in use, could be carried at the back. An example, of the close of the twelfth century, is offered by a vellum-painting of Harl. MS. 2800, vol. ii. fol. 21. It is also seen in the very curious carved church-door from Iceland, figured at page 103 of Mr. Worsaae's "Copenhagen Museum."

The Devices upon the Shields in the earlier part of the period under examination are devotional or fanciful. In the second half of the twelfth century, heraldic bearings that became hereditary, began to appear. The earlier shield-paintings consist of crosses, rounds or bezants, dragons, interlacing bands, flat tints bordered with a different hue, or simple flat tints; with some varieties which the pencil only can explain with clearness. Numerous examples of these in all their diversity will be found in the Bayeux tapestry, in Sir Frederic Madden's paper on the Isle of Lewis chessmen, (*Archæol.*, vol. xxiv.) and among the plates of Shaw's "Dresses and Decorations."

The two seals of Richard the First very exactly mark the growth of the science of heraldry. In the earliest, the monarch's shield is ensigned with the symbol of valour, a lion. (See woodcut, No. 1). But it is a rampant lion, and as the bowed shield presents only one half of its surface to view, it has been conjectured that the complete device would consist of two lions combatant. This device, whether of one or two lions, has passed away, among the serpents and knot-work of the earlier time; but the bearing on Richard's second seal, three lions passant gardant, retains its place in the royal escutcheon to the present day. In this second seal of Richard (see woodcut, No. 1, fig. 2), the lion passant appears also on the helmet of the monarch. Another example of the repetition of a royal device is afforded by the seal of Alexander II. of Scotland (circa 1214), where the lion rampant figured on the shield is repeated on the saddle. (Cotton Charters, xix. 2.)

The shields were often highly decorated with painting, and even, if we may interpret literally the evidences of chroniclers, with inlaid jewels. Examples of richly ornamented shields of the twelfth century may be seen in Shaw's "Dresses and Decorations," and in Harl. MS. 2895, fol. 82. Robert of Aix, in the eleventh century, writing of the first crusade, tells us that the European knights carried shields "auro et gemmis inserti variisque coloribus depicti."

On board ship, the knights arranged their shields along the side of the vessel, so as to form a kind of bulwark. This is very clearly shewn in Plates ii. and x. of the Bayeux tapestry.

And when at length the knight fell in battle, his kite-shield served him for a bier. The nephew of the emperor Otho having been slain before Rouen, the Germans—

> "O li cors se trahistrent el chief d'une valée;
> Sor un escu l'ont miz, la teste desarmée."
>
> *Roman de Rou*, l.
> 4024.

As we have learned from a preceding passage, the "shaven and shorn" knights of the Conqueror's time had, in the reign of his successor, fallen into disrepute as models of fashion. Long hair came into vogue, called down the anathemas of the Church, suffered a temporary discredit, and again rose into favour. Malmesbury has a curious sketch of this fluctuation of fashion. In the twenty-ninth regnal year of Henry I., he tells us, "a circumstance occurred in England which may seem surprising to our long-haired gallants, who, forgetting what they were born, transform themselves into the fashion of females, by the length of their locks. A certain English knight, who prided himself on the luxuriancy of his tresses, being stung by conscience on the subject, seemed to feel in a dream as though some person strangled him with his ringlets. Awaking in a fright, he immediately cut off all his superfluous hair. The example spread throughout England; and, as recent punishment is apt to affect the mind, almost all military men allowed their hair to be cropped in a proper manner without reluctance. But this decency was not of long continuance; for scarcely had a year expired, before all who thought themselves courtly relapsed into their former vice, vying with women in the length of their locks, and whenever they were defective, supplying their place with false tresses[206]." In 1102, at a council held in London by Archbishop Anselm, it was enacted that those who had long hair should be cropped, so as to shew part of the ear and the eyes. Compare also the well-known passage of Ordericus Vitalis, where he tells us how Bishop Serlo, preaching before Henry I. and his court, inveighed so successfully against the iniquity of long locks, that his audience saw the folly of their ways; and the prelate, seizing the favourable moment, produced a pair of scissors from his sleeve (*de manticâ forcipes*), and cropped the king and many of his courtiers with his own hand[207].

From Wace and the Bayeux tapestry we have found that the Beard was not worn by the Normans at the time of the Conquest, though in fashion among the Anglo-Saxons:—

"Li Normant * * *
N'unt mie barbe ne guernons,
Co dist Heraut, com nos avons."—*Line* 12,252.

And the Normans continued their custom till the second half of the twelfth century. The monumental effigy of Henry II. at Fontevraud represents him without either beard or moustache. "The beard," says Stothard[208], "is painted, and pencilled like a miniature, to represent its being close shaven." Among the English, however, the beard was often retained, and became a sort of protest against the new dynasty[209]. In 1196 William Longbeard, "le dernier des Saxons," as he is named by M. Thierry, became conspicuous from his opposition to the Norman rule, the inveteracy of which was manifested to the world by the excessive length of his beard[210]. At this time, however, a beard and moustache of moderate dimensions were in vogue among both races. The effigy of Richard I. at Fontevraud and that of King John at Worcester offer good examples of this change of fashion.

The WEAPONS in use among the knightly order were the lance, the sword, the mace, and, towards the middle of the twelfth century, the axe. The shaft of the Lance was of uniform thickness throughout, the swell at the grip being a much later invention. The material was usually ash or pine. Wace, in the *Roman de Rou*, has:—

"Mult i véissiez colps è de fer è d'achier,
Mainte hante[211] de sap è de fresne bruissier[212]."—*Line*
4639.

Guillaume le Breton, describing the combat of Richard I. and Guillaume des Barres, says:—

"Utraque per clypeos ad corpora *fraxinus* ibat."

115

And Albertus Aquensis, speaking of the French, tells us: "Hastæ fraxineæ in manibus eorum ferro acutissimo præfixæ sunt, quasi grandes perticæ." The heads of the lance were commonly of the leaf-form or the lozenge; more rarely barbed. All three appear in the Bayeux tapestry, and are found in many monuments throughout the twelfth century. Lance-flags (or streamers) of two, three, four, and of five points are found at the close of the eleventh and during the twelfth centuries. See Harleian MS. 603, the Bayeux tapestry, and our woodcuts, Nos. 1, 27, 28, 30 and 37. A curious Eastern example of the use of the lance-flag is found in the wall-painting of the Ajunta caves, a work referred to the first century of our era. A fine copy of this interesting monument has been placed in the Museum of the East India House. The spear was also a weapon of the inferior troops:—

> "Archiers trovent vilainz, dont la terre est planiere,
> Ki porte arc è ki hache, ki grant lance geldiere."
>
> *Rom. de Rou,*
> l. 4680.

Geldon was a name often given to the foot soldiery: "Et ceciderunt de Israël triginta millia *peditum:*" 1. Kings iv. 10. "Kar il i chaïrent trente milie de *gelde.*"

GREAT SEAL OF KING HENRY II.

No. 43.

The Sword was of the old form: straight, broad, two-edged, and pointed. The cross-piece was generally straight: in other cases, curved towards the blade. Examples of the latter fashion occur in the great seal of King Henry II., here given; in Harl. MS. 603, *passim*; and in Cotton MS., Titus, D. xvi. See also our woodcut, No. 41. The pommel was round, hemispherical, square, lozenge, trefoiled or cinquefoiled. All these forms may be seen in Harl. MS., 603, Titus, D. xvi., the Bayeux tapestry, Addit. MS. 11,695, and the effigy of Henry II., figured by Stothard. This effigy also shews very clearly the Belt with its buckle, by which the sword was fastened round the waist. Compare also the second plate of the Bayeux tapestry, where the form of this short belt is very distinctly exhibited. We have already noticed that the sword was sometimes worn with its handle projecting through a cleft in the hauberk, the scabbard being fixed beneath the hauberk. See cut 34, and Bayeux tapestry, Plate VI. As in our own day, swords attributed to ancient heroes had an especial value, and became the most cherished gifts of kings and nobles.

Thus, when Richard Cœur-de-Lion was on his way to the Holy Land, "the king of Sicily sent to him many presents of great value, consisting of gold and silver, of horses and cloth of silk. But the king of England would receive nothing from him, except a little ring, which he accepted as a token of their mutual esteem. On the other hand, King Richard gave to King Tancred that most excellent sword which the Britons call *Caliburn*, and which had been the sword of Arthur, once the valiant king of England[213]."

The Sword of William the Conqueror became the feudal instrument by which the Umfrevilles held the lordship of Riddesdale, in Northumberland:—"In the tenth year of William the Conqueror, Robert de Umfranvil, knight, obtained from that king a grant of the Lordship, Valley and Forest of Riddesdale, by the service of defending that part of the country for ever from Enemies and Wolves, with that Sword which King William had by his side when he entered Northumberland[214]."

From a very curious drawing in the Psalter of Eadwine, written at Canterbury in the middle of the twelfth century, and now preserved in the library of Trinity College, Cambridge, we learn the exact manner in which the soldiery of this day furbished and ground their swords. The implement for furbishing is in the form of an ordinary axe-head, fixed in the centre of a rod or staff, which is held by both hands. This curious subject has been engraved by Mr. Westwood in his *Palæographia Sacra*.

The Mace does not often appear in the pictorial monuments of the period. It is, however, seen in the Bayeux tapestry, in the hands of both armies. The heads are quatrefoil, or of a heart-shape. What Wace calls the "gibet" is considered to be the mace, and it is carried at the right-hand side of the knight, to be used when the lance had been broken:

"Endementrez ke il versa,
Sa lance chaï è froissa,
Et il a le *gibet* seisi,
Ki a sun *destre bras pendi*."—*Rom. de Rou*, 1. 13,456.

It was also the usual arm of Churchmen when they went to battle; who sought thus to avoid the denunciation against those "who smite with the sword." Under the name of *clava*, it is mentioned by Guillaume le Breton:—

"Nunc contus, nunc clava caput, nunc vero bipennis
Excerebrat."—*Philippidos*, p. 213.

The Axe, which in the Bayeux tapestry is never seen in the hands of the Norman knights, appears in the twelfth century to have come into favour among them, for even the kings of this race are said to have contended with it. Thus Hoveden, describing the valour of Stephen at the battle of Lincoln, in 1141, says:—"Then was seen the might of the king, equal to a thunderbolt, slaying some with his immense battle-axe, and striking down others. Then arose the shouts afresh, all rushing against him, and he against all. At length, through the number of the blows, the king's battle-axe was broken asunder. Instantly, with his right hand, drawing his sword, he marvellously waged the combat until the sword also was broken. On seeing this, William de Kahamnes, a most powerful knight, rushed upon the king, and seizing him by the helmet, cried with loud voice, 'Hither, all of you, come hither! I have taken the King.'"

In the quotation from the *Philippidos*, above, we have seen that the double-axe, the *bipennis*, was also in use at this time. Like the mace, it is of rare occurrence in the pictures of the day, but several representations of it will be found in Harleian MS. 603, a Latin Psalter of the close of the eleventh century, probably written in France.

Among the weapons in use by the common soldiery are the cultellus, the guisarme, the pike, the bisacuta, the javelin, the sling, the long-bow, the cross-bow, (at the close of the twelfth century,) and some others in which fire was the offensive agent. The Cultellus, or coustel, was a short sword or long dagger, well calculated for use of the foot-troops, rushing upon the knights who had been unhorsed in the charge of the cavalry; and equally well adapted for close fight of foot against foot. A statute of William, king of Scotland, (1165-1214,) shews the identity of the coustel and dagger: "Habeat equum, habergeon, capitium e ferro, et cultellum qui dicitur *dagger*[215]." In the fourteenth century, Knighton has: "Cultellos, quos *daggerios* vulgariter dicunt, in *powchiis* impositis[216]." And Walsingham, in the fifteenth century, writes: "Mox extracto cultello, quem *dagger* vulgo dicimus, ictum militi minabatur[217]." The cultellus, like the sica of classic times, not only became the weapon of the depredator, but gave its name to that class; as we see from a statute of the Count of Toulouse in 1152: "Si quis aliquem hominem malum, quem Cultellarium dicimus, cum cultellis euntem nocte causa furandi occiderit, nullum damnum patiatur propter hoc." The Guisarme, which we have already noticed in the previous chapter, was still in favour in the twelfth century, and is frequently mentioned by the writers of this period. A striking passage of the *Philippidos* brings before us a rich group of the weapons of this day:—

"Nunc contus, nunc clava caput, nunc vero bipennis
Excerebrat: sed nec bisacuta, sudisve vel hasta
Otia vel gladius ducit."—*Page* 213.

The contus and the sudis of these lines are pikes, of which the particular difference from each other would be a vain enquiry for our times. The clava (mace) and bipennis have been already noticed. The Bisacuta appears to have been an arm of the pick kind. Père Daniel cites from a French poet who lived in 1376, these lines:—

"Trop bien faisoit la besaguë
Qui est par les deux becs aguë."—*Mil. Franç.*, i. 433.

The phrase, *deux becs*, seems to indicate a form of the kind we have mentioned, and the exact structure of the weapon is perhaps presented to us in the well-known brass of Bishop Wyvil, at Salisbury[218]. A letter remissory of the fourteenth century appears to confirm this view: "Le dit Hue d'un gran *martel* qu'il portoit, appellé besague, getta au dit Colart," &c. The head of the martel-d'armes was constantly, on one or both sides, of this pick or beak form. The besague was also a carpenter's tool. Thus Wace, on the invasion of England by the Normans, tells us:—

"Li charpentiers, ki emprès vindrent,
Granz coignies en lor mains tindrent:
Doloères è besaguës
Orent à lor costez pendues."—*Line* 11,650.

The Sling of this time may be seen, though rudely drawn, in the group from Add. MS. 14,789, copied in our woodcut No. 37. Compare also cuts 12 and 50. The Javelin is found at the close of the eleventh century; in the hands of the English in the Bayeux tapestry, and in the French manuscript, Harl. 603, fol. 60. In the twelfth century it seems to have fallen into discredit among these nations, though probably employed to a much later period by the Spaniards[219], with whom it was always a favourite weapon, and by those races who had retained the rough fashions and the heroic traditions of their

Old-Northern ancestry.

The Long-bow was of the most simple construction: it appears frequently in the Bayeux tapestry, (Plates XIII., XV. and XVI.;) in the cotemporary manuscript, Harleian 603, and in many monuments of the twelfth century. The arrows are usually barbed. A curious variety of the arrow is seen in the Spanish codex, Addit. MSS. 11,695, written in 1109. This missile, which is frequently represented in the volume, has three pairs of barbs, fixed at a little distance from each other along the shaft; a cruel contrivance, which does not seem to have reached other nations of Europe, and, we may hope, was not long in vogue within the Pyrenees. Already in the twelfth century the English began to evince that skill in archery which afterwards gave them such celebrity. At the siege of Messina by Cœur-de-Lion, as we learn from Richard of Devizes, the Sicilians were forced to leave their walls unmanned, "because no one could look out of doors, but he would have an arrow in his eye before he could shut it." The king himself did not disdain occasionally to use the bow. When before the castle of Nottingham, which had been seized by "Earl John," the monarch, says Roger of Hoveden, "took up his quarters near the castle, so that the archers therein pierced the king's men at his very feet. The king, incensed at this, put on his armour, and commanded his troops to make an assault upon the castle; on which a sharp conflict took place, and many fell on both sides. The king himself slew one knight with an arrow, and having at last prevailed, drove back his enemies into the castle, took some outworks which had been thrown up without the gates, and destroyed the outer gates by fire[220]."

The practice of archery was encouraged and protected by statute. Among the enactments of Henry I. of England, it was provided, that if any one in practising with arrows or with darts should by accident slay another, it was not to be visited against him as a crime[221].

The Quivers, as represented in the Bayeux tapestry, are without covers; but on folio 25 of Harl. MS. 603, is a drawing of a quiver having a cap attached by cords, so that when the quiver is in use, the cap remains suspended by the strings. The dress of the archers has been already noticed.

The Cross-bow does not appear to have been recognised as a military weapon before the close of the twelfth century. The term *balista*, by which it is described in monkish annals and other writings, is indeed found at an earlier period; but there is great doubt whether this earlier balista meant a hand-weapon, or one of those "gyns" derived from classic times. The later use of the arm seems confirmed by the fact that it is not found in pictorial representations till about 1200. There appears to have been an attempt to introduce it at the beginning of this century, but it was prohibited by papal decree as unfit for Christian warfare. A council in 1139, under Innocent II., has: "Artem illam mortiferam et Deo odibilem balistariorum et sagittariorum adversus Christianos et Catholicos exerceri de cetero sub anathemate prohibemus[222]." This denunciation was renewed under Innocent III.; but by this time Richard Cœur-de-Lion and Philippe Auguste had sanctioned the use of the arm, and the cross-bow was triumphant. Both Guillaume le Breton and Guiart place the introduction of the weapon at the close of the twelfth century; and both tell us that Richard was the first to adopt it, and that Philip followed his example. Describing the siege of the castle of Boves, Brito says[223]:—

"Francigenis nostris illis ignota diebus
Res erat omnino quid balistariusarcus
Quid balista foret, nec habebat in agmine toto
Rex, quemquam sciret armis qui talibus uti."

And again, writing of the death of Richard I., he makes Atropos speak thus[224]:—

"Hac volo, non alia Richardum morte perire.
Ut qui Francigenis balistæ primitus usum
Tradidit, ipse sui rem primitus experiatur,
Quamque alios docuit, in se vim sentiat artis."

Guiart has this similar passage:—

"Ainsi fina par le quarrel[225],
Qu' Anglois tindrent à deshonneste,
Li roís Richart, qui d'arbaleste
Aporta premier l'us en France.
De son art ot mal chevance."—*Chron. Métr.*, l. 2644.

The form of the arbalest of this time may be seen in our woodcut, No. 50. It was bent by placing the foot in the loop or "stirrup" at the extremity, and then drawing the cord upwards with the hands. At a later period, the bow was made much stronger, and of steel, then requiring mechanical contrivances to bend it. The arrow of the cross-bow was shorter and stouter than that of the long-bow. As may be seen in our woodcut, No. 50, it was feathered; a particular which is noticed in the *Roman de Garin*:—

"Volent piles plusque pluie par prés,
Et les saiettes et *carriax*empennés."

This name of Carriaux (quadrelli or quarrels) was given to these missiles from the four-sided (or pyramidal) form of the head. Thus Guillaume le Breton, speaking of the death of Richard the First:—

"———Quadratæ cuspidis una
Pendet arundo."

From an ordinance of Theobald, count of Champagne, in the next century (1256), we learn that the provision of quarrels for a cross-bow was fifty: "Chascun de la commune dou Neufchastel qui aura vaillant xx. livres, aura arbaleste en son hostel et quarraus jusqu'à cinquante." The arrow of the arbalest is sometimes called *vireton*, from the French *virer*, on account of its rotary flight. Compare the classical *verutum*, a javelin which owed its name to a similar property. Though the English appear to have used the cross-bow from near the close of the twelfth to the end of the thirteenth century, in the succeeding age the long-bow obtained a signal triumph over its rival.

In the hands of a stout soldiery, indeed, the long-bow is a much superior weapon; for a dozen arrows may be discharged while the arbalester is winding up his instrument and fixing a single quarrel: and the long-bow being a vertical arm, permits a close array, which cannot be attained with the horizontal cross-bow: again, the long-bow is a weapon of very light carriage, while its rival, with its thick bow of steel and its apparatus for bending, is both ponderous and unwieldy: the size of the quarrels also permitted only eighteen of them to be brought by each man into the field, ("et auront trousses empanées et cirées de dix-huit traits du moins:" Ordinance of Charles VII. of France), while the English archer carried "twenty-four Scotchmen under his belt." "Les arbalestriers Gennevois," says Froissart, "commencèrent à traire, et ces archers d'Angleterre firent voler ces sagettes de grand' façon, qui entrèrent et descendirent si ouniement sur ces Gennevois que ce sembloit neige. Les Gennevois, qui n'avoient pas appris à trouver tels archers que sont ceux d'Angleterre, quand ils sentirent ces sagettes qui leur perçoient bras, têtes et banlèvre, furent tantôt desconfits[226]." But to handle the long-bow thus effectively, required a race strong in sinew and practised in their art: to wind up and discharge a cross-bow was the feat of a boy.

The Greek fire, still discountenanced among the Christian states of the West, was in frequent use with the enemies of the Cross in the East. All the accounts of the Crusades contain instances of its employment. Of the tubes from which it was discharged we have already spoken. In the *Bibliothèque des Croisades* of M. Reinaud[227], we have the account of a variety of this incendiary agent, from the pen of an Arabian historian of the Third Crusade, Ibn Alatir. "When Acre was besieged by the Christians," he tells us, "there came into the town a man of Damascus, to assist in its defence. He began by casting upon the towers erected by the besiegers, pots filled with naptha and other ingredients. These not being alight, fell harmlessly among the Christians, who laughed at and jeered the Mussulmans for their seeming failure. Meanwhile, the man of

Damascus waited till the mixture had diffused itself over every part of the tower. Then, casting forth a lighted missile, in an instant the tower was in flames, and so rapid and so extensive was the combustion, that the Christians had no time to descend: men, arms, all was consumed."

From a curious passage of Wace we learn what were the weapons employed by the peasantry when driven to revolt against their lords. In describing the insurrection of the "vilains" under Richard the Second, duke of Normandy, he makes these "bachelers de bele juvente" exclaim:—

"A machues è à grant peus,
A sajetes et as tineus,
As arcs, as haches, as gisarmes,
Et as pierres ki n'ara armes,
Od la grant genz ke nous avum,
Des chevaliers nus desfendum."—*Rom. de Rou*, l. 6043.

The *peus*, or *pieux*, were pikes; the *tineus* were poles used to carry the grape-tubs at the vintage, which, when converted into instruments of war, we may suppose were armed with heads of iron. The idea of contention by throwing stones is by no means a mere poetical fancy of our author. Froissart even tells us of a victory achieved by this means. A band of French knights and nobles going to attack a section of the Free Companies, these latter posted themselves on a hill, and being well provided with stones, "cast them so forcibly upon those who approached, that they broke their bassinets, however strong they might be, and wounded and maimed the men-at-arms to such an extent, that none either could or dared to advance further, however good his shield might be, (tant bien targé qu'il fut). And this first division was so thoroughly crushed that never again could it do good service." Reinforcements arriving to the Companies, a more regular onset was made: "Que vous ferois-je long parlement? De celle besogne dont vous oyez parler, les François en eurent pour lors le pieur[228]."

In the manufacture of arms, the steel of Poitou had already become celebrated. John, monk of Marmoustier, who lived in the middle of the twelfth century, in describing the knighting of Geoffry, duke of Normandy, tells us that he had a lance of ash, armed with a head of Poitou steel. Malmesbury distinguishes also Lorraine. "At the siege of Antioch," he says, "Godfrey of Bouillon, with a Lorrainian sword, cut asunder a Turk who had demanded single combat, so that one half of the man lay panting on the ground, while the other half was carried off by the horse at full speed; so firmly did the unbeliever keep his seat. Another also, who attacked him, he clave asunder from the neck to the groin; nor did the dreadful stroke stop here, but cut entirely through the saddle and the backbone of the horse."

124

Hungary had at a very early period enjoyed a celebrity for its weapon manufacture. Charlemagne, writing to Offa of Mercia, offering him presents for his churches, adds: "And for your own acceptance I send a belt, a Hungarian sword, and two silk mantles[229]." The method of hardening steel, in the eleventh and twelfth centuries, by immersion, when red hot, in cold water, may be seen in Theophilus Presbyter, lib. iii. cap. 19.

The FLAGS AND STANDARDS in use during this period were the prince's standards, the banner, the pennon, and the small lance-flag or streamer. The consecrated standard of William I., bestowed by the Pope, appears to be represented on the ninth plate of the Bayeux tapestry, where it is figured of a square form and ensigned with a cross. It was carried near the person of William throughout the day by the knight Toustain: "Turstinus, filius Rollonis vexillum Normannorum portavit[230]."

> "Et quant li Dus tournout, tournout;
> E quant arestout, arestout."—*Wace*, l. 13,807.

It was also used to indicate any danger into which the leader might have fallen. Thus, when Philip Augustus was unhorsed at the battle of Bovines, Rigord tells us that his standard-bearer signified the king's peril by depressing the Royal Standard several times over the spot.

The Dragon-standard, of which we have seen some examples in our first division, is still found among the Germans and the English. We have already observed its exact form in the pictures of Harold in the Bayeux tapestry. It accompanied the hosts of Richard Cœur-de-Lion. Richard of Devizes, in recording the attack upon the "Griffones" at Messina, says: "The king of England proceeded in arms: the terrible standard of the Dragon is borne in front; while, behind the king, the sound of the trumpet excites the army[231]." Hoveden, under date 1191, tells us that Richard "delivered *his Dragon* (*Draconem suum*) to be borne by Peter de Pratellis." Guillaume le Breton, in the *Philippidos*, gives to the Emperor Otho a standard formed of a dragon and an eagle.

> "Erigit in carro palum, paloque Draconem
> Implicat, ut possit procul hinc atque inde videri,
> Hauriat et ventos cauda tumefactus et alis,
> Dentibus horrescens rictusque patentis hiatu,
> Quem super aurata volucer Jovis imminet ala."

Guiart has a similar passage; adding that the Dragon of the emperor—

> "Vers France ot la gueule baée,
> Pour le réaume chalengier,

Come s'il deust tout mangier.
Cis Dragons soustint la Bannière
Des connoissances l'emperiere,
Qu'il porte au bel et à loré.
Desus ot un Aigle doré:
C'est *signe de guerre cuisant*."

The Car-standard, or Carrocium, of the English king Stephen has already been noticed in the sketch of the battle of Cuton Moor, (p. 107.) The Carrocio of the Milanese was still regarded as their Palladium.

Banners were carried by knights banneret, by the Church Advocati, and by the Town troops, or Communitates Parochiarum. The knight's banner, as we have already seen, was square; and, as soon as heraldic devices became settled, was ensigned with the bearing of the leader to whom it belonged. Its especial use was to muster and to rally the troops of the banneret:—

"Cil treis orent treis gunfanuns,
A ralier lur cumpaingnuns."—*Rom. de Rou*, i. 337.

Bishops and abbots appointed knights to defend their possessions, to lead their contingent, and to fight under their banner. These advocati in time made their office hereditary. The Counts of Vexin were the *avoués* of the Abbey of St. Denis, and the lands of Vexin coming into the possession of the kings of France, these monarchs acquired the office of bannerers of the abbey. Thus the plain red flag of St. Denis became, under the name of the Oriflamme, the most distinguished banner of the French monarchy.

"L'Oriflamme est une Banniere,
Aucun poi plus forte que guimple:
De cendal roujoyant et simple,
Sans pourctraiture d'autre affaire."—*G. Guiart*.

It was Louis le Gros who united the county of Vexin to the crown of France[232].

A very curious variety of the knightly banner occurs on the twelfth plate of the Bayeux tapestry; the flag is semicircular, is ensigned with a bird within a bordure, and has a fringe at the edge. Mr. Worsaae has suggested that this bird, which appears on the Norman side, may be the Raven of the Old-Northmen, retained by their descendants in honour of the deeds of their forefathers.

The banners of the communal troops bore the effigies of Saints, each parish gathering round the flag on which its particular saint was portrayed. This usage was as old as the time of Louis VI. of France: "Tunc ergo communitas in Francia popularis instituta est a præsulibus, ut presbyteri commitarentur Regi ad obsidionem vel pugnam cum Vexillis et parochianis omnibus[233]."

The word Gonfanon, Guntfano, so frequently occurring in the writings of this period, seems to be indifferently applied to the leader's standard, the knightly banner, and the lance-flag. It has been derived from the German *kunden*, indicare, and *Fahne*, vexillum; or from *Fahne* and the Old-Scandinavian *Gunna*, prœlium. Mr. Kemble inclines to the latter derivation; see glossary to *Beowulf*, in v. *Guth*. A capitulary of Charles the Bald gives the name of Gonfanon to the banner of the Church vassals: "Let our envoys (missi nostri) see that the troops of every bishop, abbot, and abbess, march forth properly equipped, and with their Gonfalonier (cum Guntfannonario)." The standard sent by the pope to William the Conqueror is by Wace named a gonfanon:—

"L'Apostoile
Un gonfanon li envéia."—*Line* 11,450.

He gives it also to the barons and more powerful captains:—

"N'i a riche home ne baron
Ki n'ait lez lui son gonfanon;
U gonfanon u autre enseigne,
U il se maisnie[234] restraigne."

In the following passages, it is the lance-flag:—

"Les lances bessent, o sont li gonfanon."—*Rom. de Garin.*
"Baisse la lance ou li gonfanon pent."—*Rom. d'Aubery.*
"Moult si siest bien au col la lance au gonfanon."
Rom. de
Duguesclin.

The Pennon, as we have before seen, (p. 95,) was the flag of those knights who had not attained to the dignity of banneret. It appears to have terminated in a point or points, but its exact form at this period has not been ascertained. It probably differed in nothing but its size from the lance-flags seen in the Bayeux tapestry and on the seals and other monuments of the eleventh and twelfth centuries. Wace, however, in the following passage, seems to use the word in a more general sense; for it is the Vicomte du Cotentin, lieutenant of the duke of Normandy, of whom he is speaking:—

"Les li fist un penun porter,
U lur gent pussent recuvrer."—*Rom. de Rou,* l. 7839.

If these various flags were found sufficient to keep together the troops of an ordinary expedition; in large armaments such as those of the Crusades, the want of some more general distinction must soon have been felt. Hoveden therefore tells us, under the year 1188, that the leaders against the Saracens, "for the purpose of recognising their various nations, adopted distinguishing signs for themselves and their people. For the king of France and his people wore red crosses; the king of England and his people, white crosses; while Philip, earl of Flanders, and his followers, wore green crosses." The existence of a mode of recognition among troops at this period is confirmed by the passage of Wace in which he names the "cognoissances" of the Norman host and their allies:—

> "E tuit orent fet cognoissances,
> Ke Normant altre conéust,
> Et k'entreposture n'éust.
> Ke Normant altre ne férist,
> Ne Franceiz altre n'océist."—*Line* 12,816.

The particular nature of the sign of recognition intended by the chronicler, it is in vain now to inquire. The note of M. Pluquet on the passage gives "Signes de convention."

The Lance-flag is found throughout the period now under notice. Many examples occur in the Bayeux tapestry, and in the royal and baronial seals of the time. The usual device upon it is a cross, a square, a number of rounds, or stripes of different colours; or the streamer is of a single tint. It is dentated in two or more cuts, and sometimes fringed at the edge. See our engraved examples.

The Musical Instruments used in war were the horn, the trumpet, and a variety of the latter called the *graisle*. Wace mentions all these in his account of the battle of Hastings:—

> "Dez ke li dous ost[235] s'entrevirent,
> Grant noise è grant temulte firent.
> Mult oïssiez graisles soner,
> E boisines è cors corner."—*Line* 13,135.

The horn of battle of this period is very clearly figured on folio 25 of Harleian MS. 603, a work of the close of the eleventh century. It is of the common semicircular form. The trumpet (boisine: buccina) is found, though in a monument of somewhat later date, on the inscribed slab of "Godefrey le Troumpour," now preserved in the library of the London Guildhall[236]. Compare also our woodcut, No. 73. The graisle (from *gracilis*) was, as its name indicates, of a slender form; its exact fashion has not been ascertained.

The Horse-furniture presents some new features; especially in the arming of the steed in chain-mail, a practice which appears to have originated towards the close of the twelfth century. Wace indeed tells us that William Fitz-Osbert, at the field of Hastings, rode a steed thus accoutred:—

"Vint Willame li filz Osber,
Son cheval tot covert de fer."—*Line* 12,627.

But we may well believe that it was rather the necessity of a rhyme to "Osber" than the usage of the period, that gives us this iron horse at so early a date. Wace, writing in the second half of the twelfth century, appears merely to have availed himself of the usual license of middle-age authorities: to depict a past generation in the lineaments of his own. The practice of arming the horse does not seem to have become general till towards the close of the thirteenth century. A pictorial example of the trapper of chain-mail will be found in our woodcut, No. 86. The Saddle had a high pommel and cantle, as may be seen in our engravings of the royal seals of this period. In many examples of the Bayeux tapestry they form volutes, (viewed laterally,) exactly like the sides of an Ionic capital. The saddle-cloth does not appear in this tapestry, but it is found on the second seal of Henry I., on the seal of King Stephen, and on that of Louis VII. of France. In these examples it is quite plain; but later it acquires an ornamental character, as in the seal of Conan, duke of Britanny, c. 1165, (woodcut 41). It is of a more enriched pattern in the Great Seal of Henry II., here given.

SECOND SEAL OF KING HENRY II.

No. 44.

From Wace we learn that the girths and breastplate were named, in the "Romance" of that day, *cingles* and *poitrail*:—

"Li peitral del cheval rompi,
E li dui cengles altresi."—*Rom. de Rou*, l. 14,674.

This poitrail has generally, in the period under examination, pendants attached to it, in the form of rounds,—perhaps grelots. See woodcuts 1, 25, 28 and 29.

Roman monuments offer similar examples, as in Trajan's Column, the Pillar of Antonine, and other remains, where the pendants are bells, crescents, trefoils, rounds, and guttæ. Such collars are found also in the paintings of the Ajunta Caves, where bells and rounds alternate. This monument is assigned to the first century of our era. In the curious Spanish manuscript, dated 1109, in the British Museum, Addit. MSS., 11,695, the circular pendants occur,

130

attached not only to the poitrail, but to the saddle (fol. 223). The Bits used for the war-horse have long cheeks, which are often of an ogee form. The rein is generally quite plain, though sometimes ornamented with studs, as in examples in the manuscript last cited.

The Spur was still of a single goad, and fastened by a single strap. The form of the goad offers some variety: it is leaf-shaped, conical, lozenge-shaped, and sometimes consists of a ball from which springs a short spike. A variety is fashioned into a sort of button, having a slender spike in the centre. The first three kinds are seen in the Bayeux tapestry and many of the seals of the period. The ball-and-spike spur is well shewn in the effigies of Henry II. and Richard I. at Fontevraud, figured by Stothard in his "Monuments." The last variety may be seen in Addit. MS. 11,695, fol. 223. The shank of the spur is sometimes straight, as in Anglo-Saxon times: sometimes curved. The curved form appears in the sculptured effigies of King Henry II. and Richard I. The spur of Richard the First seems to have been attached to the strap by rivets.

The Caltrop, or *tribulus*, an instrument derived from classic times, was in use, but not of frequent employment. Anna Comnena tells us that the Emperor Alexis strewed them in the path of the French cavalry; and at a later period, we read of knights fixing their spurs point upwards in the way of their advancing enemy, after the manner of caltrops: but this cruel device appears to have been practised very rarely, and we may venture to believe that it was generally discountenanced as beneath the dignity and generosity of true chivalry. At a later period, caltrops were used to strew over the slope of a breach, to impede the advance of a storming party.

From a very curious passage in the *Roman de Rou*, we learn that the knight sometimes went to battle *tied to his saddle*:—

"Li reis aveit un soldéier,
Brun out nom, novel chevalier.
Sor son cheval sist noblement,
Apareillié mult richement.
A sa sele fu atachiez,
E par li coisses fu liez," &c.—*Line* 16,064.

However strange such a device may appear, the mention of it by other ancient writers forbids us to regard it as a mere vagary of the poet. Matthew Paris, under the year 1243, recounting the irruption of the Tartars into Europe, says: "They have horses, not large, but very strong, and that require but little food, and they bind themselves firmly on their backs." And, in the fifteenth century, the writer of the life of Earl Richard of Warwick tells us that, at a justing-match, his hero was obliged to dismount from his horse, because some of his adversaries had accused him of being tied in his saddle.

For the Horse itself, Spain appears to have been in the highest favour for the purity of its breed. Walter Giffard had brought from Gallicia the steed on which Duke William rode at the field of Hastings:—

"Sun boen cheval fist demander.
Ne poeit l'en meillor trover.
D'Espaigne li out envéié
Un Reis, par mult grant amistié.
Armes ne presse ne dotast,
Se sis Sires l'esperonast.
Galtier Giffart l'out amené,
Ki à Saint Jame aveit esté."—*Rom. de Rou*, l. 12,673.

And in the well-known passage of the Monk of Marmoustier, where he describes the knighting of Geoffry, duke of Normandy, we are told that the young hero was "mounted upon a Spanish horse, which had been presented by the king."

How the horses of the knights were conveyed in ships and disembarked from the vessels, is curiously shewn in the ninth and tenth plates of the Bayeux tapestry.

Of the ENGINES employed in sieges, all those mentioned in our first division appear to have been still in use. The ancient Vinea (Cat or Sow) is frequently mentioned, and the moveable Tower, or *Beffroi*, becomes a prominent feature in all the great siege operations of this century. William of Malmesbury has left us an excellent description of these two contrivances in his account of the siege of Jerusalem[237]:—

"There was one engine which we call the Sow, the ancients, Vinea; because the machine, which is constructed of slight timbers, the roof covered with boards and wicker-work, and the sides defended with undressed hides, protects those who are within; who, after the manner of a sow, proceed to undermine the foundations of the walls. There was another, which, for want of timber, was but a moderate-sized tower, constructed after the manner of houses. They call it Berefreid[238]. This was intended to equal the walls in height. And now the fourteenth day of July arrived, when some began to undermine the wall with the Sows, others to move forward the Tower. To do this more conveniently, they took it toward the works in separate pieces[239], and putting it together again at such a distance as to be out of bowshot, advanced it on wheels nearly close to the wall. Meantime the slingers with stones, the archers with arrows, and the crossbow-men with bolts, each intent on his own department, began to press forward and dislodge their opponents from the ramparts. Soldiers, too, unmatched in courage, ascend the Tower, waging nearly equal war against the enemy with missile weapons and with stones. Nor indeed were our foes at all remiss, but trusting their whole security to their valour, they poured down boiling grease and oil upon the Tower, and slung stones on the soldiers, rejoicing in the completion of their desires by the destruction of multitudes. During the whole of that day the battle was such that neither party seemed to think they had been worsted. On the following, the business was decided: for the Franks, becoming more experienced from the event of the attack of the preceding day, threw faggots flaming with oil on a tower adjoining the wall, and on those who defended it; which, blazing by the action of the wind, first seized the timber, and then the stones, and drove off the garrison. Moreover, the beams which the Turks had left hanging down from the walls, in order that, being forcibly drawn back, they might, by their recoil, batter the Tower in pieces, in case it should advance too near, were by the Franks dragged to them, by cutting away the ropes; and being placed from the engine to the wall, and covered with hurdles, they formed a bridge of communication from the Tower to the ramparts. Thus what the infidels had contrived for their defence, became the means of their destruction; for then the enemy, dismayed by the smoking masses of flame, and by the courage of our soldiers, began to give way. These, advancing on the wall, and thence into the city, manifested the excess of their joy by the strenuousness of their exertions."

William of Tyre mentions also the use of the beffroi at the siege of Jerusalem; adding that the side towards the city was so constructed that a portion of it might be let down, after the manner of a drawbridge, thus enabling the assailants to enter upon the walls[240]. Philippe Auguste frequently employed this engine. At the siege of Château-Roux, in Berry,—

"Cratibus et lignis rudibus *Belfragia* surgunt
Turribus alta magis et mœnibus."—*Philippidos*, lib. ii.

And again, at the siege of Radepont, in Normandy: "Erectis in circuitu *Turribus* ligneis *ambulatoriis*, aliisque tormentis quam plurimis viriliter impugnavit et cœpit[241]."

King Richard I. constructed also in Sicily a wooden tower, which he afterwards carried with him to the Holy Land. After forcing the city of Messina, "the king," says Richard of Devizes, "having but little confidence in the natives, built a new wooden tower of great strength and height by the walls of the city, which, to the reproach of the Griffones, (Greeks,) he called *Mate-griffun*," (sub an. 1190). In 1191, "the king of England, about to leave Sicily, caused the tower which he had built to be taken down, and stowed the whole of the materials in his ships, to take along with him." And "on the third day after his arrival at the siege of Acre," continues Richard of Devizes, "the king caused his wooden tower, which he had named 'Mate-griffun' when it was made in Sicily, to be built and set up; and before the dawn of the fourth day the machine stood erect by the walls of Acre, and from its height looked down upon the city beneath. And by sunrise were thereon archers casting missiles without ceasing against the Turks and Thracians."

The name *Mate-griffon* appears to be derived from the favourite game of the courtly in these days; "donner eschec et mat" being equivalent to the "check-mate" of our modern chess-players. Ordericus Vitalis has a passage curiously illustrative of this subject: "Castrum condere cœpit, quod Mataputenam, id est, devincens meretricem, pro despectu Haduissæ Comitissæ, nuncupavit[242]."

In 1160, the Emperor Frederick besieging Crema, in Italy, employed the beffroi, filling it with chosen troops. He placed crossbowmen on the upper story, in order that, shooting down upon the walls, they might clear the parapet of its defenders; while, from the lower stage, soldiers of tried boldness might fix their drawbridges on the wall, and advance to the capture of the city[243].

At this same city of Crema, in 1159, occurred an act of patriotism, admirable from the resolution which inspired it, though terrible in its consequences. The emperor advanced a Beffroi towards the beleaguered city, in front of which he placed the youthful hostages whom he had obtained from the unhappy Cremans, in hopes of thus forcing the inhabitants to a capitulation. But the citizens, regardless of all save their liberty, continued to ply their engines against the tower, though every stone that was cast forth fell in death among their children[244].

134

The siege of Ancona, in 1174, offers another instance of heroism in connection with the belfragium, more pleasing in its circumstances. The besieged had been successful in their endeavours to beat back the towers and scatter their occupants; but as these latter still kept up a steady discharge of missiles from a short distance, no one dared venture beyond the walls to set fire to the deserted structures. At last a widow named STAMURA, seizing a torch, advanced into the plain, and regardless of the storm of bolts and arrows that fell around her, steadily achieved the task she had undertaken, and having set the towers in flames, returned in safety to the city[245].

The siege of Ancona is further remarkable for the employment by the citizens of divers; who succeeded in capturing several of the vessels engaged in blockading the port. Taking advantage of a strong wind blowing from the sea, the divers contrived to cut the cables of seven of the Venetian ships, which then drifted helplessly ashore[246].

The *Vinea* mentioned in a foregoing extract from Malmesbury, was called also the Cat. Thus Vegetius: "Vineas dixerunt veteres, quas nunc militari barbaricoque usu Cattos vocant[247]." Guillaume le Breton also mentions this machine and its use:—

"Huc faciunt reptare Catum, tectique sub illo
Suffodiunt murum."—*Philipp.*, lib. vii.

While, from the Monk of Vau-de-Cernay we learn that the contrivance was of small dimensions: "Machinam quandam parvam, quæ lingua vulgari Catus dicitur, faciebat duci ad suffodiendum murum[248]." There were, however, varieties of the Cat, one of which was used to oppose the besiegers in the beffroi. Thus Radevicus: "Magnaque audacia, super muros et in suis machinis quos Cattas appellant, operiuntur, et cum (oppugnatores) admoverentur pontes, ipsi eos vel occuparent, vel dejicerent, murumque scalis ascendere nitentes vario modo deterrent[249]." And another kind was employed by the assailants in crossing the ditch[250].

The Battering-ram, according to Richard of Devizes, was employed by Cœur-de-Lion at the siege of Messina: "In the meantime, the king with his troops approached the gates of the city, which he instantly forced by the application of the Battering-ram, and entering within, took possession of every part, even to Tancred's palace and the lodgings of the French around their king's quarters, which he spared out of respect to the king."

Among the stone-throwing machines, the Mangona and the Mangonella are discriminated as casting, the former large, the latter smaller stones. The monk Abbo has already, in his account of the siege of Paris in 886, mentioned the

"Mangana——
Saxa quibus jaciunt *ingentia*."

Guillaume le Breton, in the *Philippidos*, tells us:—

"Interea grossos Petraria mittit ab intus
Assidue lapides, Mangonellusque *minores*."

Among the effects recorded of these great projectiles, we may cite the account of Otto of Frisinga, who tells us that when the Emperor Frederic attacked Tortona in 1155, a stone was cast from one of the periers of such magnitude, that, falling before the door of the cathedral, where three of the principal citizens were in deliberation on the best means of defending the city, it killed them all[251].

The term *mangonneaux* is sometimes applied to the stones or other missiles discharged by the instrument. From the name *mangona* our word *gun* appears to be derived: a supposition that seems strengthened by the fact that the earliest "gonnes," like the mangonæ, were employed to cast stones.

The terrors of the balistæ were occasionally aggravated by their being made the instruments of a special vengeance. Thus Malmesbury informs us that, at the siege of Antioch in 1097, the Turks, irritated by losses sustained from the besieging Crusaders, "wreaked their indignation on the Syrian and Armenian inhabitants of the city; throwing, by means of their balistæ and petraries, the heads of those whom they had slain into the camp of the Franks, that by such means they might lacerate their feelings." A somewhat similar incident is reported by Froissart in his account of the siege of Thun l'Evêque in 1327[252]; so that these cruelties do not appear to be mere tales of credulous pilgrims, or inventions of monkish chroniclers.

Forts of wood were of occasional employment, the materials of which were transported from place to place, so that the structure might be speedily raised. Wace gives us a description of that brought over by William the Conqueror, and built up at Hastings:—

"Donc ont des nés mairrien[253] geté,
A la terre l'ont traîné,
Trestut percié è tut dolé:
Li cheviles tutes dolées
Orent *en granz bariz* portées:
Ainz ke il fust bien avespré,
En ont un chastelet fermé."—*Line* 11,658.

Mines were in use both by Richard I. and Philippe Auguste. At the siege of Acre in 1191, Richard attacked the city with archers and balistæ: "But more important than these," adds Devizes, "were the miners, making themselves a way beneath the ground, sapping the foundation of the walls, while soldiers bearing shields, having planted ladders, sought an entrance over the ramparts." The French king employed the mine at the siege of the Castle of Boves, as we learn from William the Breton. See also Rigord, page 185. The mines of these days were large caverns in which pillars of wood supported the incumbent mass. The posts being smeared with pitch and surrounded with combustibles, fire was then brought, and the stanchions being consumed, the walls fell in. With the mine came the counter-mine; an example of which occurs in the description by Guillaume le Breton of the siege of Château-Gaillard; where the English, countermining against the French, met them in their works and drove them back with slaughter:—

"Suffodiunt murum. Sed non minus hostis ab illâ
Parte minare studet factoque foramine nostros
Retrò minatores telis compellit abire."—*Philipp.*, lib. vii.

Later, challenges were made, to be fought out in the mines, the combatants contending over a barrier of wood fixed in the midst. And Upton tells us that the aspirant to knighthood in a besieging army, no church being at hand, performed in the mine his vigil of arms.

While the besieging force plied their attack by means of the engines and mines already noticed, they had begun, in imitation of the ancients, to construct lines of circumvallation; in order at once to cut off the citizens from all communication with the open country, and to defend themselves against the sorties of the town. An example of this may be seen in the siege of Crema by the Emperor Frederic in 1159[254].

Under the general name of Hastilude (spear-play) were in use several kinds of MILITARY EXERCISES: the joust, the tourney and the behourd. "Torneamenta, justas, burdeicias, *sive alia* Hastiluda[255]." The joust and the tourney were, in their primary sense, mere modes of attack. The joust was the charge of a single horseman against a single antagonist. The tourney was the onset of a troop, who, having made their charge, turned back to acquire the necessary speed for a fresh attack. At the siege of Rouen—

"Mult voissiez, forment armez, issir Normanz,
Querre tornoiement è joste demandanz,
E joster è férir de lances è de branz."

Rom. de Rou, i. p. 209.

Again, at the siege of Mount Saint-Michael,—

"Mult véissiez joster sovent,

Chescun jor, al flo retraiant,
Vunt chevaliers jostes menant."—*Ibid.*, ii. p. 314.

The Behourd (*Bohordicum*) was an exercise with lance and target, of which the distinctive character has not been ascertained. "Trepidare quoque, quod vulgariter *biordare* dicitur, cum *scuto et lancea* aliquis clericus publicè non attentet[256]."

Military games, whose object was to familiarize the soldier in time of peace with the usages of war, had been long known. They were practised in classic times: they were in vogue, as Tacitus tells us, among the ancient Germans: they were pursued in Germany, as we learn from Nithard[257], in the ninth century. But that splendid and costly image of battle called a Tournament is not found earlier than the epoch which we are now considering. Several nations lay claim to its invention, but none offer such good proofs as the French. The Chronicle of Tours expressly says, under the year 1066: "Gaufridus de Pruliaco (Preulli), qui torneamenta invenit, apud Andegavum occiditur." And the Chronicle of St. Martin of Tours has a similar passage: "Anno Henrici Imp. VII. et Philippi Regis VI. fuit proditio apud Andegavum, ubi Gaufridus de Pruliaco et *alii barones* occisi sunt. Hic Gaufridus torneamenta invenit." Matthew Paris, again, names the tournament "conflictus Gallicus." And Ralph of Coggeshall has: "Dum, more Francorum, cum hastis vel contis sese cursim equitantes vicissim impeterent."

Tournaments seem to have first obtained favour in England in the troublous times of Stephen[258]. They were, however, discountenanced by Henry II., and the young aspirants to military renown were forced to seek in other lands the opportunity of distinguishing themselves. "Tyronum exercitiis in Anglia prorsus inhibitis, qui forte armorum affectantes gloriam exerceri volebant, transfretantes, in terrarum exercebantur confiniis[259]." Under Richard I. they again began to flourish, and from that time to the end of the middle ages, though often discountenanced by kings and churchmen, they enjoyed the highest favour among all who practised or admired knightly deeds and military splendour. "After the return of King Richard to England," says Jocelin of Brakelond, under the year 1194, "licence was granted for holding tournaments; for which purpose many knights met between Thetford and St. Edmund's, but the Abbot forbade them. They, however, in spite of the Abbot, fulfilled their desire. On another occasion, there came fourscore young men with their followers, sons of noblemen, to have their revenge at the aforesaid place; which being done, they returned into the town to put up there. The Abbot hearing of this, ordered the gates to be locked, and all of them to be kept within. The next day was the vigil of Peter and Paul the Apostles. Therefore, having promised that they would not go forth, they all dined with the Abbot on that day. But, after dinner, the Abbot having retired to his chamber, they all arose and began to carol and sing, sending into the town for wine, drinking and then screeching, depriving the Abbot and convent of their sleep, and doing everything in scorn of the Abbot; spending the day, until the evening, in this manner, and refusing to desist, even when the Abbot commanded them. When the evening was come, they broke open the gates of the town and went forth bodily. The Abbot, indeed, solemnly excommunicated them all, yet not without having first consulted Hubert, at that time justiciary; and many of them came, promising amendment and seeking absolution."

The more regular tournaments, however, were controlled by royal ordinances. They were restricted in England to five localities: namely, between Sarum and Wilton, between Warwick and Kenilworth, between Stamford and Wallingford, between Brakeley and Mixeberg, and between Blie and Tykehill. And, as nothing in these days could be done without a fine to the king or a tax to the pope, every earl had to pay twenty marks for his privilege to appear as a combatant; every baron, ten; every knight having a landed estate, four; each knight without such estate, two; and all foreigners were excluded[260].

In France, under Philip Augustus, tournaments appear to have been held on a large scale, as Père Daniel has remarked, from the incident of Philip having suddenly procured at an assemblage of this kind, troops sufficient to repel an unexpected attack on Alençon[261].

It is not within the province (if it were in the limits) of this work, to give any detailed account of tournaments and their usages; for at this period and long after, the defensive armour used for the joust (as shewn by the pictorial monuments of the time) differed in no respect from that worn in battle[262].

In the curious sketch of London in the twelfth century by Fitzstephen, an eye-witness of the incidents he records, we have a spirited notice of the military exercises of the young citizens in these days. "Every Sunday in Lent, after dinner, a company of young men go into the fields, mounted on war-horses:—

—in equis certamine primis:

each of which

Aptus et in gyros currere doctus equus.

The lay sons of the citizens rush out of the gates in crowds, equipped with lances and shields (*lanceis et scutis militaribus*); the more youthful with blunt spears; and they engage in sham fights and exercise themselves in military combats. When the king happens to be near the city, most of the courtiers attend, and the varlets (*ephebi*) of the households of earls and barons who have not yet attained knighthood, resort thither to try their skill. The hope of victory animates every one. The spirited horses neigh; their limbs tremble; they champ the bit; impatient of delay, they fret and paw the ground. When at length

—sonipedum rapit ungula cursum,

the young riders, having been divided into companies, some pursue their fellows, but are unable to overtake them; others push their companions out of the course and gallop beyond them.

"In the Easter holidays they have a game resembling a naval conflict. A target is fastened to a post in the middle of the river: in the prow of a boat, driven along by oars and the current, stands a young man who is to strike the target with his lance: if, in hitting it, he break his lance and keep his position unmoved, he gains his point, his wish is fulfilled; but if his lance be not broken by the blow, he is tumbled into the river and his boat passes by. Two boats, however, are placed there, one on each side of the target, and in them a number of young men, to take up the tilter when he emerges from the stream. On the bridge and in chambers by the river-side, stand the spectators:—

—multum ridere parati.

"During the Summer holidays the young men exercise themselves in leaping, in archery, wrestling, stone-throwing, casting javelins beyond a mark, and in fighting with shields."

In the Winter, skaters, "binding under their feet the shin-bones of some animal, take in their hands poles shod with iron, which at times they strike against the ice, and are thus carried along with the rapidity of a bird on the wing, or a bolt discharged from a cross-bow. Sometimes two of the skaters having by mutual agreement placed themselves far apart, come together from opposite sides: they meet, and with their poles strike each other: one or both fall, not without some bodily hurt: even after their fall, they are carried along to a great distance from each other by the velocity of the motion; and whatever part of their heads comes in contact with the ice, is laid bare to the very skull. Frequently the leg or arm of the person who falls, if he chance to light on either, is broken. But youth is an age eager for glory and desirous of victory: thus, in order to distinguish themselves in real fight, these tyros contend with so much boldness in counterfeit battle."

Among the exercises glanced at in this sketch of the Londoner's sportive year, the Quintain is conspicuous. This was especially the game of the "non-noble," and might be practised either on horseback or on foot. The more ancient quintain was merely a post or a shield fixed on a pole, which the tyro attacked in lieu of a living antagonist. But a new element was soon given to the quintain, which at once brought it into favour with the populace: it was so contrived as to inflict summary punishment on the inexpert. To one kind, a bag of sand was fastened, which, whirling round from the force of the blow struck at the opposite end, buffeted the tilter who was not expeditious enough to get out of its way. Others were made in the form of a Turk, armed with sword and shield; and these, moving on a pivot as before, inflicted a smart blow on the lagging assailant. In another variety, a large tub of water was fixed on a post, which discharged its contents on the person of any clumsy jouster. Other kinds are described and figured in Strutt's Sports. And in the little village of Offham, in Kent, may still be seen an example of the quintain, which is fixed "opposite to the dwelling-house of the estate, which is bound to keep it up[263]." It now consists of a post, having a cross-piece moving on a pivot, terminating at one end with a broad perforated board, and at the other with a pendent log of wood. The log, however, seems to have been substituted for a "bag of sand," which is mentioned in old accounts of this relic.

"Besides the practice of feats of arms," says John of Salisbury, writing in the reign of Henry II., "the young knight should qualify himself for the duties of his station by a variety of toil and exemplary abstinence. From the beginning he must learn to labour, run, carry heavy weights, and bear the sun and dust: he must use sparing and rustic food: he must accustom himself to live in tents, or in the open air." Then, turning upon the luxurious and effeminate knights of his day, he upbraids them in a diatribe which gives us a singular picture of the manners of this age. "Some," he says, "think that military glory consists in the display of elegant dress, in wearing their clothes tight to the body, so binding on their linen or silken garments that they seem a skin coloured like their flesh. Sitting softly on their ambling horses, they think themselves so many Apollos. If you make an army of them, you will have the camp of Thaïs, not of Hannibal. Each is boldest in the banqueting-hall, but in the battle every one desires to be the last: they would rather assail the enemy with arrows than come to close fighting. Returning home without a scar, they sing triumphantly of their battles, and boast of the thousand deaths that wandered near their temples. If diligent idleness can procure any spears, which, being brittle as hemp, should chance to be broken in the field; if a piece of gold, minium, or any colour of the rainbow, by any chance or blow should fall out of their shields; their garrulous tongues would make it an everlasting memorial. They have the first places at supper. They feast every day splendidly, if they can afford it, but shun labour and exercise like a dog or a snake. Whatever is surrounded with difficulty, they leave to those who serve them. In the meantime, they so gild their shields, and so adorn their tents, that you would think each one, not a learner, but a chieftain of war[264]."

PORCHESTER CASTLE, HAMPSHIRE.
Built about 1150.

No. 45.

[Pg 190]

[Pg 191]
[Pg 192]

PLATE **XLVI.**

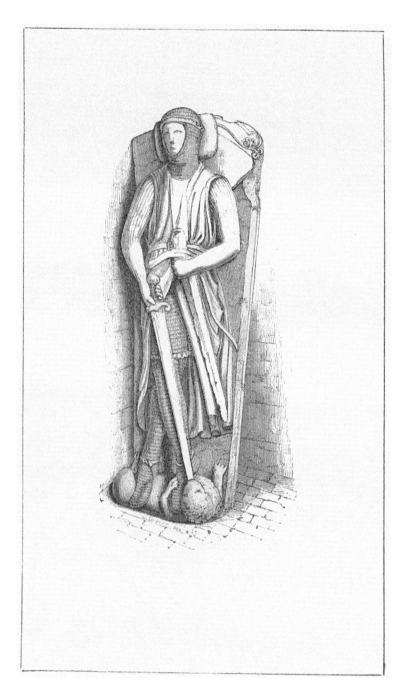

144

PART III.

THIRTEENTH CENTURY.

The authorities which throughout the last division of our inquiry have served us as guides—seals, vellum-paintings, metal-chasings, ivory-carvings, and the writings of chroniclers and poets—are still available to us: but in the thirteenth century a new and most valuable source of information is offered by the numerous knightly effigies which are found in cathedral and chantry, in wayside chapel and lofty monastery. These sepulchral figures, of the proportions of life, are of especial value to the student of military costume, permitting him to follow his inquiry into the minutest detail. Not a belt nor a lace, not a buckle nor a strap, but he can trace the exact form and assign the particular purpose of it. Whether the effigy be a statue or "a brass," he finds in it abundant material for furthering his inquiry; and while from the illuminations of cotemporary manuscripts he obtains precise information on the point of *colour*, in the effigy he sees the exact moulding of each knightly adjunct, and the smallest pattern that adorns the smallest ornament of the knightly equipment. The military brasses of this century are but few; but the statues, in stone, in wood, or in Purbeck marble, are scattered through our English counties in surprising numbers. The value of these national memorials is beginning to be understood: the crumbling figure is no longer permitted to perish in the open churchyard, to lie in fragments among the rubbish of the belfry corner, to form the ridiculous ornament of the churchwarden's grotto or the squire's glyptotheck. With pious care it is restored to the sacred fane from which it had been abstracted; it again becomes part of the chancel or chantry beneath whose pavement lie the bones of him of whom church, chantry, and statue are alike the monuments. But from the very consideration which has been newly accorded to these memorials, has arisen a fresh danger: it has, in some cases, been thought expedient to submit them to a so-called restoration. They have been patched up with Roman cement, eked out with supplementary limbs, plastered over with mock Purbeck marble. The mistakes that have been committed in costume, equipment, and art-treatment, are more fit for the pages of a jest-book than those of a sober treatise; and it is scarcely necessary to say that, for any purpose of the historian, the archæologist, or even in the more narrow view of ancestral portraiture, the statue has become, under such a treatment, utterly valueless. Yet our task is so simple. We have only to preserve. Inheritors of the finest series of national ancestral memorials that Europe can boast, let us at least transmit to after-days, in all their integrity, the admirable works that have come down to us through the troubles and turmoils of seven centuries[265].

Throughout the thirteenth century the feudal and mercenary TROOPS continued to be employed together. But towards the middle of this period, the Italian cities, combating for their liberties, began to levy their men-at-arms from the non-noble class as well as from the knightly; a force which, under the name of *Conduttitij Soldati*, obtained in the next age a very wide celebrity.

No. 47.

Besides the mounted men-at-arms or heavy cavalry, there were light-horse troops formed by the mounted archers and cross-bowmen, and the esquires attending upon the knights. The example here given is from Roy. MS. 20, D.

1, fol. 127, a work of the close of the thirteenth century[266].

The foot-troops or *Sergents de pied* consisted principally of archers, cross-bowmen and spearmen. There were also the *Sergens d'armes* or heavy-armed body-guard, Coustillers, Slingers, Bidaux, and Brigands or Ribauds; to which may be added the varlets or pages, who followed their knightly masters into the field, now fighting lustily in the *mêlée*, now bearing off the wounded body of their lord to some place of solace and safety. Clientes and Satellites were general names given to the inferior troops of the feudal and communal levy, including both horse and foot. There was nothing approaching to a uniform costume for the soldiery, though occasionally we find a leader seeking to identify his men by some addition to their dress, as a cross, a scarf, or other similar token. In 1264, Simon de Montford "ordered his troops to fasten white crosses on their breasts and backs, above their armour, in order that they might be known by their enemies, and to shew that they were fighting for justice[267]." In this case, however, the motive seems to have been, less the desire of a mark of recognition among friends, than the assumption, so common in warlike undertakings, of a holy motive for manslaughter. In the following passage from Guiart relating to the battle of Mons-en-Puelle, the object is more distinctly that of friendly recognition:—

"Pour estre au ferrir reconnuz,
Vilains, courtois, larges et chiches,
Sont de laz blans et de ceintures
Escharpés sur leurs armures.
Neis li ribaut les ont mises,
Faites de leurs propres chemises."—*Vers* 11,059.

Of the Man-at-arms and his barded charger we obtain an admirable definition from the *Chronicon Colmariense* under the year 1298: "Armati reputabantur qui galeas ferreas in capitibus habebant, et qui wambasia, id est, tunicam spissam ex lino et stuppa, vel veteribus pannis consutam, et desuper camisiam ferream, id est, vestem ex circulis ferreis contextam, per quæ nulla sagitta poterat hominem vulnerare. Ex his Armatis centum inermes mille lædi potuerunt: habebant et multos qui habebant dextrarios, id est, equos magnos, qui inter equos communes quasi Bucephalus Alexandri, inter alios eminebat. Hi equi cooperti fuerunt coopertoriis ferreis, id est, veste ex circulis ferreis, contexta. Assessores dextrariorum habebant loricas ferreas: habebant et caligas, manipulos ferreos, et in capitibus galeas ferreas splendidas et ornatas, et alia multa quæ me tæduit enarrare." The armour of these sturdy warriors we shall presently examine piece by piece.

The *Sergens à pied* (*Servientes*) included the mass of the troops beneath the knightly dignity. Guillaume Guiart arms them with the lance and crossbow:—

"———bon serjanz i a
A arbaletes et a lances."
Chronique Métrique, 2ᵉ. partie, vers 8567.

And the same weapons are assigned to those levied by the *ordonnance* of Philip of France in 1303: "Et seront armés les sergens de pie de pourpoint et de hauberjons, gamboison, de bacinez et de lances: Et des six, il y en aura deux arbalestriers[268]."

The *Sergens d'armes*, (*Servientes Armorum*,) whose establishment in the twelfth century we have already observed, (page 100,) continued to form the royal body-guard throughout the present age. In 1214 they especially distinguished themselves at the battle of Bovines, as we find recorded by the monument (before noticed) in the church of St. Catherine. The inscription of the monument, though itself not earlier than the beginning of the fifteenth century, probably relates very exactly the circumstances of their victory, and of the foundation of the church. It is as follows:—"A la priere des Sergens darmes Monsʳ. Saint Loys fonda ceste Eglise et y mist la premiere pierre: Et fu pour la joie de la vittoire qui fu au Pont de Bouines lan Mil. cc et xiiii. Les Sergens darmes pour le temps gardoient ledit pont et vouerent que se Dieu leur donnoit vittoire ils fonderoient une eglise en lonneur de Madame Sainte Katherine. Et ainsi fu il." A statute of Philippe le Bel in 1285 limits the number of these guards attending the court to thirty: "Item, Sergens d'armes, trente, lesquels seront à Cour sans plus." From the same statute we learn that one of their weapons at this time was the crossbow: "Ils porteront toujours leurs carquois pleins de carreaux."

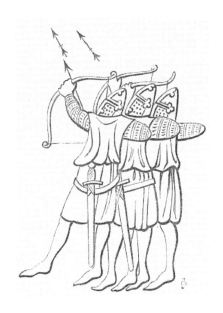

No. 48.

The Archer was becoming every day of more importance in the field; and if the bow was an efficient arm in battle, it was still more so in sieges, and the defence of strongholds and mountain-passes. From various Statutes of Arms we find that a portion of the military tenants are ordered to be provided with the longbow and arrows. The Statute of Winchester, in 1285, directs that each man "a quaraunte soudeesz de terre e de plus jeqs a cent souz, eit en sa mesun espe, ark, setes e cutel.... E tuz lez autres qui aver pount, eient arcs e setes hors de forestes, e dedenz forestes arcs e piles." Compare the statute of the 36th year of Henry III., printed in the *Additamenta* of the History of Matthew Paris[269]. The costume of the ordinary archer, defended only by his *chapel de fer*, appears to be depicted in our woodcut, No. 50, from Harleian MS. 4751, fol. 8, written at the commencement of this century. That the English occasionally mixed their bowmen with the cavalry, we have the express testimony of Matthew Paris: "Viri autem sagittarii gentis Anglorum equitibus permixti." In many illuminations of this time they appear fully armed in hauberk and helm, as in the miniature here given from Royal MS. 20, D. 1, fol. 307. See also our woodcut, No. 82, a group from the Painted Chamber of the palace at Westminster, where the archer wears a hauberk and coif of chain-mail. These examples of heavy-armed bowmen are fully borne out by written testimony. We have already observed Richard Cœur-de-Lion plying his arrows under the walls of Lincoln, (p. 157); and Otto Morena has, "Ipse Imperator optime sciens sagittare, multos de Cremensibus interfecit." (p. 58.)

149

For further pictorial examples of archers of this century, see Royal MS. 2, B. vi. fol. 10; and 20, D. i. ff. 60, 87, 150 and 285.

By a curious volume of "Proverbs" of the thirteenth century, printed from a manuscript of that date in the *Vie privée des François*[270], we learn that "the best archers are in Anjou." Other proverbial celebrities of this manuscript are: Chevaliers de Champagne, Ecuyers de Bourgogne, Sergens de Hainaut, Champions d'Eu, Ribauds de Troyes.

The provision of an equipped archer to attend the king in his wars, is the frequent sergeantry for lands at this time; and the particulars attached to the service occasionally partake of that whimsicality found in other tenures of the period. It is curious also to trace the changes which these charters undergo in a small lapse of years, as they come under the inspection of the jurors appointed to enforce their engagements. Thus, the service for the manor of Faintree, in Shropshire, in 1211, is "a foot-soldier, with a bow and arrows, for the king's army in Wales." In 1274 the soldier is bound to stay with the host only "till he has shot away his arrows." In 1284 the archer has "to attend the king in his Welsh wars, with a bow, three arrows, and a 'terpolus[271].'" This terpolus, or tribulus, was probably an "archer's stake," not the mere small iron *caltrop*, of which the provision of one only by each archer would be of little use in impeding a charge of cavalry. The duty of the bowman who had only to stay in the field till he had shot away three arrows was sufficiently easy; but on other occasions the archer did not escape so lightly. The manor of Chetton, co. Salop, supplies in 1283 an archer for the king's host in Wales, who is to take with him a flitch of bacon, and to remain with the army till he has eaten it all up[272].

No. 49.

The Cross-bowman was an essential component of the host during all this period. He was in the van of battle. "Balistarii semper præibant," says Matthew Paris[273]; and there is scarcely a conflict mentioned by this chronicler in which the arbalester does not play a conspicuous part. In the battle near Damietta, in 1237, "more than a hundred knights of the Temple fell, and three hundred cross-bowmen (*arcubalistarii*), not including some other seculars, and a large number of foot-soldiers[274]." The Emperor Frederic in 1239, giving an account of his Italian campaign to the king of England, writes: "After we had by our knights and cross-bowmen reduced all the province of Liguria[275]," &c. In 1242 the Count de la Marche, refusing to do homage to Amphulse, the brother of the French king, "swelling with anger and with loud threats, accompanied by his wife Isabella and surrounded by a body of soldiers, broke through the midst of the Poictevin cross-bowmen, and having set fire to the house in which he had dwelt, suddenly mounted a horse and took to flight[276]." St. Louis, marching to meet the English in Poitou, had an army in which there were "about four thousand knights splendidly armed to the teeth, besides numbers of others, who came from all directions, flocking to the army, like rivers flowing into the sea; and the number of retainers and cross-bowmen was said to be about twenty thousand[277]." The opposing forces of the English king consisted of "sixteen hundred knights, twenty thousand foot-soldiers, and seven hundred arbalesters."

The Cross-bowmen were of several kinds, some mounted, some on foot. The mounted balistarii in King John's time were those possessing one horse, those having two horses (*ad duos equos*[278]), and others having three horses[279]. In 1205 the king sends to the sheriff of Salop, "Peter, a balister of three horses, and nine two-horse balisters," who are to be paid 10*s*. 4*d*. per day (the whole ten). The usual pay at this time was: to the cross-bowman with two horses, 15*d*. per diem; with one horse, 7½*d*. per day; and to the foot-balister, 3*d*. per day.

The quarrels for the crossbows were carried after the army in carts. Thus Guillaume Guiart:—

"Arbaletriers vont quarriaux prendre,
A pointes agues et netes,
Qui la furent *en trois charrettes*
Venues par mesire Oudart."—*Année* 1303, p. 291.

The bows themselves, with other weapons and defences, were also carted after the host, and termed the "artillery" of the expedition:—

"Artillerie est le charroi
Qui par duc, par comte ou par roi
Ou par aucun seigneur de terre
Est charchié (chargé) de quarriaux en guerre,
D'arbaletes, de dars, de lances,
Et de targes d'une semblance."—*Guiart*, an. 1304.

Notwithstanding the services rendered in the front of the battle by the cross-bowmen, and the other foot-troops; whose post was the more perilous from their being but slightly provided with defensive equipment; the knightly body of their own party made no scruple to ride them down whenever they stood in the way of the glory or ambition of the equestrian order. At Courtray in 1302, the French foot having gallantly repulsed the Flemings, Messire de Valepayelle cried to the Count of Artois,—

"Sire, cil vilain tant feront
Que l'onneur en emporteront."—*Guiart*, pt. ii. v. 6132.

And forthwith the men-at-arms

"Parmi les pietons se flatissent,
Qu'a force de destriers entr'ouvrent:
Des leurs meismes le champ queuvrent,
Et merveilleux nombre en estraignent."

This is confirmed by the *Grandes Chroniques*: "Nos gens de pie savancent, si auront la victoire et nous ny aurons point d'onneur[280]." All our readers will remember the similar fate of the Genoese cross-bowmen at Cressy: "Or tôt, tuez toute cette ribaudaille, qui nous empêche la voie sans raison[281]."

The arbalester sometimes appears in heavy armour, as in our woodcuts, Nos. 49 and 50. And Matthew Paris has: "Arcubalistarii circiter sexaginta loricati[282]." The provision of quarrels for each cross-bowman of the communal force was fifty, as we learn from the charter of Theobald, count of Champagne in 1220: "Chascuns de la Commune de Vitré qui aura vaillant xx. livres, aura aubeleste en son ostel et quarriaux L." The office of "Master of the Arbalesters" became one of the chief dignities of the French army, and was conferred only on persons of the highest rank. Thibaut de Monleart held this charge under Saint Louis, and in the *Milice Françoise* of Père Daniel will be found a complete list of the "Maîtres des Arbalêtriers de France" till the days of Francis I., when the office ceased[283]. The little window in city or castle wall, through which the bolts of the crossbow were discharged, was called *arbalestena*. For other pictures of the cross-bowman of the thirteenth century than those given in our woodcuts, Nos. 49 and 50, see Add. MS. 15,268, fol. 122, and Roy. MS. 20, D. 1, fol. 361[b].

The Coustiller, employed, as we have seen, at Bovines in 1214, continues in request throughout this century; and will be found again in the pages of Froissart, taking part in the battles of the succeeding age.

PLATE L.

The Slinger is still of occasional occurrence. In this very curious group from

Harl. MS. 4751, fol. 8, a work of the early part of the thirteenth century, the slinger appears without any defensive armour, and his weapon differs in no particular from the sling of Anglo-Saxon[Pg 205] [Pg 206] times, as shewn in our woodcut, No. 12. Besides the ancient Cord Sling, there appears in the manuscripts of this century a variety of the arm, the Staff Sling. It seems to have been in vogue for naval warfare, or in the conflicts of siege operations. The example here engraved is from Strutt's Horda, vol. i. plate 31; the authority being a MS. of Matthew Paris of this century, preserved in the library of Benet College, Cambridge. Other examples of the Staff Sling are given in Strutt's Sports, bk. i. chap. 2.

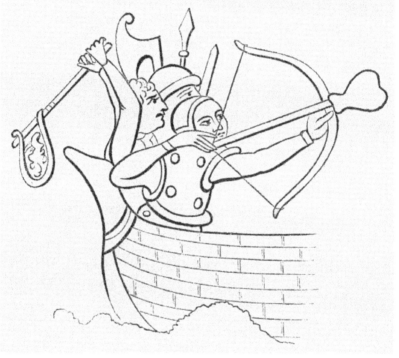

No. 51.

The Bideaux (*bibaldi*) were foot-troops fighting without defensive armour, whose usual weapons were a spear, javelins and a coutel. Guiart exactly describes them:—

"De Navarre et devers Espaingne
Reviennent Bidaux a granz routes.
En guerre par accoustumance
Portent deux darz et une lance,

156

Et un coutel a la ceinture:
D'autres armures n'ont cure."—*Pt.* ii. *verse* 10,518.

The Ribaux or Brigans were the humblest of the troops, and by their extreme poverty were driven to acts of depredation which eventually made their very name synonymous with marauder. They carried such weapons as they could obtain:—

"Li uns une pilete[284] porte,
L'autre croc ou macue torte.

L'un tient une epee sans feurre,
L'autre un maillet, l'autre une hache."—*Guiart*, v. 6635.

They are not only without armour, but their equipment altogether is in a very tattered condition:—

"Et Ribaldorum nihilominus agmen inerme,
Qui nunquam dubitant in quævis ire pericla."
Philippidos, lib.
iii.

"Leurs robes ne sont mie neuves,
Ainz semble tant sont empirées
Que chiens les aient déciriées."—*Guiart*, v. 6640.

Matthew Paris names them with but little honour: "Ribaldi et viles personæ[285]." They were, however, by no means useless members of the host. Thus, when Philippe Auguste appeared before Tours in 1189: "Dum Rex circumquaque immunita civitatis consideraret, Ribaldi ipsius, *qui primos impetus in expugnandis munitionibus facere consueverunt*, eo vidente, in ipsam civitatem impetum fecerunt," &c.[286]

They were made to assist in carrying the baggage of the army: "Inermes Ribaldos et alios, qui solent sequi exercitum propter onera deportanda[287]." And, being unprovided with defensive armour, whenever they obtained any booty, the "soudoyers," who were better equipped than they, attacked them and appropriated their prizes:—

"Mais li Soudoiers de Biaugiers,
Qui d'armes ne sont mie nuz,
De ce qu'ils portent les desrobent."—*Guiart*, v. 10,826.

The *Roi des Ribauds* was an officer appointed to restrain the excesses of the Ribaldi, and is mentioned in many documents of France from the time of Philip Augustus to that of Charles VI. At the battle of Bovines in 1214, Roger de Wafalia is named in the list of prisoners as falling to the share of the King of the Ribauds: "Rogerus de Wafalia. Hunc habuit Rex Ribaldorum, quia dicebat se esse servientem."

The names Clientes and Satellites were employed, as we have before mentioned, to indicate generally the inferior troops, whether horse or foot. At the battle of Bovines, the Clientes are a mounted corps, armed with sword and spear:—

"——Et quos Medardicus abbas[288]
Miserat immensâ claros probitate Clientes
Terdenos decies quorum exultabat in armis
Quilibet altus equo gladioque horrebat et hastâ."

Guil. le
Breton.

In the following passage, the Clientes seem to be foot-troops. It is from the History of Dauphiny, where, in 1283, Humbert promises to assist the Archbishop and Chapter of Vienne: "contra omnes homines, suis propriis sumptibus et expensis, cum centum hominibus armatis in equis, et cum tercentis balistariis, et septingentis clientibus cum lanceis."

Satellites appear at Bovines, both mounted and on foot. The horse seem to have formed a light corps, and were employed to begin the combat. They are looked upon, however, with much contempt by the opponent *knights*; who, disdaining to advance against an ignoble foe, receive the charge without quitting their post. "Præmisit," says Rigord, "idem Electus[289], de consilio Comitis S. Pauli, CL. Satellites in equis ad inchoandum bellum, ea intentione ut prædicti milites egregii invenerint hostes aliquantulum motos et turbatos. Indignati sunt Flandrenses … quod non a Militibus sed a Satellibus primo invadebantur: nec se moverent de loco quo stabant, sed eos ibidem expectantes acriter receperunt," &c. These troops, we are told, were from the valley of Soissons, and combated both on foot and on horseback. "Erant Satellites illi probissimi, de valle Suessionensi, nec minus pugnabant sine equis quam in equis."

Not only were Spies in use, but, what somewhat disturbs one's confidence in the exalted simplicity of these times, it had already been discovered that the fair sex might be employed with advantage in this office. The heroic Edward I., in his campaign against the Welsh in 1281, gives a shilling to a "certain female spy" for her services: "Cuidam spiatrici, de dono, xij. denarii[290]."

And again, a pound to another of these useful ladies, "to buy her a house:" "Cuidam spiatrici, ad unam domum sibi emendam, de dono, xx. s.[291]"

From the various Statutes of Arms of this century we learn very exactly the equipment of the military tenants. Three of these statutes for England have been preserved: that of 1252, in the Additamenta of the Historia Major of Matthew Paris, and printed in Rymer's Fœdera; that forming part of the Statute of Winchester in 1285, printed by the Record Commission in vol. i. of the "Statutes of the Realm;" and that of 1298, printed in the new edition of the Fœdera, vol. i. p. 901. The Scottish enactments will be found in Skene's *Regiam Majestatem*, and the French in the *Collection des Ordonnances*.

The Assize of 1252, 36 of Hen. III., closely resembles that of 1285; but in the first the equipment is of six varieties, while in the second there are seven classes of armed men. To avoid repetition, we shall give the earliest of these statutes in the text, and add the readings relating to the armour from the Statute of Winchester in a note.

The Sheriffs, with two knights elected for that purpose, are to go round the hundreds, cities, &c., and call before them the "cives, burgenses, liberè tenentes, villanos et alios, ætatis quindecim annorum usque ad ætatem sexaginta annorum; et eosdem faciant omnes jurare ad arma, secundùm quantitatem terrarum et catallorum[292] suorum; scilicet: Ad quindecim libratas terræ, unam loricam, capellum ferreum, gladium, cultellum et equum[293]: Ad decem libratas terræ, unum habergetum[294], capellum ferreum, gladium et cultellum: Ad centum solidatas terræ, unum purpunctum, capellum ferreum, gladium, lanceam et cultellum[295]: Ad quadraginta solidatas terræ et eo amplius usque ad centum solidatas terræ, gladium, arcum, sagittas et cultellum[296]. Qui minus habent quam XL. solidatas terræ, jurati sint ad falces, gisarmas, cultellos et alia arma minuta[297].

"Ad catalla sexaginta marcarum, unam loricam, capellum ferreum, gladium, cultellum et equum[298]: Ad catalla XL. marcarum, unum haubercum, capellum ferreum, gladium et cultellum: Ad catalla xx. marcarum, unum purpunctum, capellum ferreum, gladium et cultellum: Ad catalla novem marcarum, gladium, cultellum, arcum et sagittas: Ad catalla XL. solidarum et eo amplius usque ad decem marcas, falces, gisarmas, et alia arma minuta[299].

"Omnes enim alii qui possunt habere arcus et sagittas extra forestam, habeant: qui verò in forestâ, habeant arcus et pilatos[300]."

View of arms is to be taken by the mayors, bailiffs and provosts of the cities and towns[301]. Constables to be appointed to command the force. Tournaments and behourds forbidden:—"Clamare faciant Vicecomites, &c.

quod nulli conveniant ad turniandum vel burdandum, nec ad aliasquascunque aventuras." And none to appear armed except those specially appointed.

The distinction between the kinds of arrow to be used within and without the forest bounds, is curious, and not altogether clear at this distance from the days of archery. The fatal power of the barbed shaft upon the king's deer is indeed evident enough, but the comparatively innocuous character of the piled arrow is not so plain. The usage, however, is well attested by numerous instances. In the Statute of arms of William the Lion, king of Scotland, we have: "Et omnes alii, qui habere poterunt, habeant arcum et sagittas extra forestam: infra forestam, arcum et pyle[302]." And by an agreement made in 1246 between Roger de Quinci, earl of Winchester, and Roger de Somery, touching certain rights of chace in Bradgate Park, co. Leicester, it is stipulated "quod Forestarii sui non portabunt in bosco prædicti Rogeri de Somery et hæredum suorum sagittas barbatas sed pilettas[303]."

Shakespere, who illustrates everything, has a passage bearing on this subject among the rest. Under the greenwood tree of the forest of Arden, the Duke, in "As you like it," addresses his companions:—

"Come, shall we go and kill us venison?
And yet it irks me, the poor dappledfools
(Being native burghers of this desert city)
Should, in their own confines, with *forked heads*
Have their round haunches gored."—*Act* ii. *Sc.* 1.

And the fatal effects of the forked head are familiar to us all in the case of the

"——poor sequester'd stag,
That from the hunter's aim had ta'en a hurt,"

coming to languish away its life

"On the extremest verge of the swift brook."

The feudal levy of the Ban and Arrière-ban was of course much influenced by the pressure of the occasion requiring their armament. In 1205 King John, in a Council held at Winchester, called upon every tenth knight in the realm to accompany him into Poitou, at the expense of the other nine; and if, during his absence, the country should be invaded, every man capable of bearing arms was to join in its defence, under pain of forfeiting any lands he might hold; or, if not a landowner, of becoming, with all his posterity, a *slave* for ever, and paying a yearly poll-tax of four-pence. Each knight was to receive two shillings per day[304]. This expedition did not, however, leave our shores.

When Philip of France was preparing to attack King John in 1213, the English monarch summoned all his "liberos homines et servientes, vel quicunque sint," to aid him under pain of culvertage[305].

In 1264, when the Earl of Leicester mustered his forces on Barham Downs to resist the threatened invasion of Queen Eleanor, the military tenants were ordered, under pain of felony, to bring into the field not only the force specified in their tenures, but all the horsemen and infantry in their power: every township was compelled to send eight, six, or four footmen well armed with lances, bows, swords, cross-bows, and axes, who should serve forty days at the expense of the township; and the cities and burghs received orders to furnish as many horsemen and footmen as the Sheriff should appoint[306].

The Pay assigned to troops who, having contributed the stipulated service for their holdings or assessments, were required to render further assistance to the king in his wars, we discover in the Roll of Expenses of King Edward I. at Ruddlan Castle in Wales, in 1281-2. From this curious document, which is printed in full in the sixteenth volume of the Archæologia, we find:—

The Pay of	Per Diem.	In modern money.
A knight	12 Pence	15 shillings
An esquire	12 Pence	15 shillings
An archer	2 Pence	2s. 6d.
A cross-bowman	2 Pence	2s. 6d.
A captain-of-twenty (bowmen)	4 Pence	5s. 0d.
A constable (of 100 bowmen)	6 Pence	7s. 6d.

"Saturday the fifth day of January, paid to the Lord Engolrane, serving with the Lord John de Deynile and his four Esquires, for their wages from the first day of April to the fourth day of June, for lxv. days xix. *li.* x. *s.*

"To the same, for the pay of his fifth Esquire, for xxiv. days: xxiv. *s.*

"To the said five Esquires, for their pay, for fifteen days following the fourth of June lxxv. *s.*"

"Paid to Geoffry le Chamberlin, for the wages of twelve cross-bowmen (*balistariorum*) and thirteen archers (*sagittariorum*) for xxiv. days, each Cross-bowman receiving by the day iv. *d.*, and each Archer ij. *d.* vii. *li.* viii. *s.*"

Here the arbalester gets double the wages of the archer, but in the following and other instances, his pay is the same.

"To Guillemin and his comrade, Cross-bowmen, for their wages, for twenty-one days, at ij. *d.* by the day xxi. *s.*"

On one occasion, Guillemin and his companion receive sixpence per day: but this is altogether an unusual sum.

The archers were divided into bands of twenties, and over each was placed a Captain. To every hundred bowmen, with their captains, was appointed a Constable.

"To Master R. Giffard, for the wages of one Constable of foot, receiving *vi. d.* per day, and of fifty-three Archers, with two Captains of Twenties, for three days xxix. *s.*

"To Robert Giffard, —— for the wages of forty-three Captains of Twenties, each receiving iv. *d.* per day," &c.

There were also Constables of Cavalry, perhaps commanding mounted archers, and their pay is set down at twelve pence per day. Occasionally the constables have a command of two hundred men, and sometimes it sinks as low as fifty. The ordinary number, however, is a hundred.

Of the Armed Town-Watch in England we obtain some particulars from the "Breve Regis" of the 36th Hen. III. "Henry, king, &c. to such or such a sheriff, greeting. Be it known to you that, for the maintenance of our peace, it has been provided in our Council, that watch shall be kept in every city, borough and town of your county, from Ascension Day to the Feast of St. Michael; to wit: that in every city, six armed men (*armis munitos*) shall watch at every gate: in every borough, twelve men: in every town (*in singulis villis integris*) six men, or at least four, likewise furnished with arms, according to the number of the inhabitants. They shall watch continually throughout the night from sunset to sunrise; so that all strangers seeking to pass through, may be detained till morning. And then, if he be a loyal man (*fidelis*), he shall be set at liberty; if a suspected person (*suspectus*), he shall be delivered over to the Sheriff, to be by him kept in a place of safety. But if it happen that strangers of this latter sort refuse to allow themselves to be stopped, then the aforesaid Guards shall raise the hue against them on all sides, and shall follow them with all the inhabitants of the place (*cum tota villata*) and places adjacent, raising the hue and cry 'de villa in villam' until they be taken[307]," &c. The manner of the hue and cry is set down in the "Articuli[308]." "Pursuit by hue and cry to be made according to the ancient and proper form, so that those who neglect to follow the cry may be taken as accomplices of the evil-doers, and delivered to the Sheriff. Moreover, in every town, four or six men, according to the number of the inhabitants, shall be appointed to make the hue and cry with promptitude and perseverance, and to pursue evil-doers, if any should appear, with bows and arrows and other light weapons (*et aliis levibus armis*); which weapons ought to be provided for the custody of the whole town, and to remain for the use of the aforesaid town. And besides the foregoing, there shall be provided out of each hundred, two free and loyal men of most influence, to be over them, and to see that the watch be duly made, as well as the pursuits aforesaid."

Compare the regulations for the Watch of the city of Paris, contained in an ordinance of Saint Louis in 1254; printed in the *Collection des Ordonnances*.

The feudal constitution of armies was necessarily modified in different countries by the nature of the territory, the habits of the people, and the wealth of the state. In Germany, where the class of nobles was more restricted than in France and England, the foot-troops were at an early period regarded with consideration. In hilly countries, where the breed of horses was of a small stature, a light-armed cavalry was the most available force. While, in the fastnesses of mountains, the pikes and halberds of a sturdy infantry compensated for the want of horses and the poverty of a rugged territory.

The Scottish army in 1244, Matthew Paris[309] tells us, was "very numerous and powerful, consisting of a thousand armed knights, well mounted, although not on Spanish or Italian, or other costly horses, and well protected by armour of steel or linen; and about a hundred thousand foot-soldiers, who were all of one mind, and who, having made confession, and been encouraged by the consoling assurance of their preachers, that the cause in which they were engaged was a just one and for their country's good, had very little fear of death." In 1298 Wallace contending against Edward I. in person, formed his pikemen, who were the strength of his army, into four circular bodies[310], connected together by a number of archers from the Forest of Selkirk. Before them he planted a defence of palisades: behind them, the cavalry was stationed. In front of all was a morass, dividing them from the English. The latter, having passed the night on the bare heath, in the morning advanced to the attack. Their first division, commanded by the Earl Marshal, from its ignorance of the ground, soon became entangled in the morass. The second, led by the Bishop of Durham, wheeled round the swamp and came in sight of the Scottish cavalry, when the prelate ordered his men to await the arrival of the other bodies. "To thy mass, bishop!" exclaimed one of his knights, and rushed on the enemy. They gave way at the first charge; the bowmen were trampled under foot, but the four bodies of pikemen opposed on all sides an impenetrable front. The bravest resistance, however, could not restore the fortune of the day. Edward advanced his archers, supporting them with his military engines, an opening was made in each circle, the men-at-arms dashed in among the disordered pikemen, and the battle was won[311]. This conflict, fought near Falkirk, on the 22nd of July, 1298, affords one of innumerable instances, shewing that little reliance can be placed in the numbers of the slain given by even cotemporary writers. Trivet reports the loss of the Scotch at twenty thousand; Matthew of Westminster raises it to forty thousand.

The Welsh, keeping up their hostilities to their Norman invaders, reserved their aggressive operations till the wet and stormy season of the year, when the land was unfit for the manœuvres of a heavy-armed cavalry, and the gloomy days favourable for the sudden onslaught of mountain warriors. "Videntes tempus hyemale madidum sibi competere," says Matthew Paris[312].

The rich cities of Italy, as we have seen, began about the middle of this century to employ stipendiary men-at-arms; and it seems probable that the first of these knightly soldiers were those of the equestrian class who, from political disgust or family feuds, had become refugees in the territory of their new masters. The good wages and the booty obtained by these gentle mercenaries induced others of a more humble class to take up the trade, and under skilful leaders (the well-known Condottieri) they obtained fame, fortune and honours.

The Basques were at this time among the most prominent of the mercenary troops, acting as a light corps, for which their mountain-life rendered them very apt. They were the Swiss of the thirteenth century.

Among our northern neighbours we obtain a glimpse of the Frieslanders, through the means of the indefatigable Matthew Paris. "These Frieslanders," he says, "are a rude and untamable people: they inhabit a northern country, are well skilled in naval warfare, and fight with great vigour and courage on the ice. It is of the cold regions of these people, and their neighbours the Sarmatians, that Juvenal says, 'One had better fly hence, beyond the Sarmatians and the icy ocean,' &c. The Frieslanders, therefore, having laid ambuscades among the rush-beds along the sea-coast, (in their war with William of Holland,) as well as along the country, which is marshy—and the winter season was coming on—went in pursuit of the said William, armed with javelins, which they call *gaveloches*, in the use of which they are very expert, and with Danish axes and pikes, and clad in linen dresses covered with light armour. On reaching a certain marsh they met with William, helmeted, and wearing armour, and mounted on a large war-horse covered with mail. But, as he rode along, the ice broke, although it was more than half a foot thick, and the horse sank up to his flank, becoming fixed in the mud of the marsh. The trammelled rider dug his sharp spurs into the animal's sides to a great depth, and the noble, fiery beast struggled to rise and free himself, but without success. Crushed and bruised, he only sank the deeper for his efforts, and at length by his struggles he threw his rider among the rough slippery fragments of ice. The Frieslanders then rushed on William, who had no one to help him from his position, all his companions having fled, to avoid a similar disaster; and attacking him on all sides with their javelins, despite his cries for mercy, pierced his body through and through, which was already stiffened with wet and cold. He offered his murderers an immense sum of money for ransom of his life, but these inhuman men, shewing no mercy, cut him to pieces. And thus, just as he had a taste of empire, was the Flower of Chivalry, William, king of Germany and count of Holland, the creature and pupil of the Pope, hurled, at the will of his enemies, from the pinnacle of his high dignity to the depths of confusion and ruin[313]."

Clerics are still found participating the dangers and glories of the battle-field; not alone as councillors or leaders, but sturdily wielding the deadly mace, and clad in hauberk and helm, like the lay vassals and men-at-arms around them. We have already seen the Bishop of Durham leading a division of the English at the battle of Falkirk. At the great battle of Bovines, in 1214, the French army was commanded by Guerin, bishop-elect of Senlis; and there too, armed to the teeth, and plying the cleric weapon, the mace, contended that bishop of Beauvais, whom we have, on a former occasion, seen the prisoner of Richard Cœur-de-Lion. At the siege of Milan, in 1238, "the bishop-elect of Valentia, who knew more of temporal than spiritual arms, hastened with the knights whom the counts of Toulouse and Provence had sent to assist the emperor[314]." In 1239 the Emperor Frederic, writing to the king of England, complains of the Pope becoming a general and his monks men-at-arms, to wrest from him his crown of empire. "He hath openly declared himself the leader and chief of the war against us and the empire, making the cause of the Milanese and other faithless traitors his own, and openly turning their business to suit his own interests. Moreover, he appointed as his lieutenants over the Milanese, or rather the papal, army, the before-mentioned Gregory de Monte Longo and brother Leo, a minister of the Minorite order, who not only girded on the sword and clad themselves in armour, presenting the false appearance of soldiers; but also, continuing their office of preaching, absolved from their sins the Milanese and others, when they insulted our person or those of our followers[315]." Father John of Gatesden boldly throws aside alb and chasuble to don the knightly hauberk and chausses in good earnest. "Anno Domini 1245, King Henry passed Christmas at London, and observed the solemnities of that festival in the company of many of his nobles. At that place, on Christmas-day, he conferred the honour of knighthood on John de Gatesden, a clerk, who had enjoyed several rich benefices; but who, as was proper, now resigned them all[316]." In the contest for the empire in 1248, the army raised against Conrad by the legate, "was commanded by the archbishops of Mayence, Metz, Lorraine and Strasburg, and consisted of innumerable bands from their provinces and from Friesland, Gothland, Russia, Dacia, and from the provinces of Germany and those adjoining who had *received the cross*[317]," &c. For it was part of the papal tactics to invest the soldiers who fought in the quarrels of the Holy See with the sacred dignity of Crusaders. In the revolt of the Scots under Bruce in 1306, among the prisoners captured by the English were the Abbot of Scone and the Bishops of St. Andrew's and Glasgow, all taken in complete armour[318].

The leading principle in the TACTICS of this century was, with the exceptions already noticed, to compose the *strength of the army* of the knightly order. It was the knight who fought in the terrible mêlée of the battle-field: it was the knight who scaled the walls of the besieged fortress; who directed the discharge of perrier and mangonel; who filled the towers of assault by the city walls; who defended those walls from outward attack; and who, in sea-fights, manned the ships of war, and with pike and javelin contended against other men-at-arms battling in the adverse fleet. The remainder of the troops were looked upon as mere accessories, engines useful to clear the way for the "achievement" of the equestrian order.

The men-at-arms marched to the field of battle in squadrons so dense that, as a cotemporary writer records, "a glove thrown into the midst of them would not have reached the ground."

> "Chacun conroi lente aleure
> S'en va joint comme en quarreure,
> Si bien que s'un gant preissiez
> Et entr'eux haut le gétissiez,
> Il paroit qu'à son asseoir
> Ne duste mie tost cheoir."—*Guiart*, 2 par., v. 11,494.

They charged, however, in single line—*en haie*—the onset of the first rank being supported by the successive charges of those behind. The ancient formation of the wedge (*cuneus*) was not, however, altogether abandoned, whether for horse or foot. The particular manner in which the German cavalry composed the wedge, beginning with a front of seven men, and increasing each rank by one additional soldier, as far as to half the depth of the formation, is very clearly shewn by Fronsperger[319]. "Wie wohl bey den Alten gebraeuchlich gewesen das sie ihre Schlachtordnung (fur die Reisigen) gespitzt oder in Dreyangel gemacht haben, also das etwan im ersten Glied sieben Mann, im andern acht, im dritten neun, im vierten zehn; also fort an bis auf den halben Theil der Ordnung und Hauffen, darnach seien si durchaus geviert gemacht worden." In 1302, a body of Flemish infantry adopted a similar formation in acting against the French. "Les François virent une très grande bataille des Flamands, qui contint bien huit mil hommes; et avoient ordonné leur bataille en guise d'un escu, la pointe devant, et s'estoient entrelaciez l'un en l'autre, si que on me les peut percier[320]."

Of the circular formation we have already seen an example among the Scotch at the battle of Selkirk. Guiart furnishes another:—

> "Renaut, jadis quens de Bouloingne,
> Qui mort ne mehaing ne resoingne,
> Tant est plain de grant hardement,
> Ot fait dès le commencement
> De serjanz plains de grant prouece
> Une closture en réondèce,
> Ou, en reposant, s'aaisoit
> Toutes les fois qu'il li plaisoit;
> Et r'issoit de leanz souvent
> Quant il avoit pris air ou vent."—*Sub an.* 1214.

The entire army was usually formed into three "battles:" sometimes into four; and occasionally the whole force was gathered into one body. In 1249 the Imperialists, fighting against the Bolognese, distributed their troops into three corps, while the latter formed four[321]. And in 1266, Manfred, in a battle with Charles d'Anjou, ranged his cavalry in three bodies, while his adversary divided his army into four parts[322].

In front of all were placed the various "gyns" of the host; the mangonels, trebuchets, perdriaux, &c., serving in some degree the purpose of gunnery in our own day.

> "Près du roi devant la banière
> Metent François trois Perdriaus,
> Jetans pierres aus enniaus
> Entre Flamens grosses et males,
> Joignant d'eus rot deux Espringoles,
> Que garçons au tirer avancent."

Guiart.—2ᵉ. Par., v. 11,573.

At the battle of Mons-en-Puelle, in 1304, three espringoles were placed in battery before the French army, of which the force was so great that the quarrels discharged from them are said to have pierced four or five ranks of the enemy in succession.

"Li garrot, empené d'arain,
Quatre ou cinq en percent tout outre."—*G. Guiart.*

The Archers and Cross-bowmen were usually placed at the wings, the infantry of the communal levy in the centre, and behind these the mounted men-at-arms.

"Cil d'armes se rangent derrières."—*Guiart, Année* 1303.

Archers were sometimes intermixed with the cavalry. Thus, in the 23rd of Edward I., the Earl of Warwick fighting against the Welsh, the latter "placed their men-at-arms fronting the earl's army: they were furnished with very long spears, which, being set on the ground, had their points suddenly turned towards the earl and his company, in order to break the force of the English cavalry. But the earl had well provided against them; for between every two horsemen he had placed an archer, so that, by their missile weapons, those who held the lances were put to the rout[323]." We have already seen *bodies* of archers interspersed with other troops in the conflict between Edward and Wallace in 1298[324].

To defend themselves from the attack of cavalry, the army occasionally formed a barrier of carts and wagons.

"De chars et de charettes vuides,
Qu'à grant diligence ont atruites,
Ont entr'eus trois rengies faites,
En tel sens et par ordre commune
Que le derrière de chacune
Est mis, si com nous estimons,
A l'autre entre les deus limons."

Guiart, 2ᵉ. partie, v. 11,108.

The more usual entrenchment was the ancient one of a ditch and palissaded bank.

Stratagems were still greatly in vogue, and some of them are of so dramatic a character that they tell rather of the jongleur than of the sober historian. Others, with enough of the marvellous, are less out of the bounds of probability. In 1250, Matthew Paris informs us, the Saracens gained a victory over a body of Crusaders, whom they slew. Desiring to obtain possession of Damietta, which was in the hands of the Christians, "a strong body of them, about equal in number to the Crusaders they had slain, treacherously putting on the armour, and carrying the shields and standards of the Christians who had fallen, set out thus disguised towards Damietta; in order that, having the appearance of French troops, they might gain admission into the city, and, as soon as admitted, might kill all they found therein. When they approached the walls, the Christians on guard looked forth from the ramparts and towers, and at first thought they were Christians, exultingly bearing spoils and trophies: but the nearer they approached, the more unlike Frenchmen they seemed: for they marched hurriedly and in disordered crowds, and sloped their shields irregularly, more after the manner of Saracens than of French. And when they reached the extremities of the fortifications and approached the gates of the city, they were clearly seen to be Saracens by their black and bearded faces. But who can fully relate the heartfelt grief of the Christians when they saw the enemies of the faith giving vent to their pride and derision, clad in the armour, and bearing the standards and painted devices which were so well known to them[325]."

The device of equipping several soldiers in similar arms to the leader of the host, seems also to have been in use. At the siege of Viterbo in 1243, Matthew Paris tells us, "One illustrious soldier on the Emperor's side, and adorned with his special arms, (*armis ipsius specialibus decoratus*,) miserably expired, to the great grief of the Emperor, being pierced by the quarrel of a crossbow. His enemies raised a shout of joy, thinking they had slain the Emperor himself; but the Emperor, preceded by his trumpeters, advanced; and, though not without difficulty, disengaged his army from the fury of their opponents, who had suddenly pressed forward to crush them[326]."

The influence of the stars, the power of lucky and unlucky days over the issue of battle, were still occasionally acknowledged; not alone by the rude leaders of a company of men-at-arms, but by the commanders of armies, by crowned dignitaries. The Emperor Frederic II. had a firm faith in the predictions of astrologers; he never undertook a march until the fortunate moment for departure had been fixed by those skilled in divination; and when, in 1239, he was about to advance against Treviso, his march was suddenly arrested by an eclipse of the sun[327].

GREAT SEAL OF KING JOHN.

No. 52.

The usual BODY-ARMOUR of the knightly order was, in the early part of the thirteenth century, of interlinked chain-mail; but, in the second half of the century, portions of plate appear, in the form of shoulder-pieces, elbow-pieces, and knee-pieces. The chain-mail was of hammered iron, the art of wire-drawing not being found till about the middle of the next age. Other materials were occasionally employed for defensive purposes: leather, quilting, scale and jazerant-work, and, at the close of the century, a kind of armour which has been named Banded-mail, but of which the structure has not been exactly ascertained. There can be little doubt that, among the more humble troops, the Coustillers and the Ribauds, every kind of defensive material was in use which these men could obtain: a pectoral and a helmet of some sort were almost indispensable, to protect them from the downward flight of the arrows, which played so principal a part, whether in the field or

171

the siege. The knights themselves, indeed, did not attempt a uniform costume: on the contrary, it is often made a reproach to them, that each endeavoured to outvie the other in the magnificence of his apparel. On rare occasions we find a band of cavaliers who exhibit the marvel of a similar equipment. When Richard, earl of Gloucester, visited the Pope, in 1250, "he travelled through the kingdom of France accompanied by the Countess, his wife, and his eldest son, Henry, with a numerous suite, and attended by a large retinue, in great pomp, consisting of forty knights equipped in new accoutrements, all alike, and mounted on beautiful horses, bearing new harness, glittering with gold, and with five wagons and fifty sumpter-horses; so that he presented a wonderful and honourable show to the sight of the astonished French beholders[328]."

The usual series of knightly garments was the tunic, the gambeson, the hauberk, the chausses, the chausson, and the surcoat. With these are found various accessories: the ailettes, coudières, poleyns, and greaves.

The Tunic has already been seen in the first seal of Richard I., and other monuments. It again appears in this curious group, part of a martyrdom of Thomas à Becket, from Harl. MS. 5102, fol. 32, a work of the beginning of the thirteenth century (*overleaf.*) It is found also in our woodcut No. 63, from Add. MS. 17,687, an example of the close of the century.

No. 53.

The Gambeson, that quilted garment which we have seen was worn as an additional defence beneath the hauberk of chain-mail, is in view in the monumental effigy from Haseley church, Oxfordshire, (woodcut 46,) a figure seemingly of the middle of this century. It is again very clearly shewn in our woodcut No. 59, an effigy in Ash church, near Sandwich. In both these examples the vertical lines of quilting are plainly expressed by the sculptor. Ducange, in his Observations on the History of St. Louis, cites an account of the year 1268, which includes "Expensæ pro cendatis et bourra ad Gambesones[329]." These might, however, have been the Gambesons that formed of themselves the body-armour of the soldier. It is very clearly distinguished as a horseman's garment in a passage of the Statutes of Frejus, in 1235; where also we see the gambeson *alone* accorded to the[Pg 231]

[Pg 232]

[Pg 233] foot-fighter: "Militem sine equo armato intelligimus armatum

173

auspergoto et propuncto (with hauberk and gambeson) et scuto: peditem armatum intelligimus armatum scuto et propuncto *seu* aspergoto." The Chronicon Colmariense, under the year 1298, is still more explicit: "Armati reputabantur qui galeas ferreas in capitibus habebant, et qui wambasia, id est, tunicam spissam ex lino et stuppa, vel veteribus pannis consutam, et *desuper* camisiam ferream."

PLATE LIV.

The Hauberk of chain-mail, in the beginning of the thirteenth century, was made with continuous coif and gloves, the coif somewhat flattened at the top of the head, and the gloves not divided into fingers; it descended nearly to the knees, and at the face-opening left little more than the eyes and nose of the knight in view. A striking example of the last-named arrangement is afforded by the figure here engraved, the sculptured effigy of William Longespée, at Salisbury, c. 1227. See also the seal of King John, p. 228, and the woodcut, No. 53, from Harl. MS. 5102. The sleeve of the hauberk is sometimes secured at the wrist by a lace or strap; as in the figure of Longespée, in the brass of Sir Roger de Trumpington, c. 1289, (woodcut 73,) and the effigy at Norton, Durham, of the end of the century (woodcut 70). In order to liberate the hand occasionally from its fingerless glove, an aperture was left in the centre of the palm. This is clearly shewn in our woodcuts, No. 80 and 62; the first from the Lives of the Offas, Cotton MS., Nero, D. i.; and the other from Roy. MS. 2, A. xxii. The glove turned off and hanging from the wrist may be seen in Plate 17 of Hefner's *Trachten*, and in the sculptured effigy of a knight in Bingham church, Nottinghamshire. In the second half of the century the gloves of the hauberk were divided for the fingers; from which we may suppose that the armour-smith had by this time improved his art by making his mail-web more flexible and more delicate. Early examples occur in the sculptured effigies of knights at Rampton, Cambridgeshire, and Danbury, Essex; the former figured in Stothard's Monuments, Plate 20; the latter in Strutt's Dress and Habits, Plates 45 and 46. Instances both of the undivided and the fingered glove will be found among our engravings. Occasionally the sleeves of the hauberk terminate at the wrist, as those of the archers in cuts 47 and 48; in these instances obviously for the greater freedom in handling the bow. Where the lancer's hauberk is thus fashioned, the hand has the supplementary defence of a gauntlet. Gauntlets of scalework occur in a knightly brass, c. 1280, engraved by Waller, Part x., and Boutell[330], p. 113. To the elbows of the hauberk were sometimes affixed, but rarely in this century, plates of metal called *coudières*. An effigy in Salisbury Cathedral, circa 1260, (Stothard, Pl. xxx.,) offers a good example. There is another, a knight of the Clinton family, in the church of Coleshill, Warwickshire. The hauberk was subject to a further variety: it was made with or without a *Collar*. Matthew Paris tells us that in a hastilude "at the abbey of Wallenden" in 1252, the lance of Roger de Lemburn entered beneath the helm of his antagonist and pierced his throat, for he was uncovered in that part of his body, and without a collar (*carens collario*). Ducange cites an analogous passage: "Venitque ictus inter cassidem et collarium, dejecitque caput ejus multum a corpore[331]." The hauberk without collar may be seen in the figures of *Largesse* and *Debonnaireté* in the pictures of the Painted Chamber (Vet. Mon., vol. vi.)

The Continuous Coif was in the early part of the century nearly flat at the top; in the second half the round-topped coif was more usual. The flattened form is well shewn in the statue of Longespée (woodcut, No. 54), and in those of De l'Isle and De Braci, (Stothard, Plates xix. and xx.) The rounded crown occurs frequently in our woodcuts. The coif was drawn over the head by means of an opening in the side, and was then fastened by a lace, a buckle, or a tie. The manner in which the lace, passing through alternate groups of the links farming the coif, is made to secure the loose to the fixed part of the cap, is excellently shewn in the figures of Longespée and the so-called Duke of Normandy in Gloucester Cathedral, (Stothard, Plate xxii.) A good example of the fastening by strap and buckle is furnished by the fragment of an effigy found at Exeter, engraved in the Archæological Journal, vol. ix. p. 188. The coif adjusted by a tie is seen in our woodcut, No. 62. The side-piece hanging free is shewn in a knightly statue of this century in the Abbey Church of Pershore, Worcestershire, engraved in the Journal of the Archæological Association, vol. iv. p. 319. The coif is sometimes encircled by a fillet. See our woodcuts, No. 46, 59, and 63. The circles are of gold-colour in figures of the Painted Chamber (Pl. xxx.): in the effigy of William de Valence the band is richly jewelled, (Stothard, Pl. xliv.)

Many examples shew that the warrior often went to battle without any kind of helmet *over* the coif of chain-mail; though it is probable that some additional defence, whether of plate or of quilted-work, was in this case worn beneath it. The regular and compact form of the crown in many ancient examples favours this belief; and a modern instance from the East helps to confirm it. A suit of Birman armour in the Tower of London has a skull-cap of plate which is quite hidden from view by the outer armour of the head. In the effigy at Bingham, Notts., already mentioned, the upper part of the coif is so large that it almost gives the notion of a turban being worn beneath. The coif used in battle without any further defence over it, may be seen in our engravings, No. 80 and 82.

On other occasions, the mail-coif had the additional armament of a helmet of some kind. This may be better considered in our general notice of helmets.

No. 55.

The Hood of Chain-mail appears to have been designed as an improvement on the Continuous Coif by rendering unnecessary the side-opening and the lacing about the face. But the hood had this great disadvantage; that, as it lay on the shoulders of the knight, it permitted the lance of the adversary to pass beneath it and deal a deadly thrust on the unguarded neck. This fact is of constant occurrence, as well in the chronicles as in the pictures of the times. The hood, like the coif, is both flat-topped and round. The flattened hood is seen in the effigy of De l'Isle, (Stothard, Pl. xx.) The round appears in the brasses of Sir John D'Aubernoun (woodcut, No. 55), and Sir Roger de Trumpington (Waller, Pt. iv., and our woodcut, No. 73): in the statues of De Vere, Crouchback, and Shurland, figured by Stothard; and in our engravings, No. 59 and 63. A simple lace, passing across the forehead and tying behind, bound the hood firmly to the head. The manner of this may be seen on comparing the brass of Sir John D'Aubernoun and the statue of Sir Robert Shurland. Both hood and coif appear occasionally to have been slipped over the head and suffered to rest on the shoulders. Compare the effigy in the Temple Church (Stothard, Pl. xxxviii.), Hefner's plate 27, and our woodcuts No. 56 and 70. The hood is sometimes shewn as made of a cloth-like material, (cloth, leather, or pourpointerie?) as in the front figure of our engraving, No. 68, from a MS. in the library of Metz. Its colour is brown, while the banded mail in this drawing is iron-colour. (Hefner, Pl. LXXVII.) Plain and enriched fillets, which we have seen were worn over the mail-coif, appear also upon the hood. The plain circle occurs in the Gosberton effigy (Stothard, Pl. XXXVII.), and in our woodcuts, No. 59 and 63. Enriched examples are found in the sculptures of De Vere and Crouchback (Stothard, Pl. XXXVI. and XLII.).

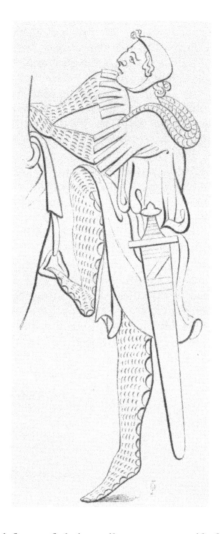

Beneath the head-defence of chain-mail was worn a coif of softer material, to mitigate the roughness of the iron-cloth; and perhaps also to assist in protecting the head by being made of quilted-work. See our woodcut, No. 56, from a miniature given by Willemin (Monumens Inédits, j. Pl. cii.) Compare also Painted Chamber, Pl. xxxv., and Willemin, j. Pl. cxliii.

Besides the Hauberk already described, which however forms in a great majority of instances the body-armour of the knights of this time, we have several varieties of defensive equipment. The Haubergeon is still mentioned, and seems to imply, not alone the smaller hauberk of chain-mail, but sometimes a garment of inferior defence and different material. There is also a chain-mail hauberk made with sleeves which reach but little below the elbows. A good example occurs on folio 9 of Roy. MS. 12, F. xiii.; a Bestiarium. See also the figures of Virtues in Plates xxxviii. and xxxix. of the Painted Chamber.

The Gambeson or Pourpoint, or *Gambesiata Lorica*, as it is called in a will of the year 1286, frequently appears as forming of itself the coat of fence. It is thus noticed in the Statute of Winchester, already quoted; where, while the first class of tenants are prescribed a "hauber, chapel de feer," &c., the third class are to have "parpoint, chapel de feer, espe e cutel." Compare also the Statute of Arms of 1252. In the eighth of Edward I. we read that "Rogerus de Wanstede tenet dimid. serjantiam ibidem per servitium inveniendi unum Valectum per octo dies, sumptibus propriis, cum praepuncto, capella ferrea et lancea, custodire castrum de Portsmut tempore guerrae[332]." In the "Ordonnances sur le Commerce et les Métiers," the duties of the pourpointers of Paris at the close of this century are very exactly defined. "Se l'on fait cotes gamboisiees, que elles soient couchees deuement sur neufves estoffes, et pointees, enfermees, faites a deux fois, bien et nettement emplies, de bonnes estoffes, soient de coton ou dautres estoffes[333]." Again: "Item que nul doresenavant ne puist faire cote gamboisiee ou il n'ait trois livres de coton tout net, si elles ne sont faites en fremes, et au dessous soient faites entremains, et que il y ait un ply de vieil linge emprez l'endroit de demie aulne et demy quartier devant et autant derriere." From these enactments we see that the counterpointers of the thirteenth century were but too apt to construct their armours of unstable materials, and to stuff them with a niggard hand.

The Cuirie (*Cuirena*) was, as its name implies, originally a defence of leather: it was also made of cloth. It covered the body alone, requiring the addition of *Brachières* to complete the coat. Thus, in the Roll of Purchases made for the Windsor tournament in the sixth year of Edward I., we have: "De Miloñ. ƚ Cuireũ (Milo the Currier) xxxiij. quire͠t, p'c peč iij. *s.*" Each took two ells ꝺ the cloth called Carda in its construction: "ſt pro qualibet quireͭt ij. ulñ card." The sleeves appear to have been of pourpointerie: "ſt pro xxxviij. pa͠r bracħ, x. bukerann[334]."

An account cited by Ducange, of the date 1239, has:—"Pro hernesio suo, videlicet baccis et cuireniis suis affecturis ix. lib. v. sol. Item pro tribus baccis et tribus cuirenis ad eosdem, iv. lib. iv. sol." See the glossarists under *Baca.* Guiart also mentions the cuirie:—

"Hyaumes, haubers, tacles, cuiries,
Fondent par les grans cops et fraingnent."

181

The Cargan seems to have been a collar or tippet of chain-mail. It occurs as part of a footman's armour in the Statutes of Frejus, A.D. 1233: "Peditem armatum intelligimus armatum scuto et propuncto, seu auspergoto, et cofa seu capello ferreo, et cargan, vel sine cargan," &c. The glossarists derive this and the cognate word, *carcannum*, from καρκίνος, genus vinculi; and, if this derivation is the true one, a gorget of chain-mail may be fairly inferred.

Other materials for armour than those mentioned above appear during the thirteenth century; but, before noticing these, it may be well to take a glance at the remaining *parts* of the knightly suit as they occur in the usual monuments of the time; then to examine the appendages which are attached to the body-armour, as the ailettes; after which we will notice the exceptional materials employed for defensive purposes; and lastly, those portions of the warrior's equipment which have not been included in the above scheme of investigation.

The Chausses, in the early part of the thirteenth century were entirely of chain-mail, covering the whole leg; as shewn in our woodcuts, No. 46, 52, and 54. Sometimes they were tightened below the knee with a lace, as in the two Salisbury effigies (Stothard, Plates XVII. and XXX., and our woodcut, No. 54.) A variety of this defence was laid on the front part of the leg, and then laced up behind. See woodcut, No. 53, from Harl. MS. 5102, fol. 32, a book of the early part of the century; and our numbers 56 and 62, towards the close of this period. Compare also Plates XXXIII. of Hefner, Plate LIV. of Strutt's Horda, and folio 10 of Roy. MS. 12, F. XIII.

To the chausses, whether of chain-mail or of banded-mail, are sometimes added Poleyns (or knee-pieces) of plate. It is often, however, difficult to determine whether the poleyns are fixed to the chausses or the chausson, from the upper edge of them being covered by the hauberk. A good example of the chausses armed with the knee-piece is offered by the knightly statue in Salisbury Cathedral (Stothard, Pl. XXX.), circa 1260. See also our woodcuts, No. 75 and 77: the first from Add. MS. 11,639, fol. 520; the latter from a glass-painting in the north transept of Oxford Cathedral. A German example given by Hefner (Pt. i. Pl. LXXVII.), from a manuscript illuminated at Metz c. 1280, is copied in our woodcut, No. 68. Poleyns are named in the Wardrobe Account of 28 Ed. I. (1300): "factura diversorum armorum, vexillorum, et penocellorum, pro Domino Edwardo filio Regis, et Johanne de Lancastria, jamberis, poleyns, platis, uno capello ferri, una cresta cum clavis argenti pro eodem capello," &c.

Towards the close of the thirteenth century the Chausses are most commonly accompanied with a Chausson of leather or quilted-work, the purpose of which was probably to obviate the inconvenience of the long chausses of metal in riding. It is found plain, gamboised in vertical lines, and sometimes richly diapered. The plain chausson is well shewn in Stothard's Plates xxii. and xxvi., effigies at Gloucester and in the Temple Church, London. The gamboised chausson is seen in this drawing of an ivory chess-piece preserved in the Ashmolean Museum. See also the effigy of a De Vere at Hatfield Broadoak, (Stothard, Pl. xxxvi.) An excellent example of the pourpointed chausson worked in a rich diaper is offered by the brass of De Bures, 1302 (Waller, Pt. 2, and Boutell's "Brasses and Slabs"). A curious variety of the chausson and chausses is found in the figure of a knight from Roy. MS. 2, A. xxii. fol. 219, given in our woodcut, No. 62; the chausson here being of chain-mail, while the chausses appear to be of rivetted plates. A chausson of chain-mail again appears in our cut, No. 86, from the Painted Chamber. To the chausson were usually attached knee-pieces of some rigid material: metal, *cuir bouilli*, or a mixture of both. See our woodcuts, Nos. 59 and 63; an effigy in Ash Church near Sandwich, and an illumination from a German manuscript, Add. MS. 17,687, both of the end of this century. Compare also the effigy at Gosberton (Stothard, Pl. xxxvii.), and those of De Vere and De Bures cited above. Among the embellishments of these poleyns are sometimes found little shields of arms; as in our woodcut, No. 70, the effigy of an unknown knight in Norton Church, Durham, c. 1300[335], and in the statue of Brian Fitz Alan, in Bedale Church, Yorkshire, engraved in Hollis's Effigies, Pt. 4, and in Blore's Monuments.

No. 58.

At the close of this century first appear the Greaves, of metal or *cuir bouilli*, covering the front of the leg from the knee to the instep. They were probably of German introduction, for their Latin name was *Bainbergæ*, from the German *Beinbergen*; and it seems likely that the Germans may have copied them from the examples of classic times with which they had become familiar during their wars in Italy. In the south of Europe, the greaves were already become of a highly ornamental character, as we may see from this sculpture of Gulielmus Balnis, 1289, from a bas-relief in the Annunziata Convent at Florence[336]; while in England they do not once appear among our monumental effigies or on our royal seals. Nor can a single example be found among the pictures that adorned the royal palace of Westminster. They are seen, however, among the illustrations of a manuscript of Matthew Paris' Lives of the two Offas, (Cott. MS., Nero, D. 1,) a work usually assigned to the thirteenth century, but perhaps not earlier than the next age. Our woodcut, No. 80, has an example from this manuscript, folio 7. On comparing the two engravings given by us, it will be seen that, while the vellum picture shews the defence below the knee only, the Italian figure has it both below and above. The abundance of ornament in the latter specimen seems to imply a moulded material—*cuir bouilli*? Antique examples, however, found at Pompeii and elsewhere, are of metal, highly ornamented with chasing and embossed-work. The name Bainberg occurs in several ancient documents. In the Lex Ripuaria we have: "Bainbergas bonas pro VI. sol. tribuat." And in the will of St. Everard, duke of Frejus: "Bruniam unam, helmum 1. et manicam 1. ad ipsam opus, *bemberga* II." &c. And again: "Bruniam unam cum halsberga et manicam unam, *bemivergas* duas." The word in the last passage being probably an error for *beinbergas*.

PLATE LIX.

In the last quarter of the thirteenth century appear those curious appendages to the knightly suit, the Ailettes. But they do not occur in any frequency till the beginning of the fourteenth century. We shall, therefore, in noticing this novelty, refer to some examples of the later period. From their name, *ailettes*, Fr.; *alette*, Ital.; and *alettæ* in the Latin of the period, they appear to have been a French or Italian invention. An early notice of them is in the Roll of Purchases for the Windsor Tournament in 1278, where they are made of leather covered with the kind of cloth called Carda. "De eodem (Milo the Currier) xxxviij. par̃ alect̃ cõr̃ p'c̃ par̃. viij. d." "ſt pro xxxviij. par̃ aleſt̃ s̃. pro q par̃ dī ulñ card. s̃. xix. ulñ." They were fastened with silk laces, supplied by "Richard Paternoster." "D Ricõ par̃ nr̃ viij. Duodeñ laqueorum serĩc pro alet̃ p̃c duodeñ viij. d.[337]" Sir Roger de Trumpington was one of the thirty-eight knights engaged in this tournament, and it is remarkable that his monumental brass furnishes one of the earliest and best pictorial examples of the ailette that has come down to us. (See our woodcut, No. 73.) There is one instance of it, and only one, in the pictures of the Painted Chamber, Pl. xxxv. It is ensigned with a bird. In monumental statues it is very rare. The figure here given is from a knightly tomb in the Church of Ash-by-Sandwich, seemingly of the close of this century[338]. The ailettes appear *behind* the shoulders, rising from the slab beneath, about the eighth of an inch. They have been quadrangular, the outer corners having become broken by accident: there is no trace of any fastening, and no remain of colour. The other monumental [Pg 247] [Pg 248] [Pg 249] statues in England exhibiting the ailette are those of a Pembridge in Clehongre Church, Herefordshire (figured, with details, in Hollis's Effigies, Pt. 5), and the so-called Crusader at Great Tew, Oxfordshire. The Clehongre figure is especially curious as shewing the ailette fastened by its "laqueus," which appears on the outside. In Switzerland there is the statue of Rudolf von Thierstein, at Basle: the ailettes here are square, and fixed on the *side* of the figure. (Hefner, Pt. 2, Pl. xli.) Our English monumental brasses furnish several examples. See those of Septvans and Buslingthorpe, given by Waller, and the Gorleston brass, Plate li. of Stothard. The curious painted windows at Tewkesbury, figured in full by Carter (Sculpture and Painting), and in part by Shaw (Dress and Decorations), afford the best illustration contributed by pictured glass. Good examples are found in the ivory carvings and seals of the period. The seals of Edward the Third, as duke and as king, are well-known instances; and the ivory casket engraved by Carter, Plates cxiii. and cxiv., offers a singular variety of this accessory. Illuminated manuscripts furnish abundant examples. See, for instance, Roy. MSS., 14, E. iii. and 2, B. vii., and Add. MS. 10,292. The Louterell Psalter has a good specimen, copied in

Carter's work named above, and in the *Vetusta Monumenta*. French monumental examples, we learn from M. Allou, are very scarce: "L'accessoire qui nous occupe est fort rare dans les monuments français. Nous en trouvons des exemples dans les dessins qui nous ont été communiqués par M. Achille Deville, des pierres sépulchrales de Robert Duplessis, 1322, de Robert d'Estouteville, 1331, et de Jean de Lorraine, Duc de Brabant, 1341[339]."

No. 60.

The forms of the ailette are various: the most frequent is the quadrangular, as in the Ash Church effigy given above, and in this example from Add. MS. 10,293, fol. 58; a book *dated* in 1316. The round form occurs on the ivory casket engraved in vol. 4 of the Journal of the Archæological Association, and in Plates CXIII. and CXIV. of Carter's Sculpture and Painting. The pentagonal is seen in an illumination of Sloane MS. 3,983, engraved as the frontispiece to Strutt's Dress and Habits; the cruciform, in the figure of a knight from Roy. MS., 2, A. XXII. fol. 219 (our woodcut, No. 62). And on folio 94vo. of Roy. MS., 14, E. iij. is an example, the only one ever observed by the writer, of a lozenge-formed ailette. It is clear, from the Cross on the shield having the same position as the other, that the ailette is not a square one worn awry.

The size of this appendage differs greatly in different monuments. In the round example of the ivory casket, cited above, it is scarcely larger than the palm of the hand: while, in an illumination of Roy. MS., 20, D. 1, fol. 18vo, it is little less than the ordinary shield of the period. Its position is generally behind the shoulder, or at the side of it: sometimes it appears in front: but too strict an interpretation must not be given to the rude memorials of these times.

The use of the ailette has somewhat perplexed antiquarian writers. The French archæologists of the present day confess that it is "difficile d'en expliquer l'usage[340]." Some writers have considered it as a simply defensive provision: others look upon it as an ensign, to indicate to his followers the place of a leader in the field. Against the supposition that it was *merely* armorial, may be urged that in many cases it has no heraldic bearing at all: sometimes it has a cross only, sometimes a diaper pattern, and sometimes it is quite blank. See examples of all these varieties in the Tewkesbury glass paintings, the Gorleston brass (Stothard, Pl. LI.), and the Buslingthorpe brass (Waller, Pt. 10). In vellum pictures it is often seen worn by knights in the tilt; where the heraldic bearings already exhibited on the shield, crest, and surcoat of the rider, and on the caparisons of the horse, would to no useful purpose be repeated on the ailette. In the case of the Clehongre example, quoted above, the outside knotting of the lace does not seem consistent with the display of armorial distinctions on the wing beneath. In Germany they are called *Tartschen* (Hefner: *Trachten*, Pt. 2, Pl. XLI.), and their purpose of shields seems most in accordance with the numerous ancient evidences in which they appear. The knights, indeed, not content with their panoply of steel, seem in the course of the middle-ages to have fortified themselves with a complete outwork of shields. Thus we have the ailettes, the shield proper, the *garde-bras*, or elbow-shield, the shoulder-shield, the *Beinschiene*, or shield for the legs, the vamplate on the lance, and the steel front of the saddle, which was in fact but another shield for the defence of the knight's body. Referring once more to the Clehongre effigy, it will be observed that, while the "défaut de la cuirasse" (where the arm joins the body) is strengthened *in front* with a steel roundel, this assailable point is covered at the *back of the arm* with the ailette. See the Details on Hollis's third plate of this monument. The analogy between these defences and those curious upright pieces of steel on the shoulders, so frequent in the armours of the sixteenth century, will at once be recognised.

Ailettes of a superb construction appear in the Inventory of the effects of Piers Gaveston in 1313: "Item, autres divers garnementz des armes le dit Pieres, ovek les alettes garniz et frettez de perles[341]." They are named also in the Inventory of the goods of Umfrey de Bohun in 1322: "iiij peire de alettes des armes le Counte de Hereford[342]."

PLATE LXII.

Besides the defences of chain-mail, which, as we have [Pg 253]
[Pg 254]
[Pg 255] seen, formed the usual armour of the knights of the thirteenth century, there were other materials occasionally employed for the warrior's habit. Scale-work still appears, though in but few monuments; and it seems to have been used for small portions only of the equipment. See the brass figured by Waller, Part x., and Boutell, page 113.

In this singular figure of a knight from Roy. MS. 2, A. xxii. fol. 219, the leg-defences are composed of a kind of Bezanted Armour: small roundels of metal, placed contiguously, appear to be rivetted to a fabric of cloth or to leather: forming a garment very similar to the "penny plate armour" of the sixteenth century. In the original drawing, the chausses are shaded with blue: but, singularly enough, the chausson is shaded with red, though it seems clearly to be intended for chain-mail. The date of the figure appears to be about the close of the thirteenth century. As a curious illustration of bezanted armour, the late Mr. Hudson Turner told the writer of these pages that he had seen in an ancient record an account of a hauberk of Edward III., studded with gold florins; though, with the usual caution of the antiquarian discoverer, he withheld the name and locality of the document.

PLATE LXIII.

In the engraving given overleaf, from Add. MS. 17,687, a German illumination of the end of this century, we have an example of Studded armour. Garments presenting an exterior sprinkled with studs are of frequent occurrence in the next age, and we shall therefore freely use the memorials of that time in illustration of our subject; and indeed we may gather some valuable evidences from existing armours of Eastern manufacture. Many a mystery of middle-age lore may be unravelled by an attentive examination of Oriental productions. As the surface only of the military studded garments is presented to our view in ancient monuments, we can seldom determine with exactness their construction: but, from the comparison of various examples, it seems probable that there were not less than four or five varieties of this kind of apparel. First, we have quilted-work, in which the studs appear to be used for holding together the component parts of the fabric. We have already noticed an example of the kind in our preceding division (woodcut, No. 37). The engraving now before us seems to represent a similar armour: the spots are coloured of a red-brown on a ground of light grey. In the fine manuscript of Meliadus, Add. MS. 12,228, not only parts of the knightly suit, but the saddles of the horses, are seeded with studs; which seems distinctly to imply a quilted covering. See also the effigies engraved by Stothard, (Plates LX. and LXIII.) And in the Tower collection will be found Chinese armour of modern date, formed of a quilted garment sprinkled with metal studs. The next kind of Studded armour is that of which a real specimen of the fourteenth century was found by Dr. Hefner in the excavations of the old Castle of Tannenberg in Germany: a relic which throws the clearest light on the costume of many a knightly effigy of that period. The defence is thus contrived: strips of metal, like hooping, are placed horizontally across the body, the upper edge of each splint being perforated for rivets. These strips slightly overlap each other: a piece of velvet, or other material of a similar kind, is then laid over the whole, and by rows of rivets fastened to the iron splints beneath. The velvet being of a rich hue, and the rivet-heads gilt[Pg 257]

[Pg 258]

[Pg 259] or silvered, the garment presents exactly the appearance of those knightly suits in which spots of gold or silver are seen studding the whole superficies of a dress of crimson or other brilliant tincture. The relic in question is figured and minutely described in the admirable tract on the results of the find by Doctors Hefner and Wolf: "Die Burg Tannenberg und ihre Ausgrabungen." The Stapelton brass, of which there is a facsimile in the Craven Ord Collection in the British Museum, and an engraving in Stothard's work, and the brass at Aveley in Essex (Waller, Pt. 1), seem to exhibit the armour in question. Foreign examples occur in the figures of Conrad von

Saunsheim and those in Bamberg Cathedral, given by Hefner in Part II. of the *Trachten*. The jazerant coats of the fifteenth century, of which several real specimens yet remain to us, are of a very similar construction. A third kind of Stud-work seems to differ from the articulated sort described above, in its basis being uniform and rigid, while the surface exhibits the same features, of a coloured ground-work spangled with bosses of gold or silver. See Stothard's Plates LXXVI. and XCIII. A fourth variety appears to be described in this passage of the Inventory of the effects of Piers Gaveston: "Item, en un autre coffre une peire de plates enclouez et garniz d'argent, od quatre cheynes d'argent, coverz dun drap de velvet vermail besaunte d'or[343]." Here we have a garment of velvet spotted with gold, covering an armour nailed with silver: clearly, therefore, differing from the preceding kinds, where the rivets unite the component materials into one vestment. A further item of the Inventory seems to shew still more clearly that the velvet coat (whether bezanted or not) was distinct from the iron defence: "Item, deux cotes de velvet pur plates coverir." Finally, another kind of studded military garment, of which we trace the existence through the examples of Modern Asia, consisted of several thicknesses of pliable stuff, held together by rivets with bossed heads which appear on the surface. In the Museum of the United Service Institution may be seen a Chinese armour constructed after this method, but having the coat lined at the breast with a few plates of iron about the size of playing-cards. In other examples, the studs are not rivetted, but only sewn down upon the garment.

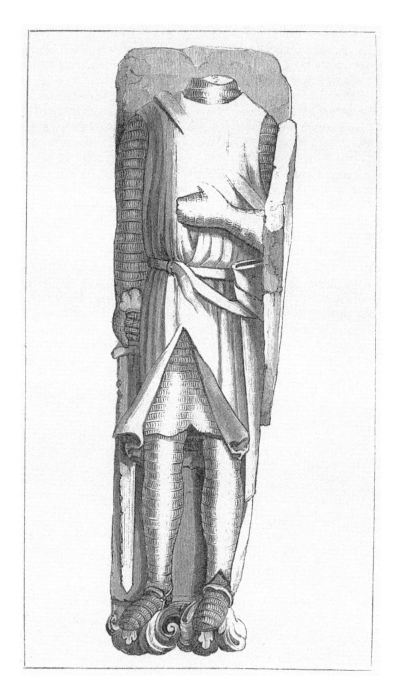

PLATE LXIV.

Towards the close of the thirteenth century we find an armour offering a new appearance, to which has been given the name of Banded Mail. Notwithstanding much careful consideration, its exact structure has not yet been discovered, though the representations of it are very abundant. For a whole century, manuscript illuminations, monumental brasses, painted windows, royal and baronial seals, metal chasings and sculptures of various kinds, afford us an infinity of examples; in none of which has hitherto been detected the exact evidence either of its material or its construction. Monumental sculptures, from their large size and the careful finish of their details, might have been expected to solve a problem which they only perplex. The effigy[344] here engraved, of a knight [Pg 261]

[Pg 262]

[Pg 263] of the De Sulney family, exhibits the warrior armed from head to foot in a suit of banded-mail; and in the following woodcut we have given a portion of the armour of this figure, of its real size. The profile view has been copied with particular care, in the hope that it might be of use in determining the structure of this very singular defence. By many writers this fabric has been described as pourpointerie; by others it has been considered as only a conventional mode of representing the ordinary chain-mail. Mr. Kerrich, whose opinions will always be received with, the greatest respect, speaking of the rows of little arcs used to express the latter defence, says: "When there are lines between the rows, whether *two* or only one, I conceive it means still but the same thing[345]." M. Pottier, in the text to Willemin's *Monuments Inédits*, does not distinguish the so-called banded-mail from the other, but names it simply "armure de mailles[346]." But it seems difficult to believe that the common chain-mail could be intended, so widely different are the two modes of representation, whether in sculpture or in painting. Observe, for instance, the details—especially the portion in profile—from the effigy at Newton Solney. And in the following subject from the Romance of Meliadus, (Add. MS. 12,228, f. 79,) there seems no assignable reason for marking one figure so differently from the rest, unless the armour itself were of a distinct kind[347].

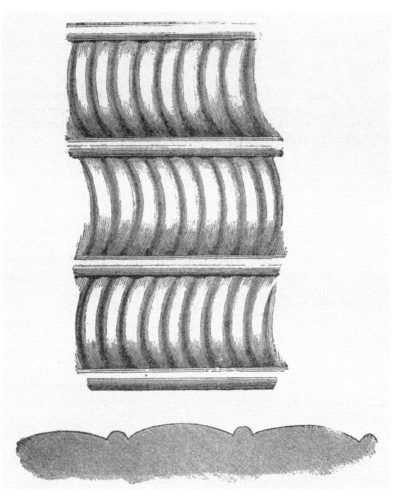

No. 65.

That the banded defences under consideration were of pourpointing is still more unlikely; for a gamboised garment, whether of velvet, silk, cloth, or whatever material, would, in painted representations, exhibit those various *colours* which are so lavishly displayed in the other portions of the knightly attire. Yet a careful examination of many hundred figures in illuminated manuscripts has failed in detecting a single instance of positive colour on banded-mail, except such as may be referred to the metals. Green, scarlet, crimson, diaper or ray, never appear. But gold or a golden tincture, silver or white, and grey of various shades, occur continually. And all these seem to indicate a fabric in which metal plays at least a conspicuous part. The examples among vellum-paintings, in which the banding is tinted grey or left white, are so numerous that one can scarcely open a manuscript of the period without finding them. Instances of it in silver may be seen in Cotton MSS., Vitellius, A. xiii., and Nero, D. vi.; in Roy. MS. 20, D. i., and Add. MS. 12,228. On folio 217vo. of the last-named book will be found the figure of a knight whose banded-mail is gilt. The same kind of armour, in gold colour, appears in the windows of Beer Ferrers Church, Devonshire, and of Fulborn Church, Cambridgeshire. See Lysons' Devonshire, p. 326, and Kerrich Collections, Add. MS. 6,730, fol. 61, for faithful copies of these examples. If from the foregoing evidences we derive the belief that the basis of this fabric was metal, from a monument figured in the superb work of Count Bastard,

Peintures des Manuscrits, &c., we gather that the lines of arcs were rings; for the fillet that binds the coif round the temples is clearly passed through alternate groups of rings, exactly as in the ordinary mail-hood. The figure is from a French Bible of the beginning of the fourteenth century, and occurs in the seventh number of the *Peintures*. In fairness we must admit that this example is not altogether inadmissible as an evidence in favour of the theory of common chain-mail. And on that side may be ranged the very curious figure of Offa the First, given in our woodcut, No. 80, from the "Lives of the Two Offas," by Matthew Paris (Cott. MS., Nero, D. i. fol. 7); where the upper part of the warrior's coif is of "banded-mail," while the lower portion is marked in the manner usually adopted to express the ordinary chain-mail.

No. 67.

Different from all these is the interpretation offered by M. de Vigne in his *Recueil de Costumes du Moyen-Age*. On Plate LVI. of that work, the author has given a series of sketches, shewing the supposed construction of various ancient armours. The banded mail is represented as formed of rows of overlapping rings, sewn down on leather or other similar material, "avec les coutures couvertes de petites bandes de cuir." Von Leber, in his sketch of medieval armour, has the same notion: "Vom 13. his nach Anfang des 14. Jahrh. der lederstreifige Ringharnisch als unschöne und unbequeme Ritterhülle[348]." This interpretation, however, is at variance with those ancient monuments where the *inside* of the defence exhibits the ring-work as well as the exterior. See our print of the De Sulney effigy. A more improbable garment, to say the least of it, than a hauberk of leather, *faced* with mail and *lined* with mail, can scarcely be conceived. Other examples of the hauberk, shewing the banding on the inside, are furnished by the brass of De Creke (Waller, Pt. viii.; Boutell, p. 39), a brass at Minster, Isle of Sheppey (Stothard, Pl. LIV.; Boutell, p. 42), in the effigy of Sir John D'Aubernoun (Stothard, Pl. LX.), and the brass at Ghent, figured in the Archæological Journal, vol. vii. p. 287.

Sometimes the knight's horse is barded with banded-mail, as in the figure from a manuscript in the Library of Cambrai, given by De Vigne in his *Recueil de Costumes*, vol. ii., plate VIII. In Roy. MS. 20, D. i. fol. 330, a work of about the close of the thirteenth century, are elephants with similar caparisons: on their backs are castles, full of fighting men.

We have already noticed that four sculptured effigies with banded-mail have been observed in England. The Tewkesbury figure is given by Stothard; an example further curious from the hauberk being sculptured as ordinary chain-mail, while the camail alone is of the banded work. In the "Memoirs," p. 125, Stothard, writing of this camail to Mr. Kerrich, says: "Amongst other curious things I have met with, is a figure which has some remarkable points about it; but, for the discovery of these, I devoted a whole day in clearing away a thick coating of whitewash which concealed them. The mail attached to the helmet was of that kind so frequently represented in drawings, and which you have had doubts whether it was not another way of representing that sort we are already acquainted with. I am sorry that I know no more of its construction now than before I met with it." The effigy at Dodford, near Weedon, is engraved in Baker's Northamptonshire, vol. i. p. 360. The knight has hauberk, chausses and coif of banded-mail, with poleyns, coutes and cervellière of plate. The figure at Tollard Royal, Wilts, has not been engraved; but from some memorandums kindly furnished by a friend, it appears that this knight is habited in hauberk, chausses and coif of banded-mail, with a skull-cap of plate.

Compare also the effigy of gilded metal in Westminster Abbey, of William de Valence, who died in 1296 (Stothard, Pl. XLIV.). In the following figures, from a German manuscript of about 1280, copied from Hefner's *Trachten*, it will be observed that each knight differs from his fellow in the manner of his equipment, though the staple defence of all is the banded-mail. Other examples of this kind of armour will be found in our woodcuts, No. 47, 48, 63, 72 and 77. At last, we can establish no definite conclusion. Our proofs are but of a negative character. Yet it is always something, to have determined what a thing is not. It seems pretty clear, then, from the absence of varied colours which we have remarked, that the Banded-mail is not pourpointerie of any kind. And, from the presence of the ring-work on the inside of the armour as well as the outside, it appears not to be of the construction suggested by the German and Belgian antiquaries. If meant for ordinary chain-mail, it must be confessed that the medieval artists never hit upon a mode of expressing this material so little resembling the original. It is to the further examination of ancient evidences, or to the discovery of monuments hitherto unobserved, that we must look for a satisfactory solution of this knightly mystery.

No. 69.

In addition to the various armours already noticed, we find in the thirteenth century the defence expressed by cross-lines which we have remarked in the earlier periods. Good examples occur on folio 9 of Roy. MS. 12, F. xiii., and in Laing's Scottish Seals, Plate ɪv.

And in a chess-piece of the early part of this century, the markings of the armour are made in a very peculiar manner: by rows of drilled holes divided by lines. (Woodcut 69.) This seems to be the device of a rude artist to express the ordinary chain-mail. The example was first brought into prominent notice in the pages of the Archæological Journal, vol. iii. p. 241.

Occasionally, but very rarely, the chain-mail was indicated in monumental statues by merely painting the links on a flat surface. The effigy of a De l'Isle in Rampton Church, Cambridgeshire, engraved by Stothard, Plate xxɪ., affords a good instance of this method.

A further singularity of the period is that the chain-mail sometimes presents a surface of a hue which does not appear consistent with a defence of steel. The effigy of Longuespée at Salisbury (woodcut No. 54) has the armour painted brown. The centre figure in our woodcut No. 53 wears a hauberk which is marked with buff on a white ground, the other hauberks being blue. The knight on woodcut No. 62 has a chausson shaded with red. And in Harl. MSS. 1,526 and 1,527 are many figures in which the chain-mail markings appear on a bright red ground. It seems probable, however, that such variations may be charged on the caprice of the artists; as in the colourings of the Bayeux tapestry, where the near legs of the horses are made blue, while the off legs are yellow.

Among the knightly effigies in the Temple Church, London, is a figure which seems to require an especial notice; the armour being of a fashion not elsewhere remarked. It consists of a back and breast-piece, each in a single part, united at the sides by straps. The sculpture being in stone, without any painting preserved, it is of course impossible to ascertain the material which the artist desired to represent. It may have been leather (the *cuirie*, of which we have already noted the existence); but there seems no good reason why it should not have been iron: and if so, it is perhaps the earliest example of a body-armour formed of a "pair of plates large[349]" that Europe has to offer. The effigy in question lies at the south-east corner of the group in the Round Church.

About the beginning of the thirteenth century arose the use of the military Surcoat. The first English monarch who, on his Great Seal, appears in this garment, is King John: 1199-1216. (See our woodcut, No. 52.) The seal of the dauphin Louis, the rival of John, (appended to Harleian Charter, 43, B. 37, dated 1216,) has it also. The earliest Scottish king who wears the surcoat is Alexander the Second: 1214-1249: a fine impression of his seal is attached to Cotton Charter, xix. 2. Imaginative writers have affirmed that this garment was first used by the Crusaders, in order to mitigate the discomfort of the metal hauberk, "so apt to get heated under a Syrian sun." Cotemporary authority, however, expressly tells us that its purpose was to defend the armour from the wet:—

"Then sex or atte[350] on assente
Hase armut hom and furthe wente

With scharpe weppun and schene,
Gay gownus of grene,

To hold thayre armur clene
And were[351] hitte fro the wete."
The Avowynge of King Arther, stanza 39.

The Surcoat was of two principal kinds: the sleeveless and the sleeved. The latter is not found till the second half of the century.

The Sleeveless Surcoat occurs of various lengths: sometimes scarcely covering the hauberk, sometimes reaching to the heels. Both the short and the long are seen throughout the century. The long appear on the royal seals noticed above. And on the seal of De Quinci, circa 1250 (woodcut, No. 87); on the sculpture from Haseley, c. 1250 (cut, No. 46); on the brass of D'Aubernoun, 1277 (No. 55); on that of De Trumpington, 1289 (No. 73); on the effigies at Ash and Norton, of the close of the century (Nos. 59 and 70); and on the statues of De Vere and Crouchback (Stothard, Plates xxxvi. and xlii.).

The shorter Surcoat occurs on the effigy of Longuespée, d. 1226 (woodcut, No. 54); the knight at Whitworth, c. 1250 (Stothard, Pl. xxiv.); the figures from the Painted Chamber and the "Lives of the Two Offas" (woodcuts, Nos. 80 and 86); the knight at Florence, 1289 (cut No. 58); De Valence, in Westminster Abbey (Stothard, Pl. xliv.); and our engravings, Nos. 47, 56, 63, 64 and 68: the last-named examples being of the close of the century.

The Surcoat is either of a uniform tint, or diapered, or heraldically pictured. Probably, in some early sculptured effigies, the surcoat, now plain, had armorial devices expressed by painting, which time has obliterated. The armorial surcoat was a necessary result of the visored helm; for when the visor was closed, it was no longer possible to distinguish king from subject, leader from stranger, comrade from foe. A similar inconvenience had already been found in the nasal helmet. At the field of Hastings, Duke William was obliged to remove the bar from his face, in order to convince his followers that he was still alive. The figure of Longuespée at Salisbury, c. 1226, still exhibits a portion of the heraldic decoration of the surcoat. And it is again found on the statue of De l'Isle at Rampton, circa 1250 (Stothard, Pl. xx.). The pictures of the Painted Chamber offer many examples. (See our woodcut, No. 86.) See also our engravings, Nos. 58 and 62. The effigy of William de Valence in Westminster Abbey, circa 1296, offers a curious variety of this garment: it is powdered with escutcheons, on each of which are the bearings of his house. A similar arrangement is seen in one of the figures of the Painted Chamber (Plate vi.)

The knightly surcoat of this time was slit up in front and behind, for convenience of riding. A singular deviation from this fashion of the garment is found in a figure in the Cathedral of Constance, c. 1220; where from the front part a portion passes under the arms, overlaps the part hanging from the shoulders behind, and then fastens at the back. See Hefner's work, Pl. IV. of Pt. i.

Occasionally the surcoat has an ornamental edge of fringe; as in the brasses of D'Aubernoun, 1277, and De Bures, 1302 (woodcut, No. 55, and Waller, Pt. ii.). In some cases, as in the Temple Church figure engraved by Stothard, Pl. XV., the garment has a rigid appearance across the shoulders, which has been taken to indicate a strengthening of the surcoat at that part. But the same treatment is seen in the enamelled effigy at St. Denis, of John, son of St. Louis; where the garment forms part of a civil dress (Willemin, vol. i., Pl. XCI., and Guilhermy's Monuments of St. Denis, p. 164). The Surcoat sometimes hangs loose, as in our woodcut, No. 86; but usually it is girt at the waist by a cord or strap. The cord is seen in the brasses of Sir John D'Aubernoun and Sir Roger de Trumpington; the strap, with its long pendent end, in the effigies at Ash Church, Norton Church, and St. Bride's (our woodcuts, Nos. 55, 73, 59, 70 and 74). The group from Add. MS. 17,687 furnishes some further examples (cut, No. 63). Rarely, the surcote is made with a "fente" at the throat, and fastened with a fibula. An effigy in the Temple Church exhibits this arrangement. (Hollis, Pt. ii.)

The Sleeved Surcoat, as we have already noticed, did not come into use till the second half of the thirteenth century. It is frequent in the pictures of the Painted Chamber. A good example is offered by the effigy at Norton, Durham (our woodcut, No. 70); and very similar are found in the statue of Lord Fitz Alan at Bedale, Yorkshire, (engraved by Hollis, Pt. iv., and in Blore's Monuments,) and the Temple sculpture (Stothard, Pl. XXXVIII.). The knightly figure on our woodcut No. 56 presents a variety, in the sleeves being "slittered." Those of the Shurland effigy (Stothard, Pl. XLI.) are divided under the arm and fastened by ties.

Plate LXX.

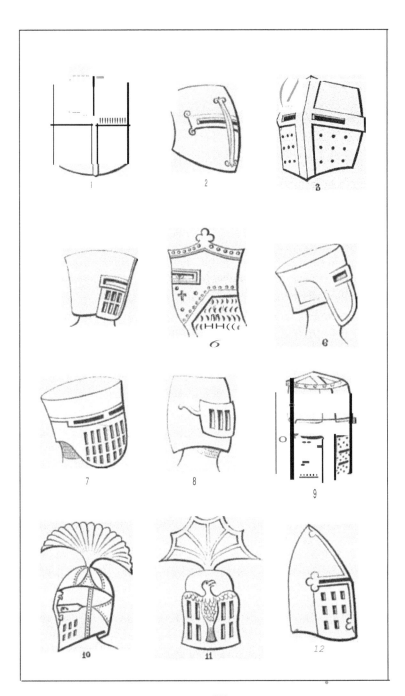

PLATE LXXI.

The HELMETS of the thirteenth century, though offering many points of difference on comparing particular examples, may yet be readily thrown into distinguishable[Pg 275]
[Pg 276]
[Pg 277]
[Pg 278]
[Pg 279] classes. The first division that Suggests itself is that of the Helm (the great, close casque of the knight) and the Helmet, a defence, as the word indicates, of diminished completeness. The Helm must again be divided into two leading kinds: that in which the plates forming it are all rivetted together, so as to make one piece; and that in which the front is provided with a moveable ventail. The successive changes of fashion supply a further division of the helms; giving us the flat-topped, the round-topped, and the "sugar-loaf" form. The Helmets may be classed as the hemispherical, the cylindrical, the conical, the wide-rimmed (Petasus form), and the nasal. Besides which are some varieties of peculiar construction, which may be better noticed after the more general forms have been considered.

The word Helm among the Northern nations merely meant a covering of any kind: the *Wærhelm* of the Anglo-Saxons was the little cap worn by the soldier, of which we have seen many examples in our previous inquiries. But from the end of the twelfth century, when the great casque enclosing the whole head, like that seen on the second seal of King Richard, came into use, the term helm or heaume was restricted to this new kind of headpiece.

The flat-topped Helm forming a single structure, appears usually in one of the following fashions. I. A cylinder having bands in front forming a cross, and sometimes similar bands crossing on the crown, which is slightly convex or conical; two horizontal clefts for vision, but without holes for breathing. Examples occur in our woodcut, No. 71, fig. 1, from the statue of Hugh Fitz Eudo, in Kirkstead Chapel, Lincolnshire; in the chess-knight (woodcut 57); in the Whitworth effigy (Stothard, Pl. xxiv.); in the carvings of the Presbytery arcade of Worcester Cathedral (woodcut 71, fig. 2); all these early in the century: and in the groups of the Painted Chamber. II. A cylinder with the cross-bands as before; but, in addition to the ocularium, having apertures for breathing. This kind is seen in our woodcut 71, fig. 3, from Hefner's *Trachten*; in the Walkerne effigy (Hollis, Pt. i.); in the sculptures of the front of Wells Cathedral, circa 1225; in the miniatures of the Lives of the Offas (Cott. MS., Nero, D.i.); and in the seal of Hugo de Vere, earl of Oxford (woodcut 71, fig. 4). III. A cylinder with ocularium and breathing-holes, but not having the cross-bands: woodcut 71, fig. 5, from the very curious drawing on folio 27 of Harl. MS. 3,244, date about 1250. IV. In this variety, the front part is rounded below, has ocularium, but not any breathing-holes: woodcut 71, fig. 6, from the seal of Alexander II. of Scotland, 1214-1249 (Cott. Charter, XIX. 2); and compare the seal of Louis the Dauphin, circa 1216. V. This kind resembles the last, except that it is provided with apertures for breathing. A good example is furnished by the seal of Robert Fitz Walter, of the second half of the century: woodcut 71, fig. 7.

We must remark also the difference existing among these helms on the point of ornament. Some are altogether plain; as in our woodcuts 57 and 71, and the Whitworth effigy (Stothard, Pl. xxiv.): others have a profusion of ornament, as in the knightly figure from Roy. MS. 2, A. xxii. (woodcut, No. 62). The term cylindrical, which has been applied to them, must not always be understood literally. In woodcut No. 57 we have a true cylinder; but in other cases, the helm swells at the sides, taking the "barrel" form, as in the second seal of Henry III. (woodcut 81); or, when viewed in profile, it presents a concave line behind, as in the seal of De Quinci (woodcut, No. 87), or, more strikingly, in the example at Worcester (woodcut 71, fig. 2).

The helm was worn over the coif of chain-mail. An ivory carving engraved in the sixteenth volume of the *Archælogia* affords an excellent illustration of this usage; the knight being there represented in the act of raising his helm from his head armed in the *coiffe de mailles*.

The flat-topped cylindrical Helm, with moveable ventail, appears about the middle of the century. The figure of Ferdinand, King of Castille, in the windows of Chartres Cathedral, affords a good example. He died in 1252: the monument is engraved by Willemin, vol. i., Pl. xcvii.: the helm is fig. 8 of our cut 71. A real helm of this type is in the Tower collection: the ventail opens by means of hinges on the side (see Archæol. Journal, vol. viii., p. 420, and our woodcut 71, fig. 9). It is entirely of iron, weighing 13lb. 8oz. And it is not unworthy of remark, that a much later helm, one with the beaked visor characteristic of the close of the fourteenth century, also in the Tower of London, differs in weight from the above example by only four ounces. (Archæol. Journal, vol. ix., p. 93.) The moveable ventail seems to be portrayed also on the second seal of Henry III., and on the seal of Edward I. (woodcuts, No. 81 and 85).

About 1270 the round-topped Helm came into vogue: not, however, to the entire exclusion of the old fashion, of which examples are found to the end of this century, and even during a portion of the next. See our Plate LXXI., fig. 10, from Cotton Roll, xv. 7. The seal of Patrick Dunbar, tenth earl of March, affords another good illustration of the helm with round crown: engraved in Laing's "Ancient Scottish Seals," p. 54. It has moveable ventail, with apertures for sight and breathing, as before. Other instances occur in the groups of the "Painted Chamber" and the "Lives of the Offas." A very curious variety of this type is furnished in the seal of Louis of Savoy, 1294; where the ventail has the form of an eagle displayed, the clefts for sight and air being contrived between the plumes of the wings. (Figured by Cibrario, in the *Sigilli de'Principi di Savoia*, Pl. xxx., and in our woodcut, No. 71, fig. 11.)

About 1280 the Helm takes the "sugar-loaf" form; having bands which make a cross in the front of it. See woodcut, No. 71, fig. 12, from Roy. MS. 20, D. i.; and the brass of Sir Roger de Trumpington, 1289 (woodcut, No. 73). It will be observed that this kind of heaume is continued so low as to rest on the shoulders.

It is not improbable that some of these casques were formed in part of leather. An early helm made of cuir-bouilli, with iron bands, is figured by Hefner (*Trachten*, Pt. ii., Pl. LXVIII.); and for the Windsor tournament of 1278, were provided "xxxviii. galee de cor."

The helm was made fast by laces. In the Romance of Perceval, the hero

"Prant ses armes et s'aparoille:
Sans atargier le haubert vest,
L'iaume lace sans nul arest," &c.—*Fol.* 237.

PLATE LXXII.

These laces are very clearly shewn in our engravings, [Pg 283]
[Pg 284]
[Pg 285] Nos. 47 and 62; from Roy. MSS., 20, D. i. and 2, A. xxii.

In order to recover the helm if struck off in the *mêlée* it was attached to some

212

part of the knight's equipment by a chain. The brass of Sir Roger de Trumpington (cut, No. 73) supplies us with an illustration. And this usage is noticed in the Romance of *Le tournois de Chauvenei*, written about 1285:—

"Chescun son hiaume en sachaaine,
Qui de bons cous attent l'estraine."

Vers 3,583.

Crests are frequently found surmounting the helm at the close of this century; but they are not of that distinctive kind, consisting of lions, griffins, eagles, wings, axes, and-so-forth, which appear in such diversity during the next age. They are merely of the fan form. The seal of De Quinci, indeed, seems an evidence to the contrary, and has been often described as an instance of a helm of the early part of the thirteenth century bearing a wyvern for a crest (woodcut, No. 87). But the wyvern in the upper part of this seal seems to be placed there merely to fill up the space between the letters, and belongs to the legend, not to the effigy; just as we see a flower occupying the space beneath the lion's feet, and in the obverse of the seal, the wyvern filling up the void beneath the horse and under the housing. Heraldic bearings do in fact appear on the casques of several figures previously to 1300. But they form part of the headpiece itself: they do not surmount it. The helm of Richard the First has a lion, but it is a figure embossed or painted on a part of the casque. The well-known effigy of a Plantagenet (Stothard, Pl. II.) is an analogous instance. The monument of Le Botiler at St. Bride's, Glamorganshire, (woodcut, No. 74,) affords another example: and in the curious helm of Louis of Savoy (woodcut 71, fig. 11) we have the heraldic eagle forming the *visor* of the casque, while the crest is composed of the usual fan ornament. This fan we have already seen on the helm of Richard I., but it does not come into general use till towards the close of the thirteenth century. See examples on our woodcuts, Nos. 71 and 72. Other instances may be found in Laing's "Scottish Seals," p. 54; in the Lives of the Offas, Cott. MS., Nero, D. i.; and in great number among the miniatures of Roy. MS. 20, D. i., where they are attached to the heads of the horses as well as to the helms. At the Windsor tournament in 1278, also, crests were provided both for man and horse:—

"If p.qualibet galea j. cresta }
If p.quolibet equo j. cresta } Sm̃. LXXVI. Cresᵗ."

And for the making of these crests, calf-skins and parchment were employed:—

"LXXVI. pell' vitul' p. cresᵗ faciend' p͞c pell' iij. d."
"Iᵗ p. qualibet cresta j. pell' parcamen⁻ rud'. Sm̃. LXXVI. p̃l' ꝺ p.cameni[352]."

Occasionally feathers supply the place of the fan ornament. A plume of seven peacock's feathers surmounts a [Pg 287]
[Pg 288]
[Pg 289] crowned helm on folio 205 of Roy. MS. 20, D. i.; and similar examples occur at ff. 60ᵛᵒ. and 239ᵛᵒ. of the same manuscript. Compare also Add. MS. 15,268: both these books being of the close of the century.

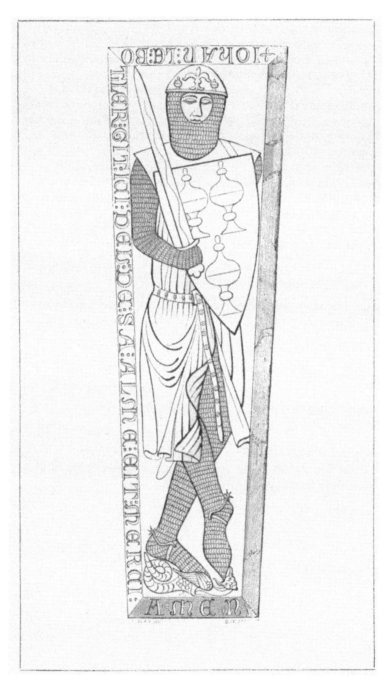

PLATE LXXIV.

Another curious appendage to the knightly helm of this time consisted of Horns; made, as we learn from Guillaume le Breton, of whalebone, and borne for the purpose of striking terror by the gigantic appearance of the wearer. The Count of Boulogne at the Battle of Bovines, in 1214, adopts this expedient:—

> "Cornua conus agit, superasque eduxit in auras,
> E costis assumpta nigris quas faucis in antro
> Branchia balenæ Britici colit incola ponti:
> Ut qui magnus erat magnæ super addita moli
> Majorem faceret phantastica pompa videri."
>
> *Philipp.*, lib. xi.
> 322.

The Helms of kings have a crown encircling them, as seen in the seals of Henry III. and Edward I. of England (woodcuts, No. 79, 81 and 85); but on the capelline of King John is no such ornament. See also our engraving, No. 72. The crown is occasionally placed on the coif of chain-mail: as on folio 7 of the Lives of the Offas (woodcut, No. 80), and in the pictures of the Painted Chamber.

Of the smaller casque—helmet, or chapel-de-fer—we have already observed that some were worn beneath the coif-de-mailles. Others were placed above it, or formed of themselves the whole arming of the head. They are cylindrical, hemispherical, conical, wide-rimmed, and of the nasal kind. The first-named appears in our woodcut, No. 53, from Harl. MS. 5,102, of the beginning of the century. It is found also on the seal of St. Louis, and in the effigy in the Temple Church, figured by Stothard, Pl. x. The rounded helmet occurs on the seal of King John (woodcut 52); in our engraving, No. 53, from Harl. MS. 5,102, early in the century; and in Nos. 49 and 74, both monuments of the close of this period. It appears plentifully in Roy. MS. 20, D. i., and in the groups of the Painted Chamber. The conical chapel is seen in our engraving, No. 58; it occurs also in Harl. MS. 1,527, and in the Painted Chamber and Lives of the Offas. The Wide-rimmed Helmet is found throughout this century. An early example appears in our engraving, No. 50, from Harl. MS. 4,751. The figure here given is from Add. MS. 11,639, fol. 520; of the close of the century. It represents Goliath, and the casque is thus painted: crown, iron-colour; rim and crest, gold. The book is in Hebrew, but believed to have been written in Germany. See also our woodcut, No. 49, from Add. MS. 15,268; and Hefner's Plate v.; and the pictures of the Painted Chamber. A good example in sculpture occurs in the arcade of the north aisle of the Lady Chapel at Worcester Cathedral. On Cotton Roll, xv. 7, a variety of this headpiece has an upright spike at the top. In the Archæological Journal, vol. viii. p. 319, is engraved a knightly effigy in which the wide and pointed iron-hat is worn over a close skull-cap of plate, to which, is joined a coif of chain-mail. The Nasal Helmet is found of three varieties: the cylindrical, the round-topped, and the conical. The first occurs on the monumental effigy of Raoul De Beaumont, in the abbey of Estival, founded by him in 1210. (Kerrich Collections, Add. MS. 6,728.) The hemispherical appears in the Lives of the Offas and the Painted Chamber, and on Plate xxxiii. of Hefner. The pointed crown is found among the subjects of the Painted Chamber, of which the following is an example. See also our woodcut, No. 82.

No. 76.

Besides the above, which are the usual types of casque found in the thirteenth century, there are some varieties of occasional appearance. Among these may be mentioned the open-faced helmet of the Temple effigy figured by Stothard, Pl. xv. In this curious example, all the head above the neck is cased in a defence of some rigid material (metal or cuir-bouilli?), and encircled by a band or turban. Another singular headpiece occurs on folio 7 of the Lives of the Offas (woodcut, No. 80); where the coif of banded-mail is covered in front with a plate, perforated for vision and breathing, and strengthened with the cross-bands already seen in the knightly heaume. Helmets formed of a framework of metal covering a cap of leather, similar to the defence noticed at an earlier period (see page 69), seem to have been in use during this century. Hefner has figured the metal portion of a real one found in the island of Negropont, which he assigns to this period (*Trachten*, Pl. LXIII.) It closely resembles the bronze example discovered at Leckhampton (woodcut 18), consisting of a hoop from which spring two arcs of metal crossing at the crown. Of similar mixed materials appear to be those helmets seen in the groups of the Painted Chamber, where a frame of gold-colour encloses a cap of crimson or purple (Plates XXXV. and XXXVI.). And compare our woodcut, No. 82, also from the Painted Chamber, in which the frame of the headpiece is of iron-colour, while the enclosed portion is painted yellow.

The Bassinet and Cervellière are named in documents of this time, but do not appear to have been anything more than the round-topped skull-cap already noticed.

The bassinet is mentioned in the will of Odo de Rossilion in 1298, cited by Ducange[353]; a monument further curious from its giving us the detail of a knight's equipment in these days:—

"Idem do et lego domino Petro de Monte Ancelini predicto centum libras Turonenses et unam Integram Armaturam de Armaturis meis, videlicet meum heaume à vissere, meum bassignetum, meum porpoinctum de cendallo, meum godbertum[354], meam gorgretam, meas buculas[355], meum gaudichetum, meas trumulieres[356] d'acier, meos cuissellos, meos chantones[357], meum magnum cutellum, et meam parvam ensem."

The Bassinet with camail *attached* is not a characteristic of this century, though isolated examples may perhaps be found. The knightly effigy at Ashington, Somersetshire, already noticed, seems to be one of these: the mail-coif being fixed to the plate-cap by rivets. (Archæol. Journ., vol. viii. p. 319.) It will be remarked in that very valuable monument, the Pictures of the Painted Chamber, that the skull-caps of plate are in many instances so placed on the coif-de-mailles as to shew very clearly that the two defences are quite distinct.

Guiart, in the *Chronique Métrique*, frequently uses the name *cervellière*:—

"Sus hyaumes et sus cervelières
Prennent plommées à descendre
Et hachètes pour tout porfendre."—*Line* 1912.

"Aucuns d'entr'eus testes desnuent
De hyaumes et de cervelières."—*Line* 5267.

"Hauberjons et cervelières,

Gantlez, tacles et gorgières."—*Line* 5467.

An amusing tale is told in the *Chronicon Nonantulanum*, of the invention of the cervellière by Michael Scot, "Astrologus Friderici Imperatoris familiaris." Having foreseen that he should meet his death from the fall of a stone of two ounces weight upon his head, he contrived a cap (*infulam*) of plate-iron. But being at mass one day, at the exaltation of the host, he reverently lifted his cap, when a little stone fell upon his head, and inflicted a slight wound. Weighing the stone, he found it to be exactly two ounces; and then, knowing his doom to be sealed, he arranged his worldly affairs and died.

From the manuscript collection of "Proverbes" of the thirteenth century, preserved in the Imperial Library at Paris, and cited by Le Grand d'Aussy in the *Vie privée des François*[358], we learn that the "Heaumes de Poitiers" had obtained the highest meed of approbation.

The ordinary SHIELD of this period was the triangular: its dimensions decreasing as the century advanced. It was bowed or flat. Other targets of this time are the kite-shaped, the pear-shaped, the heart-shaped, the round, the quadrangular, and a shield angular at the top and rounded below.

The triangular, bowed shield appears in our engravings, Nos. 52, 53, 57 and 87; all early examples. Later instances occur in the seal of Edward I. (No. 85), and our woodcut, No. 75, from Add. MS. 11,639. The flat triangular shield is found in the very curious figure on folio 27 of Harl. MS. 3,244, *circa* 1250; in the brass of Sir John D'Aubernoun, 1277 (woodcut, No. 55); in the glass-painting at Oxford Cathedral (woodcut, No. 77); and in the effigy of Le Botiler (woodcut, No. 74): the last two monuments, of the close of the century. See also Painted Chamber, Plate xxxvi. It will be observed that the shield of D'Aubernoun is curiously small. Those of Crouchback and William de Valence on their tombs are scarcely larger. (Stothard, Pl. xliii. and xliv.) The Kite-shaped shield appears very frequently in Roy. MS. 20, D. i.; a subject from which, with this form of target, is given in our woodcut, No. 72. It occurs also in Harl. MS. 1,527, and on Plate xxxvi. of the Painted Chamber. This form, like the foregoing, is sometimes bowed and sometimes flat. The Pear-shaped variety is found on the seal of Saer de Quinci, 1210—19, engraved in Laing's Ancient Scottish Seals, Pl. xi.; and on that of John de Methkil, c. 1220 (Laing, Pl. vii. fig. 3). Another Scottish seal gives us the Heart-shaped shield, a rare and early example (Laing, Pl. x. fig. 11). The Round target supported by its guige appears in a group of fighters in Harl. MS. 1,527; again in the Malvern effigy (Stothard, Pl. xix.); in the Lives of the Offas; and among the pictures of the Painted Chamber. The quadrangular bowed shield is figured in our woodcut, No. 88, from a Tower Roll, commemorating a wager of battle in the reign of Henry III. The shield made angular at top and rounded below may be found on Plate xxxi. of the Painted Chamber, and occurs again on the seal of a Melros charter of 1285, engraved on page 30 of Laing's Scottish Seals. It is scarcely necessary to say that the types which we have endeavoured to distinguish will be found somewhat varied in particular examples: to describe every modification of the general forms we have detected, would be a tedious and a useless task.

The Boss is still retained in some of the shields of this time, though but rarely. It appears in our woodcuts, Nos. 75 and 88, and on folio 4 of the Lives of the Offas. The Enarmes, or straps by which the knight sustained his shield in combat, are well shewn in the effigy of De Shurland (Stothard, Pl. xli.), and receive some further illustration from the statues of De Vere at Hatfield Broadoak, Essex, and of Brian Fitz Alan at Bedale, Yorkshire. Compare also folio 4 of the Lives of the Offas, and Plate xxxviii. of the Painted Chamber. The Guige, or strap by which the shield was hung round the neck, is a usual adjunct to this defence during the whole of the century, and is sometimes of a highly enriched character. Many of our woodcuts shew the manner of its use.

From a passage of "The Ancren Riwle," lately printed by the Camden Society, from a MS. of the thirteenth century, we learn that the materials of the shield at this time were "wood, leather, and painting." (p. 393.) These ingredients frequently reappear in the real targets of a later time which have been saved from the destruction of passing centuries.

No. 77.

Armorial bearings are the usual adornment of the knightly shield throughout this period; and the field was sometimes richly diapered, as in this example from the window of the north transept of Oxford Cathedral. Compare the monument of De Vere at Hatfield (Stothard, Pl. XXXVI.) Where heraldic devices are not found, a "pattern" generally takes their place: a cross, a rosette, a star, a fret, or some such simple ornament. In other cases the face of the shield is painted of a single colour. In the effigies placed over the tombs of the knights, the shield is usually represented as borne on the arm. The figure of William de Valence in Westminster Abbey has it slung at the hip; an arrangement frequently adopted in French monuments, and occasionally in those of other continental countries.

Another continental custom sometimes imitated by our own countrymen, was that of adorning the walls of the banqueting-hall on great occasions with the shields of distinguished heroes. When, in 1254, the English king entertained the French monarch in the Temple in Paris, "the banquet was given," says Matthew Paris, "in the great hall of the Temple, in which were hung up, according to the *continental custom*, as many bucklers as the four walls could hold." Amongst others was seen the shield of Richard, king of England, concerning which a witty person present said to King Henry, "Why, my Lord, have you invited the French to dine with you in this house? See, there is the shield of the noble-hearted English king, Richard! your guests will be unable to eat without fear and trembling[359]."

From the curious volume already cited, the *Ancren Rule*, we learn that at the demise of a brave knight, his shield was hung aloft on the church walls, in honour and remembrance of his valorous deeds.

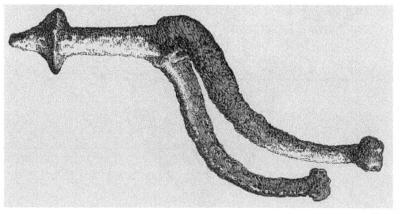

No. 78.

The Spur of this century is of three kinds: the simple goad, the ball-and-spike, and the rowel. The goad is sometimes straight, sometimes curved. The straight spike is seen in this example of an iron spur found in the churchyard of Chesterford, Cambridgeshire, and now preserved in the collection of the Hon. Richard Neville. Compare our engravings, Nos. 58 and 85. The curved goad appears in woodcuts 55 and 73. Our engravings, Nos. 62, 72 and 81 shew the ball-and-spike kind; of which we have already seen examples in the statues of Henry II. and Richard I. at Fontevraud. The rowel spur is found but in one or two instances during this century. It is represented on the seal of Henry III., here given; where, in order to bring up the rowel to the middle of the heel, the seal-engraver has resorted to the singular expedient of raising the field into a sort of hillock, on the top of which he has sculptured the star-like rowel. See Harleian Charter, 43, C. 38. The rowel spur again appears on the effigy of Le Botiler (woodcut, No. 74). It is, however, rather a characteristic of the fourteenth than of this century; and, generally speaking, its presence alone should lead one to hesitate long before assigning a monument to the earlier period, even though it should exhibit all the other features of the more ancient costume. The monument of Johan Le Botiler, just named, is by no means exempt from the operation of this rule.

GREAT SEAL OF KING HENRY III.

No. 79.

The shank of the spur is curved, each end being formed into a loop to receive the strap. The strap itself is single, buckling over the instep. See Stothard's Plates XVII. and XXII. Some exceptions occur to this usual arrangement. In the effigy of a De L'Isle, figured by Stothard, Plate XX., the outer shank is flattened into a trefoil and rivetted upon the leather. In the figure at Norton, Durham, (woodcut, No. 70,) the shanks terminate in rings, and two straps are employed to fix the spur to the foot. Both straps and spurs are occasionally shewn of an enriched character. On folio 27 of Harl. MS. 3,244, the spur is ornamented with a row of studs or bosses. In the brass at Acton, Suffolk, 1302 (Waller, Pt. ii.), the pattern consists of rosettes.

The gilded spurs of the knights occasionally became the trophy of a victory; as in the case of the battle of Courtray, in 1302. More than five hundred pairs, Froissart tells us, were suspended in a chapel of the church of Our Lady of Courtray: "Et ces éperons avoient jadis été des seigneurs de France, qui avoient été morts en la dite bataille; et en faisoient ceux de Courtray tous les ans, pour le triomphe, très grand solemnité[360]."

The Beard during this century appears to have been usually worn by the aged only. The young knight has commonly neither beard nor moustache: indeed, this imberbed state of the Western cavaliers is made a reproach to them by the Saracens. The Sultan, we are told by Matthew Paris, under 1250, addressing his chiefs, in arms against the forces of St. Louis, exclaimed: "What rash madness excites these men to attack us and endeavour to deprive us of our inheritance, who have inhabited this noble country since the Flood? A certain motive, however slight, urges the Christians to covet the land which they call Holy: but what have they to do with Egypt? Unfit indeed are they to lord it over a land which is watered and enriched by the river sent from Paradise: beardless, shorn men, unwarlike and imbecile, more like women than men, what rash daring is this[361]!"

For the arrangement of the beard of this time, see the effigies of King John and Henry III. (Stothard, Plates XI. and XXXI.), and Plate XXXIX. of the Painted Chamber.

The fashion of the Hair differs considerably in the first and second portions of the century. In both it was cut short at the forehead: but in the first half it was allowed to fall in its natural flow to some length at the sides of the head and behind; while, in the second, it was most carefully arranged in large curls, which cover the ears, and give a strongly marked character to the monuments of this time. In the effigy of King John at Worcester, the side hair is cut sheer off just below the ear. In the figure of Prince John, the son of St. Louis, in the Abbey Church of St. Denis, the hair falls in a natural ringlet to the neck[362]. The large and formal curl of the later period is well shewn in the knightly sculpture from Norton Church, Durham (woodcut, No. 70). See also the statue

226

of Henry III. (Stothard, Pl. xxxi.), and the series of monumental figures sculptured in 1263-4 by order of St. Louis, to perpetuate the memory of his ancestors entombed at St. Denis. (Guilhermy, pp. 218, 223, 225 and 228.)

The SPEAR for war of the thirteenth century offers no change from that of the preceding age. The shaft of it is still uniform from end to end, not yet being hollowed out for the grip, as in the lance of a later date. The head is of three forms: the lozenge, the leaf, and the barbed. The lozenge spear-head is the most usual, and appears in the accompanying group from the Lives of the Two Offas, Cott. MS., Nero, D. i. fol. 7. See also our woodcuts, No. 62 and 75. The leaf-shaped head occurs on fol. 4 of Nero, D. i.; on fol. 27 of Harl. MS. 3,244; and on the Shurland monument (Stothard, Pl. xli.) The barbed spear was probably not considered a knightly weapon, but carried by soldiers of an inferior grade. At all events, we occasionally find men-at-arms furnished with it, as in Roy. MS. 20, D. i., a book of about the close of this century. And earlier in the period, at the battle of Bovines in 1214, we have the curious account of Rigord, shewing the jeopardy in which the life of King Philip was placed through the attack of a soldier armed with a spear of this description. This soldier of the emperor's host struck at the neck of the king, the usual point of attack, and though the gorget of the monarch prevented the weapon from inflicting any wound, the barbs of the spear became so firmly fixed between the hauberk and the head-defence, that the sturdy German was enabled to pull Philippe Auguste from his horse and lay him prone at his feet. The king managed to raise himself again, but the soldier held firm. The

emperor, who was near at hand, rushed forward to terminate the strife by the death of his rival, and all seemed over. Galon de Montigny meanwhile, the Bannerer of the king, proclaimed the danger of his master by incessantly *raising and lowering* the Standard over the spot where this contest was taking place. The French were animated to new exertions: a band of seigneurs and gentlemen cut their way to the spot where the king was struggling in[Pg 303]
[Pg 304]

[Pg 305] unequal conflict with his foes: the spearman, struck down or slain, let go his hold: the fight continued, furiously as ever, but in numbers less disproportionate than before: Etienne de Longchamp, one of the bravest of the French nobles, is slain by the side of the king: Pierre Tristan, another distinguished knight, leaps from his steed, and gives it to his monarch: Guillaume des Barres at this moment comes up with reinforcements, charges the German host with impetuous bravery, and turns their triumph into a rout.

The Lance is occasionally furnished with a streamer, as at a former period. It is seen in our last engraving (No. 80), from the Lives of the Offas; and again in woodcuts, Nos. 55 and 62. Compare also Harl. MS. 3,244, fol. 27, and other groups from the Lives of the Offas. In some of these examples, the lance-flag is ensigned with a cross only; in others it is quite blank: in others, again, as the brass of D'Aubernoun, it bears a device clearly heraldic.

In a few rare instances the spear is represented on the tomb of the knight. The necessity of reducing it far beneath its legitimate proportions, in order to be comprised within the narrow limits of the sepulchral memorial, would furnish a sufficient reason for its being generally excluded from the monumental design: but it is not improbable that mere fashion (for the tomb has its fashions) contributed in some degree to this exclusion; because we find that the royal and knightly seals, which at a previous date constantly exhibited the lance with its streamer, now more usually represent the warrior armed with the sword. The lance is found on the brass of D'Aubernoun (woodcut, No. 55), on the sculptured effigy of a knight in the churchyard of Ruabon, in Wales, and in the incised slab at Ashington, Somersetshire, figured in the Archæological Journal, vol. viii. p. 319.

For the hastilude, the spear-head was blunted, and "about the breadth of a small knife;" as we learn from Matthew Paris, in his account of the Round-Table Game held at the Abbey of Wallenden in 1252. Here, one of the knights, Roger de Lemburn, aimed his weapon, the point of which was not blunted as it ought to have been, in such a way that it entered under the helm of his adversary, Arnold de Montigny, and pierced his throat; for he was uncovered in that part, and without a collar (*carens collario*). The Earl of Gloucester with the other knights immediately sought to extract the fragment of the lance, and when he had succeeded in withdrawing the wooden shaft of it, the iron head remained behind: on this being at length extracted, and examined by the surrounding knights, it was found to be very sharp at the point, like a dagger; though it ought to have been blunt, and about as broad as a small knife. Its shape was like that of a ploughshare on a small scale, whence it was commonly called a little plough (*vomerulus*), and in French, *soket*[363]. We have here the description of two spear-heads very distinct in character: one rebated for the Jousts of Peace, seemingly the prototype of the coronel which afterwards replaced it; and the other a sharp instrument, the form of which we may perhaps recognise among the tilting weapons of the *Triumph of Maximilian*. See, for instance, the group of knights armed for the "Course appelée Bund."

When, in battle, the charge had been made with the Lance, and that weapon was no longer available in the *mêlée*, it was cast aside, and the conquest carried on with the Sword:—

> "Aprés le froisseis des Lances,
>   Qui ja sont par terre semées,
>   Giettent mains à blanchesespées,
>   Desquels ils s'entr'envaissent,
>   Hyaumes e bacinets tentissent
>   E plusieurs autres ferreures.
>   Coutiaux trespercent armeures."—*Guiart.*

SECOND GREAT SEAL OF KING HENRY III.

No. 81.

The knightly SWORD of this day resembled in its essentials that of the preceding century: indeed, it did not materially change during the whole Gothic period. The blade was straight, broad, double-edged, and pointed. The type is well shewn in the second seal of Henry III. (woodcut, No. 81).

The cross-piece was usually curved towards the blade, as represented in several of our engravings. Sometimes this curved guard threw out a kind of cusp in the middle, as in the sculpture at Haseley, (woodcut 46,) and the effigy figured by Stothard, Plate xx. The cross-bar was at other times straight, as in the seal of King John (woodcut, No. 52), and in our other woodcuts numbered 53, 56, and 63. Compare the sword of De Vere (Stothard, Pl. xxxvi.). A variety of the straight guard forms also a cusp over the centre of the blade, as in the example given in our engraving, No. 80. The knightly effigy in Walkerne Church (Hollis, Pt. i.) has a sword-guard in the form of a chevron. Edward I., on his great seal, (woodcut, No. 85,) offers us a further variety, in which the outline somewhat resembles that of the Greek bow.

The pommel of the sword during this century takes many forms: the round, the trefoil, the cinquefoil, the rosette, the lozenge, the conical, the pear-shaped, the square, and the fleur-de-lis. The round is either plain or ornamented on its sides: in the latter case the ornament is usually a cross, or a shield of arms. The plain round pommel is generally wheel-formed; that is, it has a projection in the centre something like the nave of a wheel. See Journal of Archæological Association, vol. i. p. 336. The sacred symbol of the Cross is very frequently found on the circular pommel; as in our woodcuts, No. 55 and 77. The shield of arms appears in our engraving, No. 70. Compare the Fitz-Alan monument (Hollis, Pt. iv.). The trefoil pommel is represented in our cuts, No. 56 and 74; the cinquefoil, on our engraving, No. 64, and in Plate xx. of Stothard's Monuments. The rose form occurs in our woodcut, No. 62; the lozenge on the effigy of King John (Stothard, Pl. xi.); the conical, in our print, No. 63; the pear-shaped, in Stothard's 37th Plate; the square, on Plate xxxv. of the Painted Chamber; and the fleur-de-lis on the seal of Edward I. (woodcut, No. 85).

The sword-handle is sometimes of a highly enriched character. That of King John, on his monument in Worcester Cathedral, represents a weapon in which both pommel and cross-bar were inlaid with precious stones. Ornamental grips are seen in the monument of Crouchback (Stothard, Pl. xliii. fig. 4), and the brass of De Bures, 1302 (Waller, Pt. ii.).

The Sheath also occasionally exhibits enrichments. These are either metal harnessings, of Gothic patterns, similar to the architectural designs of the day, as in our woodcut, No. 70, and the effigy of Brian, lord Fitz-Alan (Hollis, Pt. iv.); or the scabbard is embellished from end to end with a series of shields of arms, as in our engraving, No. 73, and the statue of De Montfort (Stothard, Pl. xxxix.). These escutcheons were probably tinctured by means of enamel.

The characteristic Sword-Belt of this century consisted of two straps, a long and a short one. The long strap was looped to the scabbard about two hands-breadths from the top, passed round the waist, and fastened to the buckle in front, leaving a long end tipped with a metal tag. The short strap held the buckle, and was split into two thongs, one of which was laced into the top of the (leather) scabbard; the other, passing obliquely across the sheath, being laced into the loop of the long strap below. See our woodcuts, Nos. 55 and 73. A variety of this mode consisted in attaching the long and short straps to the scabbard by ring-lockets of metal, in lieu of the loop and lacings. This occurs late in the century. See woodcut, No. 70, and the effigy of Brian Fitz-Alan (Hollis, Pt. iv.). The common sword-belt of the soldiery was formed on the old plan: at one end of a broad strap were two clefts, through which the two thongs into which the other end was split were passed and tied into a knot. See woodcut, No. 63. The figures there given represent the soldiers of Herod engaged in the Massacre of the Innocents. The knightly sword-belt is often highly enriched; being covered with elaborate patterns, worked in the most brilliant colours, and harnessed with bars and bosses of gilt metal, or perhaps of gold itself; the bosses, towards the end of the period, taking not unfrequently the form of lions' heads. The ornament of bars only, appears on a Temple Church effigy, figured by Hollis, Pt. i.; of bars and rosettes, in Stothard's 15th and 45th Plates; of a painted pattern, in Plate xxi. of Stothard's work; of bosses in the form of lions' heads, in Part iv. of Hollis. The sword-belt of Edmund Crouchback is enriched with heraldic bearings. See Stothard, Pl. xliii. detail 1.

Minute variations from the above types of Sword-belt may be found, but do not seem to require a particular description. We must not omit to remark, however, that, in some early monuments of this period, the sword is represented as worn at the right side of the warrior. Three effigies in the Temple Church, London, exhibit this arrangement.

At York, on Christmas-day, 1252, King Henry III. conferred knighthood on the young king of Scotland; who, the day following, espoused the Princess Margaret, daughter of Henry, amidst great rejoicings and a splendid ceremonial. To obtain a detailed description of the Sword used by the king of England on this occasion was scarcely within the hope of the archæologist; but, singularly enough, such an account, of curious minuteness, has come down to us. It is preserved in the Tower, (Close Rolls, 36 H. III. m. 31,) and has been Printed in Walpole's "Painting in England" (vol. i. chap. 1):—

"Mandatum est Edwardo de Westm. quod cum festinatione perquirat quendam pulchrum gladium et scauberg. ejusdem de serico, et pomellum de argento bene et ornate cooperiri, et quandam pulcram zonam eidem pendi faciat, ita quod gladium illum sic factum habeat apud Ebor., de quo Rex Alexandrum Regem Scotiæ illustrem cingulo militari decorare possit in instanti festo Nativitatis Dominicæ. Teste Rege apud Lychfeld xxi. die Novembr. Per ipsum Regem."

Besides the ordinary knightly sword of the thirteenth century, the size of which is authenticated by many existing monuments, we have the evidence of cotemporary writers that swords of differing sizes were employed by different nations. The Germans affected a large brand, the French a shorter weapon. Thus Guiart:—

"A grans espées d'Allemagne
Leur tranchent souvent les poins outre."

"Là Francois espées reportent
Courtes et roides, dont ils taillent."

And again, under 1301:—

"Epées viennent aux services
Et sont de diverses semblances,
Més Francois, qui d'accoutumance
Les ont courtes, assez legieres,
Gietent aux Flamans vers les chieres."

In the description of the Battle of Benevento, in 1266, Hugues de Bauçoi, an eye-witness of the conflict, tells us that the troops of Manfred, Germans and Saracens, fought with long swords, axes and maces; but the French, coming to close quarters, pierced them with their short swords: "ex brevibus spathis suis eorum latera perfodiebant[364]." Guillaume de Nangis gives similar testimony[365]. How far these German weapons approached the great two-hand swords of later times, or the French reverted to the short blade of the Romans, it is vain to inquire. Commentators have seen in the above descriptions both the types here named; but the evidence of pictorial monuments does not confirm the conclusion. As large and small are but comparative terms, it is probable that the swords of the French and Germans differed in no great degree.

Other varieties of Sword which appear in the thirteenth century are the Falchion, the curved Sabre, the Espée à l'estoc, the Cultellus, and the Anelace.

The Falchion (*fauchon*, Fr., from the Latin *falx*) is of two kinds: the first a broad blade, becoming wider towards the point, the edge convex, the back concave; as in this example from the Painted Chamber:

the other differing from it only in having the back quite straight. The latter is figured on Plate xxxi. of the Painted Chamber; and of this form is the curious tenure sword of the lordship of Sockburn, co. Durham, engraved in the Archæologia, vol. xv. Plate xxvi. See, in Blount's "Antient Tenures," an account of this weapon; of the "monstrous Dragon, Worm, or flying Serpent, that devoured Men, Women, and Children," which fell at last under its keen edge; and of the "tomb of the great Ancestor of the Conyers, having carvings of the falchion, and of a dog, and of the monstrous Worm or Serpent, lying at the Knight's feet, of his own killing, of which the History of the Family gives the above account." The passage is too long for extract[366].

The falchion is a weapon of very remote antiquity. It appears among the paintings on the tomb at Thebes of Rameses III., B.C. 1230. See Plate III. of Wilkinson's "Ancient Egyptians" (ed. 1837). And it is found, almost identical in shape, in the wall-paintings of the Ajunta Caves, of the first century of the Christian era; of which a careful copy has been made for the Museum of the East India House. Guiart often mentions it in the *Chronique Métrique*, as in this passage:—

"Là ou les presses sont plus drues
Est le chaple[367] aux espees nues,
Aux fauchons, aux coutiaus à pointes,
Si merveilleus que les plus cointes
N'ont ores soing de vanteries."

The curved Sabre is of very rare appearance. It occurs among the pictures of the Painted Chamber, Plate xxxv.

The Epée à l'estoc (Stabbing Sword) is named in a judgment of the Parliament of Paris in 1268: "Sufficienter inventum est quod dictus Boso dictum Ademarum percussit cum Ense a estoc in dextro latero propria manu, et de ipso ictu cecidit dictus Ademarus." It appears also to be the weapon which Rigord assigns to some of the imperial troops at the battle of Bovines: "Habebant cultellos longos, graciles, triacumines, quolibet acumine indifferenter secantes, a cuspide usque ad manubrium, quibus utebantur pro gladiis."

The Cultellus, as we have seen[368], was a weapon partaking of the character of the sword and the dagger. It clearly varied in size; for Odo de Rossilion, in 1298, names in his will "meum magnum cultellum et meam parvam ensem." Being the chief arm of the coustillers, it must have been of some considerable size: and of this larger kind must also have been the weapon assigned, in the "Outillement du villain," to the peasant, for the defence of his home:—

"Si le convient armer
Por la terre garder,
Coterel e hauvet,
Macue e guibet,
Arc e lance enfumée," &c.

In other places, it appears as a mere secondary arm, a knife or dagger; as in the Statutes of Arms already cited, where the various classes of proprietors are directed to have "espe, cutel e cheval," or "espe e cutel," or "espes, arcs, setes e cutel."

The particular construction of the Anelace, as well as the derivation of its name, has hitherto eluded the most careful examination of antiquaries and glossarists. Some have referred the name to the Latin or Italian, *annulus*, or *annello*. Others to the Old-German, *Laz*, from *latus*; the weapon being therefore a "side-arm." Matthew Paris often uses the word, and tells us that the arm was worn at the girdle: "Loricâ erat indutus, gestans anelacium ad lumbare." Without hoping to settle this question, we may venture to point out that a weapon of the dagger kind, carried at the belt, and having a chain with *a ring running loosely upon the grip*, to prevent its being lost in the *mêlée*, was certainly in use during the middle-ages; an example of which may be seen in the effigy of William Wenemaer, at Ghent, dated 1325; engraved in the Archæological Journal, vol. vii. p. 287. We may note also that the wheel-like form of the *guard* may have supplied the name; for Florio, in the sixteenth century, defines "Annelle" to be "thin plates of iron made like rings, called of our gunners washers," &c. Guiart also mentions the anelace: under the year 1298, he has:—

> "Aucuns d'entr'eus testes desnuent
> De hyaumes e de cervelieres,
> E plantent alenaz es chieres
> En pluseurs lieus jusques es manches."

In the manufacture of Swords at this period, Cologne seems to have had the palm. The volume of Proverbs already noticed gives the highest place to the "Espees de Cologne." And Matthew Paris, under 1241[369], relating how certain wicked German Jews, wishing to assist the Tartars, sent them certain barrels, (filled, as they told the Christians, with poisoned wine,) adds that, on the toll-man suspiciously scrutinizing the contents, "all the casks were found to be filled with Cologne swords and daggers, without hilts, closely and compactly stowed away. The Jews were, therefore, at once handed over to the executioners, to be either consigned to perpetual imprisonment, or to be slain with their own swords."

The Exercise of the Sword and Buckler (*Eskirmye de Bokyler*) was in vogue in this century, and schools were established for teaching it. But disorders arising from the practice, the schools were ordered to be closed. Thus the "Statuta Civitatis London" of the 13 Edw. I. has: "Primerement pur ceo qe multz des mals com des murdres robberyes e homycides ont este fetz ca en arrere deinz la Citee de nuyt e de jour, e gentz batues e mal tretes e autres diverses aventures de mal avenuz encontre sa pes (du roi), defendu est qe nul seit si hardi estre trove alaunt ne batraunt parmy les ruwes de la Citee apres coeverfu parsone a seint Martyn le grant, a espey ne a bokuyler ne a autre arme pur mal fere ne dount mal suspecion poet vienir, &c....

"Ensement pur ceo qe fous qe sei delitent a mal fere vount aprendre eskirmye de bokyler e de ceo plus sei abaudissent de fere lour folyes, purveu est e defendu qe nul ne tiegne eskole ne aprise de eskirmye de bokyler de deinz la Citee de nuyt ne de jour, e si nul le faceo, eit la prison de xl. jours."

Representations of the Sword-and-buckler contest occur in Roy. MSS. 14, E. iii. and 20, D. vi., both engraved in Strutt's Sports. See also Hefner, Pt. ii. Plate VII. All these, however, are miniatures of the fourteenth century; though

14, E. iii. is early in the period. From these examples we learn that the buckler was about a foot and a half in diameter, had a boss in the centre, and was held at arm's length by a bar crossing the hollow of the umbo, exactly in the manner of the Anglo-Saxon shields described and figured in a former page. (See woodcut, No. 20.)

No. 83.

Occasionally the figure of a Sword was carved on the tomb of the knight, to indicate his calling, as in this incised slab from Brougham Church, Westmoreland, commemorating one of the Brougham family. The example is further curious from its including also the round shield of the period; differing, as we see, from the buckler named above, in having no boss. The sword is usually, on tombs of this kind, accompanied by a Cross: sometimes it forms itself the cross on the monument, as in the Gorforth memorial, engraved on page 84 of Mr. Boutell's work on Incised Slabs. At Aycliffe, Durham, is a tomb on which appears a cross, having on one side a sword, on the other a hammer and pincers. This group of emblems has been thought to indicate a weapon-smith. The monument is figured in the Archæological

Journal, vol. v. p. 257. Not the sword only, but the spear, the axe, the dagger, and other weapons, are found on the incised slabs of the thirteenth and fourteenth centuries; many examples of which may be seen in the works on these memorials by the Rev. Mr. Cutts and the Rev. Mr. Boutell.

The Dagger by no means filled that prominent place in the knightly equipment during this century which it is found to occupy in the fourteenth; though, towards the close of the period, it is seen to be coming into vogue. It is worn by the knights represented in our engravings, Nos. 58 and 72; and the Ash Church effigy (woodcut, No. 59) shews us the lace by which the dagger, now destroyed, was fastened to the waist-belt. The figure of De Montford (Stothard, Pl. xxxix.) has the dagger. It appears also in the Shurland monument (Stothard, Pl. xli.), worn by the knight's attendant; and in this example the guard of it is formed of two knobs, a fashion occasionally found up to the sixteenth century. In Durham Cathedral is preserved a real dagger, which is believed to have belonged to one of the retainers of Bishop Anthony in 1283. It is entirely of iron, and the blade, which is sixteen inches in length, is inscribed "ANTON: EPS: DUNOLM.[370]"

Under the name of *Misericordia*, the dagger has an early mention in the Charter of Arras, in 1221: "Quicumque cultellum cum cuspide, vel curtam sphatulam, vel misericordiam, vel aliqua arma multritoria portaverit," &c. Under 1302, Guiart speaks of it by the same name:—

> "Plusieurs piétons François ala,
> Qui pour prisonniers n'ont pas cordes,
> Mais coutiaux et misericordes,
> Dont on doit servir en tiex festes."

And under 1303:—

> "Fauchons trenchans, espées cleres,
> Godendas, lances émoulues,
> Coutiaux, misericordes nues."

This name of misericorde appears to have been given because, in the last struggle of contending foes, the uplifted dagger compelled the discomfited fighter to cry for mercy. In this view, the murderous misericorde was by the middle-age poets assigned to "Pity," as an emblem of her benevolence. Thus Jean de Méun in the Romance of the Rose:—

> "Pitiez, qui à tous bien s'accorde,
> Tenoit une Misericorde
> Decourant de plors e de lermes."

The Short Axe is very rarely given to the knightly combatant by the artists of the thirteenth century. It appears to have been resigned to the less dignified order of soldiery. The form of the head exhibits three principal varieties: the single blade, of which we have a good example in Harl. MS. 4,751, fol. 8 (woodcut, No. 50); the double weapon, in which one side has a vertical axe-blade and the other a pick (see Strutt's Dress and Habits, Pl. LXV.); and the double weapon, in which one side has a horizontal blade and the other a pick (see Stothard's Monuments, Pl. XIX.). Guiart, under 1264, mentions the axe mingling in the strife of battle with the mace and the sword:—

> "Le chaple commence aus espees,
>   Dont là a de maintes manieres.
>   Sus hyaumes e sus cervelieres
>   Prennent plommees à descendre,
>   E hachetes, pour tout porfendre."

And when, in the same year 1264, the Earl of Leicester assembled his army on Barham Downs, in addition to the ordinary military levy, every township was required to send eight, six, or four footmen well armed with spears, bows and arrows, swords, cross-bows, and hatchets. (New Rymer, 444.)

From the collection of thirteenth-century Proverbs, which has already supplied us with several curious particulars of this early time, we learn that the "Haches de Dannemark" held the first place among the axes of the period: but whether this distinction is accorded for the form or the manufacture of the weapon, is not clear. Matthew Paris speaks of it under 1256: "Cum jaculis ——Danisque securibus et gesis[371]——hostiliter insequuntur."

The "Danish Axe" is mentioned in several military tenures of this century; but a more remote antiquity is usually assigned to the origin of the grant itself. The weapon (more or less original) was always exhibited with great pride in the family mansion. Dugdale tells us that Plumpton in Warwickshire "was possest in *Henry* 3. time by one *Walter de Plompton*, who held these lands by a certain weapon called a *Danish Axe*: which, being the very Charter whereby the said land was given unto one of his Ancestors, hung up for a long time in the Hall of the capitall messuage belonging thereto, in testimony of the said tenure; untill that the said House was seized upon by Sir *John Bracebrigge*, Knight, Lord of KINGSBURIE in *Edward* 3. time, and pulled to the ground: After which it remained a great while in the Hall of the mansion belonging to *William de Plompton*, in HARDRESHULL (about two miles distant), being commonly reputed and called *the Charter of* PLOMTON[372]."

And in the 12th Edw. I.: "Robertus Hurding tenet unam acram terrae et unum furnum in villa Castri de Lanceveton (Launceston, co. Cornwall) nomine serjantiae essendi in Castro de Lanceveton cum uno Capello ferreo et una

Hachet Denesh per XL. dies tempore guerrae ad custum suum proprium, et post XL. dies, si Dominus Castri velit ipsum tenere in eodem Castro, erit ad custus ipsius domini[373]."

The Mace is both named and pictured in evidences of this century. Matthew Paris, describing the disasters of a tournament near Hertford in 1241, adds: "Many other knights and men-at-arms were also wounded and seriously injured with maces (*clavis*) at this same tournament, because the jealousy of many of those concerned had converted the sport into a battle[374]." This and similar mishaps led to the mace, with other weapons, being interdicted at these pastimes; for in a "Statutum Armorum ad Torniamenta" of this century, it is ordered by the king "qe nul Chivaler ne Esquier qe sert al Turney ne porte espeie a point, ne cotel a point, ne bastoun, ne mace, fors espee large pur turneer[375]." Pictured examples of the mace occur in Roy. MS. 20, D. i., ff. 12 and 69; and on Plate XXXIII. of the Painted Chamber. The striking part is formed in the manner of a cogged wheel: the top sometimes terminates in a knob; sometimes it is prolonged into a pike.

The Bâton named in the above Statute was probably no more than a stout cudgel. The form of the tournament bâton of a later time is given in full detail in the "Tournois du roi René."

The long-handled weapons of the infantry named in this century are the Guisarme, the Godendac, the Croc, the Faus, the Faussar, and the Pilete.

The Guisarme, or Pole-axe, has already been described, (ante, p. 50). It is named by Matthew Paris: "Gestabant autem gladios, bipennes, *gaesa*, sicas et anelacios." It occurs also in the Statute of Winchester: "E que ad meyns des chateus de XL. soudes, seyt juree as faus, gysarmes, coteaux e autres menus armes." The Pole-axe with a single vertical blade is seen in a miniature of the thirteenth century, inserted into the Gospels of Mac Durnan in the Lambeth Library (figured in Westwood's Palæographia); and it appears again in the Lives of the Offas, Cott. MS., Nero, D. i.

The Godendac was the name given by the Flemings to the Halbard. Guiart, describing the battle of Courtrai, in 1302, has this very curious passage:—

"A grans batons pesans ferrés
Avec leur fer agu devant
Vont ceux de France recevant
Tiex baton qu'il portent en guerre
Ont nom Godendac en la terre.
Goden-dac, c'est *Bon jour* à dire,
Qui en Francois le veut décrire.
Cil baton sont long e traitis,

Pour férir a deux mains faitis."

Should the axe-stroke fail, then the skilful halbardier repairs his mishap with a prompt thrust of the piked head:—

"Et quand l'on en faut au descendre,
Si cil qui fiert y veut entendre,
Et il en scache bien ouvrer,
Tantot peut son cop recovrer,
Et férir sans s'aller moquant,
Du bout devant en estoquant
Son ennemi."

The halbard, consisting of an axe-blade balanced by a pick, and having a pike-head at the end of the staff, is figured on Plate XXXI. of the Painted Chamber.

The Faus (*falso*: from *falx*) appears to have been a kind of spear with a broad, cut-and-thrust blade. It is made synonymous with the spear in this passage of the Synodus Nemausensis, in 1284: (de Clericis) "Enses non deferant, nec cultellos acutos, nec lanceas *seu falsones*," &c. But in the Statuta Eccles. Cadurcensis, in 1289, it is distinguished from the spear: "balistas et arcus, lanceas, falsones, costalarios seu alia arma non deferant." In the Statute of Winchester, as we have seen, (ante, p. 211,) it was placed at the head of the humbler class of weapons prescribed to the militia of small means.

The Faussar, a kindred word, was probably a kindred weapon. Like the falso, it most likely presented some variety in the exemplars turned out from the village weaponers' smithies. One kind was three-edged, and had a second name, the Trialemellum. At Bovines, "Ante oculos ipsius regis occiditur Stephanus de Longo Campo, in capite percussus longo, gracili Trialemello[376], quem Falsarium nominant[377]." The faussar appears to have been sometimes used as a missile: thus, in the Chron. de Duguesclin (of the fourteenth century) we are told that the combatants

"Gettent dars et faussars, moult en vont ociant."

The Croc was probably the Bill. It is named by Guiart among the weapons of the Ribauds in 1214:—

"Li uns une pilete porte,
L'autre croc ou macue torte."

The fashion of the Bill of this time, a broad, cutting blade, forming a beak near the top and terminating in a pike, may be seen in Plate XXXI. of the Painted Chamber.

The Pilete (dimin. of *Pilum*) named in the above passage of Guiart, was a pike, the exact form of which, like that of so many of the weapons of this period, has not been ascertained. The "macue torte" is a knotted club.

The missile weapons of this day were the javelin, the long-bow, the cross-bow, the cord-sling and the staff-sling.

The Javelin is mentioned by Matthew Paris: "cum jaculis Danisque securibus et gesis[378]."

The Long-bow has already been noticed in our examination of the troops of this century. Its form is seen in our woodcuts, Nos. 47, 48, 49 and 50. The fashion of the Quiver appears in the engraving from Roy. MS. 20, D. i. (No. 47). The feathering of the arrows is shewn in the same print; the shaft and head in woodcut, No. 82, from the Painted Chamber. Besides the ordinary arrows, shafts armed with phials of quick-lime were occasionally discharged from the long-bow. Strutt, in his *Horda*[379], has furnished an example of this missile, from a MS. of Matthew Paris in Benet College, Cambridge (copied in our woodcut, No. 51); and in the Additamenta to the printed History of Matthew Paris, page 1091, is given the letter of Sir Guy, a knight of the household of the Viscount of Melun, in which, recounting the capture of Damietta, he says: "We discharged fiery darts (*spicula ignita*) and stones from our sea mangonels, and we threw small bottles full of lime (*phialas plenas calce*), made to be shot from a bow, or small sticks like arrows against the enemy. Our darts, therefore, pierced the bodies of their pirates, while the stones crushed them, and the lime, flying out of the broken bottles, blinded them."

The Cross-bow, as we have seen, (ante, p. 201,) was in general use throughout this century. It is figured in our woodcuts, Nos. 49 and 50. In both these examples there is a provision for holding down the bow with the foot, while the cord was drawn up to the notch. The bow might thus be bent by the hand: but there appears also to have been, at this early date, some apparatus similar to the moulinet of later days, by which a stouter bow might be easily bent by mechanical appliance. Such a bow was called an "arbaleste à tour," and the instrument by which it was wound up was named "la clef." No delineation of this little engine has yet been noticed among the monuments of the time. Guiart has:—

> "Messire Alphonse un jour ataignent,
> Qui armez iert[380] de son atour,
> D'un quarrel d'arbaleste a tour."

And again:—

"En haste vont les clefs serrant des arbalestes."

2^e. Partie, vers
8,625.

Several further varieties of the Cross-bow are named about this time:— Balistæ corneæ; ad stapham[381]; ad viceas[382]; de torno vel de lena[383]; ad unum pedem; ligneæ ad duos pedes; de cornu ad duos pedes; a pectoribus; a pesarola[384]; and among the rest, a *Double Cross-bow*, discharging two quarrels: "Balista sine nuce, quæ duos projicit quarrellos." See Ducange and Adelung, v. *Balista*.

The Quarrel (*carreau*), as its name indicates, was an arrow with a four-sided or pyramidal head. This distinctive form of the arbalest shaft is carefully kept in view in the illumination from Add. MS. 15,268 (our No. 49); where, while the archer plies his barbed arrow, the cross-bowman discharges his angular quarrel. The feathering of the quarrel is seen very clearly in woodcut, No. 50; where the markings shew that *feathers* are really intended, and not slices of wood, leather, or metal. These last-named materials being found in later monuments, it seems not unlikely that they may have been used thus early; and we have the distinct evidence of cotemporary writers that the *larger* quarrels discharged from the engines called espringales were "empennés d'airain[385]."

The Slings of this period have already been noticed (page 204): the cord-sling is figured in our woodcut, No. 50, the staff-sling in No. 51.

The Military Flail appears in the following woodcut from Strutt's *Horda* vol. i., Plate xxxii. The original miniature is in the MS. of Matthew Paris, at Benet College, Cambridge, which has already furnished us with examples of the Staff-sling and other weapons of this time. The flail-man in our engraving is engaged in the assault of a castle: other assailants in the same vessel are armed with bows and slings. Adelung cites the following passage, in which the flail is mentioned under the name of *flaellum*: "Cum ducentis hominibus in armis, electis et gleatis, et cum flaellis[386]."

No. 84.

The Greek Fire, still rejected among the nations of Western Europe, for the reasons assigned in a former page, was in frequent use among the Saracens. In 1250, the Christians, advancing towards Damietta by water, were intercepted by their enemies. "The Saracens in their vessels met the Christians sailing down the river, where a most fatal naval conflict ensued, the missiles of the combatants flying like hail. At length, after an obstinate battle, rendered more dreadful by the Greek fire hurled on them by the Saracens, the Christians, being worn out by grief and hunger, suffered a defeat[387]." The letter "to his respected lord, Richard, earl of Cornwall," from "John, his Chancellor," gives a similar account of this terrible fight; from which one only of the Christians escaped, "Alexander Giffard, an Englishman of noble blood." "The Saracens, by throwing Greek fire on the Christians, burnt many of their boats and killed the people in them, thus obtaining the victory. The Christians were drowned, slain, and burnt[388]." The authors of the treatise, *Du feu grégeois*, Captain Favé and M. Reinaud, remark that during the fifty-seven years of the reign of French princes at Constantinople (taken in 1204), the secret of the Greek fire could not have remained concealed from men who had made some advances in the science of chymistry. "Mais alors les préjugés de l'ignorance se joignaient aux idées religieuses et aux sentimens chevaleresques, pour repousser l'emploi d'un art qui semblait rendre inutiles la force et le courage individuels[389]."

In the East, however, the employment of incendiary weapons was constant, and the variety of them very great. An Arabic treatise of this century, published in the work named above by MM. Reinaud and Favé, gives us the most curious information relating to them, and the interest of the manuscript is heightened by its containing drawings (somewhat rude, it is true) of the principal instruments and engines described. From this "Treatise on the Art of Fighting," by Hassan Alrammah, we learn that the Arabs of the thirteenth century employed their incendiary compositions in four different ways: they cast them by hand; they fixed them to staves, with which they attacked their enemies; they poured forth the fire through tubes; and they projected burning mixtures of various kinds by means of arrows, javelins, and the missiles of the great engines resembling the trebuchets and mangonæ of their Western neighbours. Among these fire-weapons we have—"Balles de verre; Pots à feu; La Maison de feu; Massue de guerre; Massue pour asperger; Lance de guerre; Lance à fleurs; Lance avec massue; La lance avec la flèche du Khatay; Flèches en roseau; Flèches du mangonneau; Flèches de la Chine; Marmite de l'Irac; Marmite de Mokharram; Vase de Helyledjeh; Cruche de Syrie (the last four for the mangonel); L'œuf qui se meut et qui brûle (Captain Favé takes this to be a projectile on the principle of our rockets); Dard du Khatay; Des Coupes; Des Volants; Des Lunes," &c.

The vessels of glass and pottery, discharged by hand or by machines, were so contrived that on striking the object at which they were aimed, their contents spread around, and the fire, already communicated by a fusee, enveloped everything within its reach. A soldier on whose head was broken a fire-mace, became suddenly soaked with a diabolical fluid, which covered him from head to foot with flame; and a flame of so terrible a nature that it was believed to be absolutely inextinguishable. The receipt for making the Massue de Guerre is given with great particularity: "Tu feras faire par le verrier une massue, &c. Ensuite tu feras les mélanges usités, &c. Tu mettras le feu à la massue et tu la briseras pour le service de Dieu[390]." One of the lances is furnished with a firework "so that the spear shall burn the enemy, after having wounded him with its point." Another lance "brulera bien et s' étendra à plus de mille coudées." It will be remembered that the Arabic superlative is commonly expressed by "a thousand." What we learn, therefore, is that this fire-missile was contrived to wound at a distance. In applying the Massue à asperger, you are to break it against the person of your antagonist, "but keep out of the current of the wind, lest the sparks return upon and burn you." The machines for casting forth the fire-pots and vases of larger dimension bear so close a resemblance to the trebuchets and mangonas in use by the Christian nations, that Captain Favé is inclined to think that the latter warriors copied their engines from those of the Arabs during the Crusades (p. 49).

On the second plate of the treatise are given examples of two of the Arabian mangonels. One is formed of a sling and weighted lever, like the instruments represented in Roy. MS. 16, G. vi., engraved in Shaw's "Dresses and Decorations," and on the ivory casket figured in the fourth volume of the Journal of the Archæological Association. The other differs only in having, in lieu of a weight, a number of cords hanging from the end of the lever; from which it would appear that the lever was in this case moved by men acting together by means of the cords. Captain Favé remarks that the expressions, La flèche de la Chine, La fleur de la Chine, in shewing us that the Chinese practised the fabrication of incendiary agents and contributed these names to the Arabs at so early a period, may permit us to suppose that this mode of warfare received its chief development from them, and even that to them may be ascribed its invention (p. 44).

The various STANDARDS and FLAGS found in the last period are continued throughout the present. But the advancement of the science of heraldry gave to the devices of this age a permanence which has in many cases subsisted to the present day. The Dragon Standard was still in use in England. At the battle of Lewes, in 1264, between the king and his barons, "the king, being informed of the approach of his enemies, soon set himself in motion with his army, and went forward to meet them with unfurled banners, preceded by the royal ensign, which was called the Dragon[391]." In the same battle, on the barons' side, we find the ancient Carrocium. When the revolted nobles, with De Montford at their head, "had reached a place scarcely two miles distant from the town of Lewes, Simon with his friends *ascended an eminence* and placed his Car thereon, in the midst of the baggage and sumpter horses. There he displayed his Standard, fastening it securely to the car, and surrounded it with a great number of his soldiers[392]." The Milanese still held their Carrocio in the utmost veneration. When the Emperor Frederic, in 1236, crossed the Alps to attack them, "the citizens sallied forth from the city in great strength, to the number of about fifty thousand armed men, and proceeded with their Standard, which they call Carruca, or Carrochium, to meet the emperor, sending word that they were ready to fight him[393]." In 1237 the Milanese again placed their defiant Carrocium in front of the imperial host. They went forth with an army of about sixty thousand men, and fixed their Carrocium where their ranks seemed to be strongest. At sight of this, the emperor summoned his counsellors, and, animating them by warlike words, said: "Behold how these insolent Milanese, our enemies, dare to appear against us, and presume to provoke me, their lord, to battle; enemies as they are to the truth and to Holy Church, and borne down by the weight of their sins. Cross the river, unfurl my Banner, my victorious Eagle! and you, my knights, draw your formidable swords, which you have so often steeped in the blood of your enemies, and inflict your vengeance on these mice, which have dared to creep out of their holes, to cope with the glittering spears of the Roman Emperor[394]." From the letter of the emperor himself, addressed to "Richard, earl of Cornwall, his beloved brother-in-law," we learn that the Standard-Car was drawn by horses: "quod apud Crucem-Novam (*Nuova Croce*) in equorum celeritate præmiserant." And further on he writes: "We now directed our attention to the attack and capture of this standard, and we saw that some of our troops, having forced their way over the top of the trenches, had penetrated almost to the mast of the Carrocium. Night, however, coming on, we desisted from the attack till the following morning; lying down to rest with our swords drawn, and without taking off our iron hauberks. When day broke, however, we found the Carrocium deserted, left amidst a crowd of vile wagons, entirely undefended and abandoned, and from the top of the staff where the Cross had been, the Cross was now severed: but, being found too heavy for the fugitives to carry off in safety, they had left it half-way[395]."

The Car with its Dragon and Eagle, forming the standard of the Emperor Otho at Bovines, has already been noticed, (page 164). The Oriflamme of the French monarchs maintains its illustrious position. Captured by the Mahometans, with Saint Louis and his equipage, it still miraculously subsists; and when destroyed by the Flemings at the battle of Mons-en-Puelle, it is discovered that the banner which has been torn to pieces is, after all, only a counterfeit oriflamme, the real one being still intact under the guardianship of the Abbot of St. Denis. Thus Guillaume Guiart:—

"Aussi li Sire de Chevreuse
Porta l'Oriflamme vermeille,
Par droite semblance *pareille*
A *cele* s'élevoit esgarde
Que l'Abbé de Saint Denis garde.

Et l'Oriflamme *contrefaite*
Chaï à terre, et la saisirent
Flamans, qui après s'enfuirent."

Chron. Mét., ann. 1304.

The "Royal Standard" of the French monarchs is described as of blue, adorned with fleurs-de-lis of gold. That of Philip Augustus at Bovines is thus noticed by Guiart:—

"Galon de Montigni porta,
Ou la Chronique faux m'enseigne,
De fin azur luisant Enseigne
A fleurs de lys d'or aornée,
Près du roi fut cette journée
A l'endroit du riche Estendart."

An ordinance of Philip IV. in 1306, quoted by Père Daniel (Mil. Fran. j. 520), under the heading, "L'ordonnance du Roy quant il va en Armez," directs: That the chief Ecuyer Tranchant shall have charge of the Royal Standard: that the chief Chamberlain shall carry the Banner of the king: and that the chief Varlet Tranchant shall follow close behind the king, bearing his Pennon; and his duty is to accompany the king wherever he may go, in order that all may know where the monarch is stationed.

The knightly Banner of this time may be seen in Roy. MS. 20, D. i.; in the Lives of the Offas (Cott. MS., Nero, D. i.); and in many of the plates of the Painted Chamber. In all these examples it is quadrangular, but *not square*: its height is double its breadth. The effigy at Minster, Isle of Sheppey, (Stothard, Pl. xli.) gives us in sculpture a large specimen of the banner, and shews very distinctly how it was fastened to the staff by tasselled cords.

The office of Bannerer of the City of London was filled in the thirteenth century by the family of Fitz Walter, who held the castlery of Baynard's Castle in fee for the performance of this duty. The services and privileges attached to the office are laid down in a curious document printed in Blount's "Antient Tenures," from a MS. preserved by Dugdale. They are recorded under two heads: the rights in time of war, and the rights in time of peace. We give the first in full: a mere note will suffice for the other, which are privileges rather of a civil than a military character:—

"These are the rights which Robert Fitz Wauter, Castellan of London, Lord of Wodeham, has in the city of London: That is to say, the said Robert and his heirs ought to be, and are, Chief Bannerers of London, by fee, for the said Castlery, that *his ancestors* and he have of Castle Baynard in the said City. In time of War the said Robert and his heirs are to serve the city in manner following. The said Robert is to come on his barded horse (*sus son Destrier covert*), he the twentieth man-at-arms, all with horses housed with cloth or iron (*coverts de teyle ou de fer*), as far as the great gate of the minster of St. Paul, with the Banner *of his arms* displayed before him. And when he is come to the great gate of the aforesaid minster, mounted and equipped as aforesaid, then ought the Mayor of London, with his Sheriffs and Aldermen (*ove touz ses Viscountz et ses Audermans*), armed in their arms, to come out of the minster of St. Paul as far as the said gate, with his Banner in his hand; all being on foot. And the Banner shall be red, having an image of St. Paul in gold, the feet, hands and head of silver, with a silver Sword in the hand of the said image. And as soon as the said Robert shall see the Mayor and his Sheriffs and his Aldermen come on foot out of the said minster, bearing this Banner, then the said Robert, or his Heirs, who owe this service to the said City, shall dismount from his horse, and shall salute the Mayor as his companion and peer, and shall say to him: 'Sir Mayor, I am come hither to fulfil the service which I owe to the city.' Then the Mayor, Sheriffs, and Aldermen shall say: 'We deliver to you, as the Bannerer by fee of this City, this Banner, to bear and govern to the honour and profit of our City, to the best of your power.' Then the said Robert or his Heirs shall receive the Banner. Then the Mayor of the said City and his Sheriffs shall follow him to the gate, and shall deliver to the said Robert a horse of the value of twenty pounds[396]. And the horse shall have a saddle of the arms of the said Robert[397], and shall have a housing of Cendal silk of the same arms; and they shall take twenty pounds sterling, and shall deliver them to the Chamberlain of the said Robert, for his expenses this day. And the said Robert shall mount the horse which the said Mayor has given to him, holding the Banner in his hand. And as soon as he is mounted, he shall require the Mayor to cause to be elected a Marshal out of the troops of the City. And as soon as the Marshal is elected, the said Robert shall direct the Mayor and Citizens to have the Tocsin of the said city rung (*que facent soner le Sein communal de la dicte Citee*); and all the commonalty shall go with the Banner of St. Paul, which the said Robert shall carry, as far as Aldgate. Beyond that, the Banner shall be borne by one approved of the said Robert and the Mayor. If so be (*si issint soit*) they have to go forth out of the city, then ought the said Robert to elect two of the most discreet persons from each ward of the city, to provide for the safe keeping of the city during their absence. And this council shall be held at the Priory of the Trinity by Aldgate. And for every town or castle that the host of London shall besiege, the said Robert shall receive from the commonalty of London a hundred shillings for his pains, and no more, though the siege should last for a year. These are the rights that the said Robert shall have in London in time of War."

The rights of the Chief Bannerer in time of peace were the possession of one of those jurisdictions called a Soke, the power of imprisoning and punishing certain offenders within his district, the privilege of taking part in every "Great Council" held by the Mayor, and some others of a similar kind. And if the culprit within his jurisdiction has deserved death for treason, "then shall he be tied to the post which is in the Thames at the Wood Wharf, where boats are fastened, there to remain for two floods and two ebbs of the tide. And if he be condemned *pur commun larcin*, then is he to be taken to the Elms[398], and there undergo his punishment like other common thieves."

Not less in honour than was the gold-and-silver Banner of Saint Paul in the south, was the Banner of Saint John of Beverley in the north of England. It accompanied the heroic Edward the First in his wars in Scotland; and, besides the military bannerer, appears to have had a clerical custodian: as we learn from this curious document preserved in the Tower:—

"Rex dilecto et fideli suo, Johanni de Warenna, Comiti Surr', custodi suo regni et terræ Scotiæ, salutem.

"Cum nos, ob reverentiam Sancti Johannis de Beverlaco, gloriosi confessoris Christi, concesserimus dilecto clerico nostro Gileberto de Grymesby, qui Vexillum ejusdem Sancti ad nos usque partes Scotiæ, detulit, et ibidem de præcepto nostro cum Vexillo illo, durante guerra nostra Scotiæ, moram fecit, quandam ecclesiam, viginti marcarum vel librarum valorem annuum attingentem, ad nostram donationem spectantem, et in regno Scotiæ proximo vacaturam.

"Vobis mandamus quod præfato Gileberto, de hujusmodi ecclesia, in prædicto regno Scotiæ, provideri faciatis, quamprimum ad id optulerit se facultas.

"Teste Rege, apud Kyrkham xiij. die Octobris." (1296[399].)

The triangular Pennon occurs in many of the groups of the Painted Chamber.

It is not always heraldically charged; but this may have arisen from the partial decay of the colours.

The Lance-flag, of one, of two, or of three points, may be seen in our woodcuts, Nos. 55, 62 and 80.

The Horns and Trumpets used in battle are not frequently represented in the pictures of the time; but good examples occur in Roy. MS. 20, D. i., and on Plate xxxvi. of the Painted Chamber. The trumpets are of two kinds, straight and slightly curved; and are figured as of four or five feet long. The straight trumpet appears on folio 222vo. of Roy. MS. 20, D. i.; and is borne as a heraldic charge on the shield of Sir Roger de Trumpington (woodcut, No. 73). The long, curved trumpet occurs on folio 21vo. of Roy. MS. 20, D. i. Both kinds are pictured in Plate xxxvi. of the Painted Chamber. The smaller semicircular Horn is drawn on folio 70 of 20, D. i.

GREAT SEAL OF KING EDWARD THE FIRST.

From the collection of medieval "Proverbes" already cited, we learn that Spain was still the favourite mart for the knightly CHARGER. Denmark and Brittany had also a celebrity for their breeds of horses of a different character. The fiat of popular approval is given to the

"Dextriers de Castille.
Palefrois Danois.
Roussins de Bretagne."

Such was the noble nature of the high-bred dextrarius that, when two knights had been dismounted and were continuing the fight on foot, their horses, left to themselves, instantly commenced a conflict of their own of the most gallant and desperate character. A representation of a double battle of this kind is given on folio 42 of Roy. MS. 12, F. xiii., a treatise *"De natura Pecudum, Volucrum,"* &c. The form of the Saddle of this time, with its high pommel and cantle, may be seen in the Royal seals engraved on Plates 52, 79, 81 and 85; and again in the figure numbered 58. It was sometimes heraldically decorated. In the purchases for the Windsor Tournament[400], in 1278, we have:—

"D Feliŝ Le Seler. viij. sell' de arm̄ Angł. p'c̃. Lxiiij. łi. Pⁱis.

"D Eodem. iiij. selle brond' de filo auri et argent̄ tract̄ videlicet una de arm̄ Rob'ti Tibetot una de arm̄ Joħis de Neele. j. de arm̄ Imb'ti Gिbet una de arm̄ Comitis Cornub' p'c̃ ˣˣ/ᵢᵢᵢⱼ. viij. łi.

"D Eodem. j. sella brond' eodem modo de arm̄ Joħis de Grely. c̃ scalŏp argent' p'c̃. xxxviij. łi." &c.

On the seal of Alexander II. of Scotland, 1214—49, the king's saddle is ensigned with a lion rampant (Cotton Charter, xix. 2). And the seal of Robert Fitz-Walter, 1299, presents an analogous example (Plate xvii. of vol. v. of the *Archæologia*). The Stirrup of the period is shewn by numerous examples to have been triangular. See woodcuts, No. 47, 48 and 56. The Peytrel or breastplate was sometimes of plain fashion, as in the first seal of Henry III. (woodcut, No. 79): sometimes it had the pendent ornaments of the preceding period, as in the example on Plate xxxvii. of the Painted Chamber, where the pattern is a string of golden trefoils. From the Windsor Roll quoted above we find that the poitrail was of leather, and that this leather was occasionally gilt:—

"De Stephano de Perone xi. par̄. strep̃ et xi. pectoral' deaurat̄ p'c̃. xxij. łi.

"De eodem. iiij fren̄ cū pector̃ et strepis de corea. p'c̃. vi.ł

"De eodem. ij. fren̄ ij. pector̃ et ij. strep̃ deaũr. p'c̃. iiij. ł"

The Bridle presents two kinds of bits: one has the cheeks joined by a bar from their lower end, as in woodcut, No. 80; the other has no such cross-bar (see fol. 27 of Harl. MS. 3,244). The last quotation from the Windsor Roll shews us that the bridles were sometimes gilt. The group from the Painted Chamber on our woodcut, No. 82, offers a curious arrangement of the brow-band. The rounds in the original are gold-colour.

The Caparison of the knightly steed appears to have been of five kinds. 1. The horse has a "couverture" of chain-mail only. 2. The couverture is of quilted work. 3. The housing is of a light, fluttery material, probably covering an armour of chain-mail. 4. A light housing, heraldically decorated, which seems to have no armour beneath. 5. The horse has no furniture beyond the ordinary war-saddle, peytrel and bridle.

Of the mailed dextrier we have already had some notice in the preceding century (see page 169). The example here given is from the Painted Chamber.

The trapper of chain-mail occurs on two of the plates of that work: those numbered 31 and 37. A fragment of a similar defence is seen on the Shurland monument at Minster (Stothard, Pl. XLI.). But representations of this kind of armament are of the greatest rarity. It is, however, often mentioned by the writers of the time; though, perhaps, not without some exaggeration of the numbers of mail-clad steeds gathered in the host. At the battle of Nuova Croce in 1237, between the imperialists and the Milanese, Matthew Paris tells us that: "A credible Italian asserted that Milan with its dependencies raised an army of six thousand men-at-arms with iron-clad horses[401]." The *Chronicon Colmariense*, under the year 1298, describing the force of "Australes, qui armis ferreis utebantur," brought against the duke of Austria, says: "Habebant et multos qui habebant dextrarios, id est, equos magnos. Hi equi cooperti fuerunt coopertoriis ferreis, id est, veste ex circulis ferreis contexta." An ordinance of Philip the Fair in 1303 provides that every holder of an estate of 500 livres rental, shall furnish for defence of the realm "un gentilhomme bien armé et monté à cheval de cinquante livres tournois et couvert de couvertures de fer ou de couverture pourpointé[402]." The particular use of the barding of steel or pourpointerie was to defend the horses against the missiles of the enemy. Sutcliffe's "Practice of Arms," written in the sixteenth century, when the musquet was rapidly supplanting the long-bow, has: "Use of late times hath brought in divers sorts of Horsemen, which, according to their armes and furniture, have divers names. Some Horse are barded; others without bardes. The French Men-of-armes, in times past, used barded Horses, for feare of our Arrowes. Nowe, since Archerie is not so much reckoned of, and Bardes are but a weak defence against Shotte, Lanciers, leaving their bardes, are armed much like to the Albanian Stradiots."

The pourpointed housing is named in the ordinance of Philip IV. quoted above, and it may probably be implied in most cases where we read of a "cheval couvert." Rigord, under 1214, (battle of Bovines,) describes the approach of the Imperialists on their barded horses: "Dixit quod viderat equos militum coopertos, ... quod erat evidentissimum pugnæ signum." In a roll of expenses, of 1294, given by Du Cange[403], "Pour les gages de Monsieur Bertran Massole, retenu aux gages accoustumez pour lui et deux Ecuyers," we read: "Et estoit luy et autre à chevaux couverts, et un autre sans cheval couvert:" and again: "Pour onze Ecuyers à chevaux couverts, à chacun vii. sols vi. deniers par jour, et pour deux qui n'ont point chevaux couverts, chacun v. sols."

In England, the armed horse came into use between the years 1285 and 1298; for, while the Statute of Winchester in 1285 makes no mention of any defence for the steed, the Statute of 27 Edw. I. in every case requires such an armament:—

"Le Rey ad ordene qe sire Thomas de Furnivall voit en les contees de Notingham et de Derb', de eslire, trier, ordener et asseer gentz d'armes en meismes les contez, aussi bien a chival come a pie, de toutz ceus qui sont de age d'entre vint anns e seissaunte: ensi qe chescun qe eyt xxx. liverees de terre, seit mis a un *chival covert*: e de seissaunte liverees, a deux *chivaux covertz*: e se vers mount de chescune xxx. liveree de terre, a un *chival covert*. E s'il eit plus avant qe xxx. liveree de terre e ne mie seisaunte, qe en ceo qe il avera entre les xxx. livereez, seit joint e mis a un autre qe serra de meisme la condicion.

"E de ceus qui averont meins de trente liveree de terre en aval jusqes a seisaunte soudes, e de ceus qe out seisaunte soudees, e de seisaunte soudees en amount, soient enjoingnz e mis as autres qe serront de meisme l'estat, de si qe il seient a xxx. liverees, e adunkes soient assis a un *chival covert*: ensi qe chescune trente liveree de terre, aussi de greindres come de meindres, face un *chival covert*.

"E face le dit sire Thomas mettre en roulle les nouns de touz ceaus qi serront assis as chivaux covertz, e le noumbre des chivaux par eus severeaument de chescun wapentakel, e aussi les nouns de gent a pe par eus.

"E ausitost come il avera ce fet, distinctement e apertement de ce certifie le Rey.

"Don' a Noef Chastel sur Tyne, le xxv. jour de Novembre[404]."

The housing of a lighter material seems to be presented to us in the engravings, Nos. 47, 72 and 80. The folds of the drapery in these examples have in no degree the character of a stiff quilted garment. The last of the three miniatures (from the Lives of the Offas) is further curious from its exhibiting in the same group the horse with and without its housing. The caparisoned steed in front is that of King Offa the First, who leads his troops to the defeat of the Scots. A very early example of the trapper is found in the seal of Saer de Quinci, earl of Winchester, 1210—19: engraved in Laing's Scottish Seals, Plate xi. In this monument, too, the housing is armoried; which seems to shew that the heraldic and the plain housing were introduced simultaneously. Neither of them was at this early time a necessary concomitant of knightly dignity; for we find no English royal seal exhibiting the caparisoned steed till the time of Edward I. (See woodcut, No. 85.) Another early instance of the armorial trapper is afforded by the seal of Hugo de Vere, earl of Oxford, 1221-63[405]; and in this, as in other examples, it will be remarked that, while the couverture of the horse is decorated with heraldic devices, the surcoat of the knight is altogether plain. The seal here given, of Roger de Quinci, earl of Winchester from 1219 to 1264, has the same arrangement.

PLATE LXXXVII.

Other examples of the armoried housing will be found in the Lives of the Offas, the Painted Chamber, in the seal of Patrick, earl of March, 1292 (Laing, p. 54), in the monument of Edmund Crouchback, 1296, (Stothard, Pl. XLIII.) and in our engravings, Nos. 47 and 85.

Towards the end of the thirteenth century came in the fashion of ornamenting the head of the horse with a Fan Crest, similar to that fixed on the helm of the knight. This fan crest for the horse is a decoration of very high antiquity: it appears among the Assyrian sculptures, and again among the Lycian marbles in the British Museum. See the engravings at page 159 and page 285 of Mr. Vaux's able work on our national collection. The seal of Patrick Dunbar, earl of March, 1292, affords a good example of knight and steed decorated with the fan crest: it is figured in Laing's Ancient Scottish Seals, page 54. In the provision for the Windsor Tournament in 1278, crests are furnished for every knight and every horse[406]:—

> "It p̲ qualibet galea j. cresta }
> It p̲ quolibet equo j. cresta } S̃m. LXXVj. Crest."

They were in this case made of parchment, and fastened by means of nails or rivets and "chastones":—

> "It p̲ qualibet cresta j. pell' parcamen̄ rud'.
> It p̲ qualibet cresta j. par̃ chaston̄ et j clauon̄."

The clavones are again mentioned in the Wardrobe Accounts of King Edward I. in 1300[407]: "factura diversorum armorum, vexillorum, et penocellorum, pro Domino Edwardo filio Regis et Johanne de Lancastria, jamberis, poleyns, platis, uno capello ferri, una Cresta cum *clavis argenti* pro eodem capello," &c. The chasto (Fr. *châton*) was a kind of socket or cavity, but the particular arrangement of it in fixing the crest has not been ascertained.

About the same time we first hear of a defence for the horse of the nature of the later chanfrein. The same Windsor Roll of 1278 gives us the earliest notice of these "copita" of leather, made after the fashion (*de similitudine*) of horses' heads:—

> "D Milon̄ le Cuireur̃. xxxviij. copita cor̃ de similitud' capit̄ equoȝ ꝑij. s."

They appear again in 1301, under the name of *testaræ* (or *testeræ*) in the Indenture of Delivery of the Castle of Montgomery to William de Leyburn (Cott. MS. Vitell. C. x. fol. 154): "Item liberavit eidem iij. par̃ coopertorum ferri et ij. Testaras et v. loricas cum capite et v. sine capite," &c.

The thirteenth century appears to have retained all the ENGINES for the approach and attack of towns that were in use during the preceding age. In this century we first obtain pictorial evidence of the form and principle of the mangona or trebuchet of the middle-ages, and from this valuable testimony we learn that the motive power of *torsion* employed during the classic period is no longer in favour; but instead, we have a machine from which, by means of a counterpoised beam, a large stone is cast forth from a sling fixed at one end of the beam. We have already (page 330) referred to the drawings of these instruments in an Arabic manuscript of this century, used by Captain Favé and M. Reinaud in their work, *Du feu grégeois, &c.* Other early representations occur in Roy. MS. 16, G. vi., copied in Shaw's "Dresses and Decorations;" in the ivory carving figured in the fourth volume of the Journal of the Archæological Association, and in the *Études sur l'Artillerie* of the Emperor of the French, Vol. ii. Plate III. In the work of Gilles Colonne[408], written for his pupil, Philip the Fair of France, we have a distinct account of four varieties of the trébuchet: "Of pierriers," he says, "there are four kinds, and in all these machines there is a beam which is raised and lowered by means of a counterpoise, a sling being attached to the end of the beam to discharge the stone. Sometimes the counterpoise is not sufficient, and then they attach ropes to it, in order to move the beam. The counterpoise may either be fixed or moveable, or both at once. In the fixed counterpoise, a box is fastened to the end of the beam, and filled with stones or sand, or any heavy body. These machines, anciently called *trabutium*, cast their missiles with most exactness, because the weight acts in a uniform manner. Their aim is so sure that one may, so to say, hit a needle. If the gyn carries too far, it must be drawn back or loaded with a heavier stone: if the contrary, then it must be advanced or a smaller stone supplied. For without attention to the weight of the stone, one cannot hope to reach the given mark.

"Others of these machines have a moveable counterpoise attached to the beam, turning upon an axis. This variety was by the Romans named *biffa*. The third kind, which is called *tripantum*, has two weights: one fixed to the beam and the other moveable around it: by this means, it throws with more exactness than the *biffa*, and to a greater distance than the trebuchet. The fourth sort, in lieu of weights fixed to the beam, has a number of ropes; and is discharged by means of men pulling simultaneously at the cords. This last kind does not cast such large stones as the others, but it has the advantage that it may be more rapidly loaded and discharged than they. In using the perriers by night, it is necessary to attach a lighted body to the projectile: by this means, one may discover the force of the machine, and regulate the weight of the stone accordingly[409]."

The trebuchet arranged with cords is represented in the treatise *Du feu grégeois* noticed above, and in the *Études sur l'Artillerie*, vol. ii. Pl. III. Those familiar with the sights of the Thames will not fail to be struck with the curious resemblance between this ancient engine of warfare and the apparatus by which a gang of colliers raise the cargo from the hold of their ships.

Matthew Paris mentions the plying by day and by night of the terrible trebuchet. Under 1246, he gives us the letter of Master Walter de Ocra, a clerk of the Emperor, to the king of England, recounting the events of the Italian campaign: "About eight days before the end of last July, my Lord laid siege to the Castle of Capaccio, in which were (certain knights) traitors to him, and who had attempted his life, with a hundred and fifty others, including knights, cross-bowmen, and other friends of theirs; all of whom my said Lord, by uninterrupted discharges of missiles, day and night, from seven well-ordered Trebuchets, and by vigorous and unceasing assaults, also made night and day, reduced to such a helpless state that they could not assist one another[410]." The castle was finally taken and destroyed, the garrison punished by loss of eye-sight and other mutilations; and the six leaders who had attempted the life of the Emperor, having partaken the punishment of their comrades, were by the imperial order "sent to all the kings and princes throughout the various countries of the world, with the impression of the papal bull, which was found there, stamped on their foreheads, to give public notice of their treachery."

The trebuchets were sometimes distinguished by particular names, a fancy already begun in the "Mate-Griffon" of Cœur-de-Lion's war-tower, and afterwards largely indulged in the great bombards of the fifteenth and succeeding centuries. In 1303, when the Bernese besieged Wimmis, they had two trebuchets, one of which was named *La fille de bois*, the other *L'Âne*[411].

In 1850, under the direction of the present Emperor of the French, a trebuchet of large dimensions was constructed after the ancient monuments, and set up at the École d'Artillerie at Vincennes. A minute account of its formation and the experiments made with it, has been given in the Report to the Minister of War by Capt. Favé: this report is printed in the *Études sur l'Artillerie*, vol. ii. page 38.

The projectiles thrown from the ancient trebuchets were rounded stones, barrels of Greek fire or other incendiary compositions, and occasionally the putrid bodies of animals, when the siege was obstinately prolonged, or the combatants were greatly exasperated. The rounded stones are particularly mentioned by Guiart:—

"Giétent mangonniaus et perrières:
La grosse pierre areondie
Demainne a l'aler grant bondie."

Chron. Métr., Par. i. vers 3,296.

The English seem to have been somewhat behindhand in the construction of their perriers, for Matthew Paris tells us that in 1253 the Gascons hurled stones and darts of such wonderful size on the army of the king, that many of them were carried into England, to be exhibited as curiosities[412].

The mangonel was used also in sea-fights. In the Additamenta to the *Historia Major* of Matthew Paris, we have an account of the taking of Damietta, in which occurs this passage: "Et lapides de *mangonellis navalibus*, qui sic parabantur ut quinque vel sex lapides simul longo jacerent[413]." It does not seem, however, (as it has been suggested,) that we have here the description of an engine which threw five or six stones at once: we must rather understand that five or six mangonels were so managed as to shoot in volleys.

Another variety of the trebuchet was the Biblia or Bible; but its distinctive character has not been ascertained. It is mentioned in 1238: "adducens secum Bibliam, Petrariam et caetera bellica instrumenta[414]." And in the *Roman de Claris*:

> "Li rois fait ses engins drecier
> Et vers les haus murs charroier;
> Bibles et Mangoniaux geter,
> Et les Chats aux fossez mener,
> Les Berfrois traire vers les mur:
> Cil dedens ne sont pas à sur."

And again, in the same romance:—

> "Et pierres grans et les Pierriers,
> Et les Bibles qui sont trop fiers,
> Getent," &c.

Other names occur at this time, indicating machines for casting stones: some of these are probably mere synonyms of the words already noticed; and of the particular mechanism implied by others, it is vain, in the absence of cotemporary drawings, to hope for an exact idea.

Besides the engines of the mangona kind, formed by a sling and weight, there was another class constructed on the principle of the cross-bow. The Spingarda and Spingardella (*Espringale*) appear to have been arbalests mounted on frames with wheels, somewhat after the manner of the field-pieces of our own day. The French used them against the Flemings at the battle of Mons-en-Puelle in 1304:—

> "Joignant d'eus rot deux Espringales,
> Que garçons au tirer avancent."—*Guiart.*

They shot forth, not only stones, but darts or quarrels:—

"Et font getter leurs espringales:
Ça et là sonnent li clairain:
Li garrot, empené d'airain,
Quatre on cinq en percent tout outre."
Guiart, année 1304.

They were also called *Arbalestes à tour*, and under this name are included by Christine de Pisan (in the fourteenth century) in the armament for a strong siege: "Deux cens arbalestres, *trente* autres *arbalestes à tour*, et cent autres à croc, ... douze tours tous neufs, à tendre arbalestres," &c. From the last item we see very clearly that the distinctive name of this arbalest was derived from the instrument used to bend its powerful bow. The figure of an espringale mounted on its carriage is given in the *Études sur l'Artillerie*, vol. i. Plate I.

The old contrivances to cover the sappers as they approached the walls of a besieged place, still continued in use: the Cat, the Cat-castle (CHAT-CHASTEL) the Vinea, and other varieties of the mantlet occurring frequently in the chronicles and poems of the time. The king, in the *Roman de Claris*,

"———fait ses engins drecier,
Et les Chats aux fossez mener."

In 1256, the Papal troops, led by the Archbishop of Ravenna, attack Padua, defended by the partisans of the tyrant Eccelino; the archbishop, surrounded by a medley of knights and monks, soldiers and priests, assaulted the city at the gate of the Ponte Altinato: they had made their approaches under cover of a "kind of moveable gallery which they called *Vinea*." The defendants from their walls poured burning pitch and boiling oil upon the wooden vinea, so that it took fire; but the city gate being also of wood, the besiegers pushed the machine close to the gate, burnt it down and entered the place[415].

The Moveable Towers also were still in vogue. Under the name of *berfrois*, they are mentioned in the passage on a preceding page from the *Roman de Claris*. Under the year 1204 they are named by Guiart:—

"Un fort Chastel se fust drécié:
Le sommet plus haut en repose
Que les murs de Gaillart grant chose."

In Roy. MS. 20, D. i., of about the close of this century, the wooden Tower occurs in several of the miniatures. It is constructed in the manner of a scaffolding, having at the top an open platform filled with archers: its height, that of the city walls, close to which it is placed. Examples will be found on folios 305, 306 and 317. The besieged, when they were able to discover the point to which the assaulting tower was to be moved, loosened the soil in that spot by digging; so that, when the ponderous machine arrived, it was overturned by its fore-wheels sinking into the soft earth[416]. The *Chat-Chastel* combined the *beffroi* and the *cattus*.

But the best account that can be offered of the Siege operations of this time, is furnished by a cotemporary writer, the Seneschal of Carcassone; himself the commander of the defending forces. This very curious document is preserved in the Archives of France, and has been published in the *Bibliothèque de l'École des Chartes*, vol. vii. p. 363. Carcassone was besieged in the autumn of 1240 by the son of the Vicomte de Béziers; and the defender of the city, Guillaume des Ormes, sends to Queen Blanche, regent of the kingdom during the absence of Saint Louis, an exact account of the proceedings. Carcassone was surrounded with a double wall, furnished as usual with towers, and having several barbicans in advance of its various gates. The object of the Barbican was to afford the besieged the means of a flanking attack: it was formed something like a street, with a wall on each side, terminating in a kind of open tower: and it thus became necessary that the enemy should act in the first instance against this outwork; for, by assaulting the curtain, they would be exposed to a flank attack from the barbican, and might also be assailed in the rear by sorties from the head of the work.

"To his most excellent and highly illustrious mistress, Blanche, by the grace of God, Queen of the French, William des Ormes, Seneschal of Carcassone, her humble and devoted servant, greeting and faithful service.

"Madame, this is to let you know that the city of Carcassone was besieged by him who calls himself the Viscount, and by his accomplices, on the Monday following the Octave of the Nativity of the Blessed Mary[417]. And immediately we who were within the city took from them the suburb *Graveillant*, which is before the Toulouse gate; and thence we obtained much timber, which was of great use to us. The said suburb extended from the Barbican of the city as far as the corner of the said city. And the same day, our enemies, through the multitude of their forces, took from us a mill. Afterwards, Olivier de Termes, Bernard Hugon de Serre-Longue, Géraud d'Aniort, and those who were with them, lodged themselves between the corner of the city and the water; and there, on the same day, by means of the ditches in that spot, and by breaking up the roads which lay between them and us, they so fortified themselves that we could by no means get at them.

"On another side, between the bridge and the Castle Barbican, Pierre de Fenouillet and Renaud de Puy, Guillaume Fort, Pierre de la Tour, and many others of Carcassone, established themselves. And at both these places they had so many Cross-bowmen[418], that no man could stir out of the city without being wounded. Afterwards they set up a mangonel before our barbican, when we lost no time in opposing to it from within an excellent Turkish petrary[419], which played upon the mangonel and those about it; so that when they essayed to cast upon us, and saw the beam of our petrary in motion, they fled, utterly abandoning their mangonel. And in that place they made ditches and palisades. Yet, as often as we discharged our petrary, we drove them from it, still being unable to approach the spot on account of the ditches, the pits, and the bolts from their bows(?)—*propter fossata, quarellos et puteos qui ibi erant.*

"Moreover, Madame, they began to mine at the barbican of the Narbonne gate; and we, having by listening ascertained where they were at work, proceeded to countermine; and we built within the barbican a strong stone wall, so as still to retain half the barbican in surety: they then set fire to the props of their mine, and a breach was made in the outer part of our barbican.

"They also began to mine against another tower (*tornellam*) of the outer ballium, but by countermining we succeeded in dispossessing them of the work. Afterwards they began (to mine) beneath another wall, and destroyed two of our battlements (*cranellos de liceis*): but we speedily set up a good strong palisade between us.

"They mined also at the corner of the city, towards the bishop's house, and beginning their mine from a very great distance, they came beneath a certain Saracenic wall (*murum sarraceneum*[420]) to the wall of the *ballium*, which, when we perceived, we forthwith made a good strong palisade between us and them, and countermined. Then they set fire to the props of their mine, and brought down about ten fathoms of our battlements. But we speedily made a good strong palisade, on the top of which we constructed a good *bretèche*[421], with good loopholes for arrows; so that none of them dared to come near us in this place.

"They began also to mine at the barbican of the *Porte de Rhodez*, working underneath in order to reach our wall; and in that place they formed a wonderfully large passage. But when we perceived this, we immediately made, on each side of their work, a great and strong palisade; and we also countermined, and having broken into their mine, speedily dispossessed them of it.

"Be it further known to you, Madame, that, from the beginning of the siege, they have never ceased making assaults. But we had such good store of cross-bows, and of brave fellows determined to resist to the utmost, that they never assaulted us but with very great loss to themselves.

"At length, on a certain Sunday, they got together all their men-at-arms, cross-bowmen, and others, and in a body made an assault on the barbican below the castle: but we went down into the barbican, and discharged so many stones and quarrels against them that we forced them to retire; many being killed or wounded. On the following Sunday, after the Feast of St. Michael, they made a very fierce assault. But we, thanks to the brave defence of our men, repulsed them, killing and wounding many: on our side, not one was either slain or mortally wounded.

"The day after, towards the evening, hearing, Madame, that your troops were approaching to relieve us, the enemy set fire to the suburb of Carcassone. They have entirely destroyed the buildings of the Friars Minor, and those of the monastery of the Blessed Mary, in the suburb, using the timber from them to construct their palisades. But at night all the besiegers furtively withdrew; and, with them, those of the suburb.

"In sooth, Madame, we were well prepared to hold out much longer; for, during the whole siege, not one of your people, however poor his estate, ever suffered for want of food; and we had corn and meat enough for a much more obstinate resistance, if need had been. Be it known to you, Madame, that these evil-doers, on the second day of their coming, slew thirty-three priests and other holy men whom they met on entering the suburb. Know also, Madame, that the Seigneur P. de Voisin, your Constable of Carcassone, R. de Capendu, and Gerard d'Ermenville, have greatly distinguished themselves in this affair. But the Constable, by his vigilance, his bravery and his daring, is entitled to the chief praise of all. On other matters concerning the district, we can better render a faithful account, Madame, when we shall be in your presence. In a word, they began mines against us in seven different places: but we in most cases countermined them, and offered a stout opposition. They commenced their mines at their own quarters, so that we knew nothing of their approach till they were near our walls.

"Given at Carcassone, 13 Oct. 1240.

"Know, Madame, that the enemy burned the castles and towns which they passed in their flight."

The town of Carcassone in its present state is probably the most perfect fortification of the middle ages in existence. The whole of the walls, towers, barbicans, ditches, and even the drawbridges, are still in being, and wonderfully little injured, considering that they date from the thirteenth and fourteenth centuries. Enough remains to restore the whole perfectly, without doubt or hesitation. An admirable series of plans and drawings of these interesting fortifications has been made by M. Viollet-Le-Duc for the French Government, shewing every part in its actual state, and an equally complete series of designs for their restoration, representing them exactly as they appeared at the siege so well described by the Seneschal. The accounts relating to the building of these walls and the preparations for their defence, are preserved in the French archives. The very valuable and interesting series of drawings named above was exhibited by the French government in the Architectural Gallery of the *Exposition des Beaux Arts* in 1855, and a great part of them are beautifully engraved on a reduced scale in the "Essai sur l'Architecture Militaire du Moyen-Age," already noticed. In these plans the situation of the castle on one side of the town, and of the different barbicans as described by the Seneschal, are very clearly marked. There are a few barbicans remaining perfect in England, as at Warwick and Alnwick.

The siege of Bedford Castle in 1224 affords another good example of the mode of attacking a stronghold at this period. The garrison in this instance were rebels to the king; their leader, one Fawkes, a foreigner, a partisan of the Bishop of Winchester; though not himself present at the time of the siege. The castle was invested by the king himself. Two lofty towers of wood, of the kind already described, were raised by the walls and filled with archers. Seven mangonæ cast forth ponderous stones from morning till night. Sappers approached the walls under cover of the Cat. First, the barbican, then the outer ballium, was taken. A breach in the second wall soon after gave the besiegers admission to the inner bailey. The donjon still held out, and the royalists proceeded to attack it by means of their sappers. A sufficient portion of the foundations having been removed, the stanchions were set on fire, one of the angles sank deep into the ground, and a wide rent laid open the interior of the keep. The garrison now planted the royal standard on the tower, and sent the women to implore mercy. But a severe example was required, in order to strike terror among the disaffected in other quarters of the realm. The knights and others, therefore, to the number of eighty, were hanged; the archers were sent into Palestine, to redeem their fault by fighting against the enemies of the faith; while their leader, Fawkes, who now surrendered himself at Coventry, was banished from the island[422].

Matthew Paris records the existence of a singular and somewhat poetical Monument of Victory, left to celebrate the capture of a castle in the Campagna of Rome. The emperor "had taken a castle near Montfort, belonging to the nephews and other relatives of the pope, which he, the pope, had newly built with the money of the Crusaders. The emperor destroyed the fortress, hanged all whom he found therein, and in token of the destruction of it, left a sort of *tower half-destroyed*, that the memory of the offence, as well as of his vengeance, might never die[423]."

Sea-fights were still achieved by the same knights, men-at-arms, archers and "satellites," as contended in land warfare. A good pictorial example of a naval battle of this time occurs on folio 357 of Roy. MS. 20, D. i. See also fol. 23vo of the same MS., for the picture of an armed fleet. Further examples of a similar kind will be found in this very curious volume, as well as of Tents and many other objects of military use.

TOURNAMENTS continued to enjoy a large amount of favour among the nobles and knights, and their retainers: but princes began to see that these great armed meetings of their powerful vassals, in the facilities they afforded for combinations against the royal power, and in the imposing exhibition of the baronial force and dignity necessarily involved in these pageants, were full of danger to the kingly order; and, in consequence, forbade their celebration except under express permission of the sovereign[424]. The plea was, the dangers incurred by the competitors at these mock battles, and the disorders to which they sometimes led. And indeed it was not difficult to justify the prohibition on these grounds. Among many instances that might be quoted of the tumultuous termination of a tournament, we may notice that of Rochester in 1251. "In this same year," says Paris[425], "on the Feast of the Conception of the Blessed Virgin, a fierce Tournament was held at Rochester between the English and foreigners, in which the foreigners were so shamefully beaten that they disgracefully fled to the city for refuge; but, being met by knights coming in an opposite direction, they were again attacked, despoiled, and soundly beaten with sticks and staves: and thus they returned with much interest the blows and injuries they had received at the tournament of Brackley. The anger and hatred between the English and foreigners increased in consequence, and became daily more fearful." Another striking example of this century is the hastilude between King Edward I. and the Count of Châlons in 1274, which was of so serious a nature as to receive the name of "La petite Bataille de Châlons." The king, returning from the Holy Land, to take possession of his crown, was invited by the Count to participate in a tourney which he was preparing. The king's company is said to have been a thousand only, while those engaged on the Count's side are estimated at double the number. But this is the estimate of English chroniclers. The tourneyers met near Châlons, some on horseback, others on foot, armed with swords. The Count, who was a very powerful man, singled out the king for an antagonist; cast aside his sword, threw his arms round the neck of the monarch, and used all his force to drag him from his horse. But the king, taking advantage of the tight hold by which the Count had fixed himself to his person, and relying on his own strength, suddenly clapped spurs to his horse, carried away the Count out of his saddle, and then by a violent shake tumbled him to the ground. Being remounted, the Count renewed the attack, but with no greater success than before. His knights, meanwhile, exasperated at the discomfiture of their leader, began to assail the English with all the rancour of real warfare. The English returned wound for wound: the "Joust of Peace" became a "Joûte à outrance:" Edward's archers plied their terrible arrows, routed the troops opposed to them, rushed upon the knights, slew their steeds or cut their saddle-girths, so as to bring to the ground many a sturdy baron and rich prisoner[426].

Of the mandates issued for the suppression of tournaments, many examples have come down to us. The Fœdera contains a considerable number. Some were sent forth by the temporal prince, others were launched by the spiritual arm; for it was no difficult matter in these days to obtain the pope's aid in any scheme of this nature, where a benevolent intention could be assigned, and a liberal douceur had been supplied. In 1220, Pandulf the legate forbids a tournament in England, under pain of the forfeiture of goods and of excommunication[427]. In 1234, the king of England charges his subjects that they offend not by tourneying or behourding (*buhurdare vel torneare*[428]). In 1255 the royal inhibition is again sent forth, and the reason given for its publication is the peril of Prince Edward in Gascony: "eo quod Edwardus, filius Regis in gravi periculo existit in Wasconia[429]." 1265 is the date of another[430]. In 1299, the king again issues his mandate: this time with penalties of peculiar severity. The knight is forbidden "sub forisfacturâ vite et membrorum, et omnium que tenet in dicto regno, torneare, bordeare, seu justas facere, aventuras querere, aut aliàs ad arma ire, quoquo modo, sine nostrâ licenciâ speciali." Should any dare to disobey, then they are forthwith to be arrested and placed in safe custody, "corpora ipsorum, unà cum equis et hernesio suis[431]."

Whilst, however, the monarch of timid character and jealous of his baronage, looked with disrelish on the Tournament, the prince of an enterprising disposition and skilled in military exercises, naturally regarded with more complacency a pastime in which his own achievements were placed in the most brilliant light, and the respect and attachment of his nobles secured, by the exhibition of those qualities on which they themselves founded their chief claim to power and distinction. Thus, in the thirteenth century, when the king (Henry III.) had created eighty new knights, the gallant Prince Edward accompanied them to a tournament which had been proclaimed on the continent, "that each might try his strength, as was the custom with newly-made knights[432]." In 1253, the Earl of Gloucester with a companion also went abroad, to take part in a marriage festivity and in a tournament which followed it: an adventure in which they were so roughly handled by the antagonist knights as to require daily fomentations and bathing to restore them to health[433].

Regarding the equipment of the knights and their assistants at the

Tournament, there are two documents of this century which are of the highest interest and afford the most curious information. These are the "Statutum Armorum ad Torniamenta," compiled previous to 1295; and the roll detailing the "Empciones facte contra Torniamentum de Parco de Windsore," in the 6th year of Edward I.; from the latter of which we have already extracted some passages illustrative of various portions of the knightly armament.

By the tournament statute we learn that there existed at this time a sort of Court of Honour, to judge all disputes and delinquencies that might arise during the celebration of the games; and the members of it were the king's eldest son, Prince Edward; Edmund, earl of Lancaster; William de Valence, earl of Pembroke; Gilbert de Clare, earl of Gloucester; and the earl of Lincoln. As De Valence, the last of his name, died in 1296, and the earl of Gloucester in 1295, the date of this document cannot of course be later than the year last quoted[434]. It is not unworthy of note that the effigies of two of these Judges of the Tournament, fully equipped in the trappings of armed knighthood, have been preserved to our days: the monuments of Edmund Crouchback and of William de Valence in Westminster Abbey are among the most curious memorials that can be consulted by the student of ancient military costume. There are several copies of the statute extant. The following, from a manuscript in the Bodleian Library, has been selected by the Record Commission as the most trustworthy[435]:—

"A la requeste de Contes e de Barons e de la Chivalrie de Englet're, ordine est e p nostro Seign^r le Rey comaunde: qe nul ne seit si hrɑ̄ desoremes, Conte ne Baron ne autre Chivaler, qe al Torney voysent de aver plus qe treys Esquiers armez, pur li servir al Turney: e qe chescun Esquier porte chapel des armes son Seignur qe il servira a la jornee pur enseygne.

"E qe nul Chr ne Esquier qe sert al Turney ne porte espeie a point, ne cotel a point, ne bastoun, ne mace, fors espee large pur turneer. E qe tuz les baneors, qe baners portent, seent armez de mustilers[436], e de quisers[437], e de espaulers, e de bacyn[438] sanz plus.

"E sil avent qe nul Conte ou Baron ou autre Chivaler voyse encontre le estatut p le assent e le comaundemt nostre Seign^r Sire Edward, ê ê Rey, e Sire Eumond frere le Rey, e Sire Willeme de Valence, e Sire Gilbt de Clare, e le Cunte de Nichole[439], qe celi Chivaler, qe issint s'ra trove en forfetaunt en nul poynt encontre le estatut, seyt encurru cele peyne: qe il perde chival e armes, e demeorge en prison a la volunte   de avaūtdiz Sire Edward, Sire Eumond, e le autres. E qe le Esquier   qe serra trove fesaunt encontre le estatut, qe issi est devise, en acun poynt, perde chival e herneys[440] e seyt iij. aunz en la prison. E qe nul sake[441] Chivaler a terre, fors ceus qe serrunt armez pur lur Seign[r] servir, qe le Chivaler pusse recovrir son chival, e cely seit en la forfeture des Esquiers avaunt diz.

"E qe nul fiz de graunt Seignur, ceo est asaver, de Conte ou de Baron, ne seit arme fors de mustilers, e de quisers, e de espaulers, e de bacynet, saunz plus, e qe nul aporte cutel a poynte, ne espeye, ne mace, fors espee large. E si nul seit trove qe, en ascun de ceos poynz, alast encontre le estatut, qe il perde son chival le quel il serra munte a la jornee, e seit en la prison un an.

"E qe ceus qe vendrunt pur veer le turnemīt ne seent armez de nīmanere de armure, ne qe il ne portent ne espee, ne cutel, ne bastun, ne mace, ne perre, sur la forfeture des Esquiers avauntdiz. E qe nul garson, ne homē a pee ne porte espee, ne cutel, ne baston, ne perrer: e si il seīttrovez enforfetaunt, qe il seyent emprisonez vij. aunz.

"E si acun graunt Seign[r] ou autre teygne mangerie, qe nul esquier ne ameyne eynz fors ceus qe trencherunt devaunt lur Seignurs.

"E qe nul Roy de Haraunz ne Menestrals[442] portent privez armez, ne autres forz lur espees saunz poynte. E qe le Reys des Harraunz eyent lur huces des armes saunz plus." &c.

This document affords us some curious glimpses at the customs of the time; not less by what it forbids than by what it ordains. A tournament in which the combatants are liable to be pelted by the stones and slings of the varlets and other lookers-on, does not give us a very exalted idea of these festivals; and, for a holiday game, the rules seem oddly severe which decree that the poor squire who infringes them shall lose horse and armour, and "demeorge iij. aunz en la prison."

The Roll of Purchases made for the Tournament of Windsor Park, "per manum Adinetti *cissoris*," is preserved in the Tower of London, and bears date 9th of July in the sixth year of Edward I. (1278). The jousts were of the kind called "Jousts of Peace," and the knights for whom armour is provided are thirty-eight in number. Of these, twelve are styled "digniores," and wore gilded helms, while the remainder had head-pieces that were silvered only. A "memorandum" informs us that each suit consisted of one coat-of-fence, one surcoat, one pair of ailettes, two crests (of which, one for the horse), one shield, one helm of leather, and one sword made of whalebone. "M[d] q[d] in quo p fīnēs fu'unt j. Tunic' ārm: j. cooptōr: j. pār aleīt. Itm̄ ij. Crest̄ & j. Bōn&una galea cōr & j. ensis de Balōn." Each coat-of-fence was composed   of a

Cuirass and Arm-defences. The cuirasses (*quirettæ*) being supplied by "Milo the Currier," were probably of leather, as the helms were: "De Miloñ ł Cuireũr. xxxviij. quire̅t: p̃c pe̅c iij. s." For each of them were furnished wells of the cloth called "Carda;" while eight pieces of "Diaper" contributed to the formation of the whole thirty-eight:—

"Pro qualibet quireſt ij. ulñcard.
Pro eisd' ſinẽs armand' viij. diaspeř."

The carda is charged at fourpence an ell; the diaper at eight shillings the piece. "Ten buckrams" are supplied to form the arm-defences: "Item ꝓxxxviij. pař bracſ x. bukerann." And the whole of these are painted: "Item ꝓſcuř & pictuř xxxviij. pař Brach' de Bokeran pᷓc pař iiij. d." These body- armours must have differed very widely in their structure or embellishment; for while the Harness-of-Arms of Walter de Sancto Martino only cost seven shillings, that of the Earl of Lincoln amounted to thirty-three shillings and fourpence. Little bells were added to the equipment either of the knights or their horses; perhaps both: and they were purchased of Richard Paternoster: "De Ricō pat'nř DCCC. Nola3 sive Tintunabul' pᷓc ceñt. iij. s." This decoration of bells obtained great favour in the next two centuries.

The surcoats of the four earls[443] were of Cindon silk, the remaining thirty-four of Carda: "Pro iiij. cooptoř ꝓ iiij^or Comíτ ij. Cind' & dī. Item ꝓ xxj cooptoř. CXIX. ulñ. card." The ailettes were made of leather and carda, being fastened by laces of silk: "D. Miloñ le Cuireuř. xxxviij. pař aleſt coř pᷓc pař viiij. d.... Item pro xxxviij. pař aleſt xix. ulñ. card.... viij. Duodeñ ꝗꝓɜerīc ꝓ aleſt pᷓc duodeñ viij. d." Each helm and each horse had a œτꝟn was made of calf-skin, and fastened by the *chastones* and *clavones* already noticed at page 347. Stephen the Joiner supplied thirty-eight shields of wood at fivepence each: "De Stephō Junctoř xxxviij. scuſt fustiñ pᷓc scuti. v. ꝺ̓ Being elsewhere called *blazonæ*, we may conclude they were heraldically ensigned. The helms were of leather, supplied by Robert Erunnler in their crude state at sixteenpence per helm; but afterwards embellished by Ralph de la Haye, who gilt twelve of them with pure gold for the chief knights at a shilling apiece, and silvered the remainder at eightpence each: "De Rob'o Erunnler xxxviij. galee de coř ꝓ pᷓc galee xvj. d. Item Raꝺo de la Haye ꝓ Bixij. galea3 de auro puř ꝓ dingmoř arñ prēc galee xij. d. Eidem pro Batuř xxvi. gal' de argento, pᷓc gal' viij. d." The swords were made of whalebone and parchment, their blades silvered, the hilt and pommel gilt: "De Petro le Furbeuř (the furbisher) xxxviii. glad' fact de Baleñ & Parcomeñ, pᷓc pēc vij. d. Itñ ꝓ Batuř ꝺco3 glad' de argent' xxv.s. Itñ ꝓ Batuř pomell' & ſteo3d' de auro puř iiij. s. vi. d."

The sum-total paid for these thirty-eight equipments, including their carriage from London to Windsor, was £80 11*s.* 8*d.* Other purchases were made at Paris, of which a portion appears to have been for the tournament, as the horse furniture, already noticed at page 340. Other articles are of a miscellaneous character, as hawking-gloves, furs for mantles, carpets, and "a hundred *fromages de Brie* for the King and Queen" (c. casei de Bria pro Rege et Regina, precium xxxv. s.). The whole of the document, however, deserves a careful investigation, though we have extracted the chief particulars which illustrate the subject of our inquiry. It is printed in full in the seventeenth volume of the *Archæologia*.

There was a variety of the tournament in vogue during this century, called the Round Table; of which, though some curious details have been preserved, the particular characteristic has not been ascertained. Matthew Paris[444] has noted with especial distinctness that the *Tabula rotunda* was not a mere new name given to an old sport, but that it was a pastime of a different kind. "In this year, 1252, he says, the knights of England, in order to prove their skill and bravery in military practices, unanimously determined to try their powers, not in the sport commonly and vulgarly called a Tournament, but in that military game which is named The Round Table: (non ut in hastiludio illo quod communiter et vulgariter Torneamentum dicitur, sed potiùs in illo ludo militari qui Mensa Rotunda dicitur:) therefore, at the Octave of the Nativity of the Blessed Virgin, they assembled in great numbers at the Abbey of Wallenden, flocking together from the north and from the south, and some also from the continent. And, according to the rules of that warlike sport, on that day and the day following, some English knights disported themselves with great skill and valour, to the pleasure and admiration of all the foreigners there present. On the fourth day following, two knights of great valour and renown, Arnold de Montigny and Roger de Lemburn, came forth completely armed after the manner of knights, and mounted on choice and handsome horses. And, as they rushed onward to encounter with their lances, Roger aimed his weapon, the point of which was not blunted, as it ought to have been, so that it entered under the helm of Arnold, and pierced his throat: for he was unarmed in that part of his body, being without a collar (*carens collario*)." Montigny expired on the spot, and the festivities were turned to mourning; so that "those who had come thither in joy and gladness, separated on a sudden amid grief and lamentation; De Lemburn at once making a vow to assume the Cross and undertake a pilgrimage for the release of the soul of Arnold."

From this relation we learn that the knights, fully armed, contended with lances on horseback, and that it was an especial rule of the combat that the lance-heads should be blunt or "rebated."

In 1280, the eighth of Edward I., earl Roger de Mortimer held a Round Table at his Castle of Kenilworth. "It was," says Dugdale, "a great and famous concourse of noble persons called the *Round Table*, consisting of an hundred Knights and as many Ladies, whereunto divers repaired from foreign parts for the exercise of Arms, viz., Tilting and martial Tournaments: the reason of the

Round Table being to avoyd contention touching precedency; a Custome of great antiquity, and used by the antient *Gauls*, as Mr. *Cambden* in *Hantsh.* from *Athenæus* (an approved Author) observes." The original authorities for this description of the Kenilworth Round-Table festival are Trivet and Walsingham, and the passages may be seen either in their histories, *ad an.* 1280, or in Ducange, *sub voce* Tabula Rotunda. Dugdale seems to have had the notion that, to avoid disputes about precedency, all the jousters dined together at the Round Table; but it must have been a large table to have accommodated "an hundred Knights,"—to say nothing of the hundred Ladies. It seems more probable, comparing this institution with others of an analogous character, that a certain number of knights, representing (and perhaps assuming the names of) King Arthur and his far-famed band of warriors, held the field "against all comers." This view receives some support from the well-known relic at Winchester, "the rownde table of Kyng Arthur and hys Knyghtes," which is painted in compartments, each bearing the name of one of the fraternity. The table in question is not, indeed, more ancient than about the beginning of the sixteenth century; but, as the Hall at Winchester in which it is preserved is of the thirteenth century (the very period in which the sport of the *Tabula Rotunda* came into vogue), it seems likely that this table represents some more ancient one which time has destroyed. The existing "King Arthur's Round Table" is figured in the Winchester volume of the Archæological Institute; and in the notice of it in that volume is cited a curious passage from Leroux de Lincy (himself quoting Diego de Vera, who was present at the marriage of Philip and Mary), by which it appears that tradition had assigned to a particular compartment the name of "the place of Judas or the perilous seat:" "Lors du mariage de Philippe II. avec la reine Marie, on montroit encore à Hunscrit[445] la table ronde fabriquée par Merlin: elle se composoit de 25 compartimens en blanc et en vert: dans chaque division étoient écrits le nom du cavalier et celui du roi. L'un de ces compartimens, appelé *Place de Judas* ou *Siége périlleux*, restoit toujours vide." Judas appears to have been interpolated from one of the Mystery Plays of the Middle-Ages, and it must be confessed that a table "made by Merlin" and surrounded by King Arthur and his knights, with Judas for a boon-companion, has in it a certain boldness of concatenation which might well strike with awe the solemn mind of Don Diego de Vera, on the occasion of his visit to Hunscrit. A passage in the *Faits de Bouciquaut* seems to imply that holding a Round Table meant a hastilude in which the challengers kept open house: "Ainsi fit là son appareil moult grandement et très honnorablement Messire Bouciquaut, et fit faire provisions de très bons vins, et de tous vivres largement et' à plain, et de tout ce qu'il convient, si plantureusement *comme pour tenir table ronde à tous venans* tout le dict temps durant, et tout aux propres despens de Bouciquaut[446]."

If the nobles of the land retained their fondness for the military pastimes of their order, the commonalty were not less attached to the cognate sports of their class. Indeed, their enthusiasm sometimes led them to an excess of ambition which resulted in an armed contest between the two bodies of knight and craftsman: they dared to practise the exercise of the quintain for the prize of a peacock! the peacock, that noble bird, every feather in whose tail was an eye of disdain contumeliously glowering upon the whole generation of plebeians.

The inexhaustible Matthew Paris again furnishes us with an illustration:—"In the first fortnight of Lent (1253), the young men of London tested their own powers and the speed of their horses in the sport which is commonly called the Quintain, having fixed on a Peacock as the prize of the contest. Some attendants and pages of the king's household (he being then at Westminster) were indignant at this, and insulted the citizens, calling them rustics, scurvy and soapy wretches, and at once entered the field to oppose them. The Londoners eagerly accepted their challenge, and, after beating their backs with the broken spear-shafts till they were black and blue, they hurled all the royal attendants from their horses or put them to flight. The fugitives then went to the king and with clasped hands and gushing tears besought him not to let so great an offence go unpunished; and he, resorting to his usual kind of vengeance, extorted from the citizens a large sum of money."

Figures of the quintain and the tilters may be seen in Strutt's Sports: the manuscripts he has used are of a somewhat later date, (that is, fourteenth century,) but the forms of the quintains may be fairly taken as similar to those of the preceding age.

In the thirteenth century we first obtain a pictorial representation of the LEGAL DUEL, or wager of battle: rude, it is true, but curiously confirming the written testimony that has come down to us of the arms and apparel of the Champions.

This drawing has been carefully traced from one of the "Miscellaneous Rolls" in the Tower, of the time of Henry III. The combatants are Walter Blowberme and Hamun le Stare, the latter being the vanquished champion, and figuring a second time in the group as undergoing the punishment incidental to his defeat. The names of the duellers are written over the figures, the central one being that of the victor. Both are armed with the quadrangular bowed shield and a "baston" headed with a double beak. Britton (De Jure Angliæ, fol. 41) exactly describes their arming: "Puis voisent combattre armés sans fer et sans longe arme, à testes découvertes et à mains nues (à pié?) ovesque deux bastons cornuts d'une longueur, et chascun de eux d'un escu de quatre corners, sauns autre arme dont nul ne puisse autre griever." The exact length of the bâtons we learn from a statute of Philip of France in 1215: "Statuimus quod Campiones non pugnent de caetero cum baculis qui excedant longitudinem trium pedum." They might, however, continues the statute, use staves of shorter dimensions, if they thought proper.

The arming "sans fer" mentioned above is made more clear by a passage of the "Coustumier of Normandy," chap. 28: (Les champions doivent être) "appareillez en leurs cuiries, ou en leurs cotes, avec leurs escus, et leurs bastons cornus, armez si comme mestier sera de drap, de cuir, de laine et d'estoupes. Es escus, ne es bastons, ne es armures de jambes, ne doit aver fors fust ou cuir, ou ci qui est pardevant dit; ne ils ne peuvent avoir autre instrument à grever l'un l'autre fors l'escu et le baston." The bare heads and cropped hair of our duellers are in conformity with another ordinance of the Camp-fight: "Les Chevaliers qui se combate por murtre ou por homicide, se doive combatre à pié, et *sans coiffe*, et estre *roignés à la reonde*[447]." Compare the figure of the champion of Bishop Wyvil, which appears on the

276

monumental brass of the prelate in Salisbury Cathedral: date 1375. It is engraved in Waller's Brasses, Part ix., and in Carter's "Painting and Sculpture." For an extended series of evidences relating to the custom of Wager of Battle, see Ducange or Adelung, *v. Campiones*, and compare Henault, *ad an.* 1260.

CAERPHILLY CASTLE, GLAMORGANSHIRE.

Built about 1275.

No. 89.